Class Matters:
'Working-Class' Women's
Perspectives on Social Class

Edited by

Pat Mahony
and
Christine Zmroczek

Taylor & Francis
Publishers since 1798

UK Taylor & Francis Ltd, 1 Gunpowder Square, London EC4A 3DE

USA Taylor & Francis Inc., 1900 Frost Road, Suite 101, Bristol, PA 19007

First published 1997

A Catalogue Record for this book is available from the British Library

ISBN 0 7484 0540 2
ISBN 0 7484 0541 0 (pbk)

Library of Congress Cataloging-in-Publication Data are available on request

Typeset in 10/12 pt Times
by Best-set Typesetter Ltd, Hong Kong

Printed by SRP Ltd, Exeter

Contents

Contents

Chapter 1

Why Class Matters

Pat Mahony and Christine Zmroczek

This collection represents, for us, a celebration of ten years of work on the subject of women and social class and in particular on the experiences of women from working-class backgrounds now living and working in a variety of contexts.

In this chapter we will briefly review our work to date, concentrating on the main reasons for our interest and the processes through which our understandings have developed. We will identify the major themes which have emerged, many of which are explored in greater depth by the authors in this volume, and point to those areas where, in our view, further work needs to be done.

There were three main reasons for our initial interest in women and social class. First, as two women from working-class backgrounds, the experience of going through university as students and then working in the academy as teachers and researchers left us confused about our own class positioning. Though both of us were told repeatedly that by virtue of our education and our 'position in the labour market' we were not working-class, we did not *feel* middle-class nor believe that we had necessarily 'gone up in the world'. While we believed that it was insulting to other working-class people to pretend that our lives were the same as theirs, given the relative privileges bestowed on us by our middle-class occupations, neither did we feel that we inhabited the world of the university in the same ways as the majority of our colleagues (including other feminists). In addition, the social and cultural assumptions underpinning and permeating some of our worlds seemed to be very different from those of our middle-class feminist colleagues and friends. As we began talking about these issues in the mid 1980s, we discovered that we shared a massive sense of confusion about where we fitted in (if anywhere) and as we talked more, we were relieved to learn that we tended to have similar reactions (outrage) to the subtle reminders of our 'difference', sometimes ascribed as inferiority.

The second stimulus to our work occurred at a conference where we heard, yet again, that 'radical feminism is middle-class and not interested in exploring difference between women'. Our objections to this assertion were twofold. First, the statement was made from a position described by the speaker as 'one perspective within postmodernism', the virtues of which were, apparently, to avoid the theoretical inadequacy of radical feminism with its alleged 'tendency to deal in universalizing truth claims about all women'. This is not the place to enter into debate about the merits or otherwise of postmodernisms (Mies and Shiva, 1993; Bell and Klein, 1996) but the irony was not lost on us in this instance, of the tendency of postmodernism to deal in universalizing truth claims about radical feminism. Our second objection related to our own work. We had spent some twenty years as radical feminists, during which we had attempted to explore differences in women's social, cultural and political circumstances through our own teaching and writing (for example, Mahony, 1989, 1992; Zmroczek, 1992). We were not pleased (to put it mildly) to have our contribution rendered invisible; we may have been confused about our own complicated social class positioning, but the claim that we were middle-class simply did not fit with our experiences.

The third impetus for our work came from our dissatisfaction with writing on social class. Although a great deal has been written, much of it is by and about men and it did not have the power or resonance of feminist writing. We could find only a few books (hooks, 1981; Steedman, 1986 and later Taking Liberties Collective, 1989; Walkerdine, 1990) about the experiential level of class oppression which would enable us to grasp the nature of the influences on the formation of working-class women's identities and the ways in which these in turn affect our possibilities, real and perceived. Some people have mistakenly taken our project to be an exploration of identity. It is more than that. It is a search for theory which can begin to describe the relationships between the classed nature of our lives and our positionings within the broader material structures. For if we do not understand the processes which undermine us, steal our creativity and marginalize us, we cannot interrupt or challenge them. Our exploration is based on a feminist perspective which seeks to understand how class power both structures our lives and is reconstituted through them.

For all these reasons it seemed urgent to find out how to place ourselves as two white women distanced from our undoubtedly working-class backgrounds but certainly not always comfortable in and at times positively enraged by the oppressive behaviour of the largely middle-class world which we now inhabited.

We knew two more women who were also concerned about these issues and in the mid 1980s we formed a group. We consisted of three ex-Catholics (an African/Asian Scot, an English Pole and an English Irish woman) and an Asian Muslim woman. One of us had children, two identified as heterosexual, one as (sort of) heterosexual and one as lesbian. Our ages ranged from late forties to early twenties, all of us had working-class backgrounds which seemed to live on with us into the present, all of us had been to university and were in middle-class occupations. In such a group the two of us who described ourselves as radical feminists had little difficulty in resisting any urge to universalize our experience.

We learned a great deal about our similarities as well as the very real differences for black and white, lesbian and heterosexual women, living in a racist and heterosexist society. We began to clarify the ways in which the constant drip of negative and oppressive experience operates at a personal level to re-create gendered class and race divisions in Britain. We shared our strategies for coping with and overcoming the obstacles which had faced us at school and in higher education, at home and in our workplaces and we rediscovered and revalued some of the strengths we had developed by virtue of our working-class backgrounds. We had been meeting for two years when new jobs, house moving, family illness and pressure of work combined to make it impossible for the group to continue.

Some time later the two of us attended a workshop for working-class women, given by Jo Stanley at a Women's Studies Network conference (Stanley, 1995). We were inspired by the energy, strength, anger and humour of the women we met and resolved to resurrect our own work and develop it.

The major themes which emerged from this stage of our work have been discussed elsewhere (Zmroczek and Mahony, 1996a, 1996b) and it has been particularly exciting to see many of them explored further in this volume. The authors here write powerfully on the basis of their own experiences, of their confusion and ambivalence in locating themselves as 'working-class'. Others contest the category itself while still giving voice to their dissatisfaction with the claim that Britain is not a class-ridden and class-determined society. How to find a place (or places) within the variety of worlds we inhabit, what counts as a place and a desire to make a place of one's own are all discussed in ways which will take the debate further.

The ways in which the lack of material resources not only affected us while we were growing up, but linger on into the present, shaping our consciousness, attitudes and behaviour, is another theme which is developed in the book. Closely related to this are the differences in cultural capital, awareness of which persists long after we have acquired many of the trappings of a middle-class lifestyle. The part that language and accent play in signifying our histories is particularly complex. Some black women of African and African-Caribbean origin, for example, have told us that despite their middle-class accents, it is frequently presumed that they are working-class and that all kinds of assumptions follow from this. In this volume, issues of class difference between black women are discussed and questions raised which clearly need to be pursued in a future volume. The ways in which white women from working-class backgrounds continue to be marked out by accent (if the enforced elocution lessons failed) also constitute areas of particular sensitivity. It is surely no accident that many of us have learned to play with accent, to 'use' it in quite self-conscious ways as a political tool to expose the pompous, to undermine the snobbish and to challenge the stereotypes about us.

And stereotypes there are, in plenty. In the course of preparing a conference paper (Zmroczek, 1996) in which she wanted to explain current conceptions of class in Britain to an international audience, Chris was surprised to notice the plethora of offensive, stereotyped representations of working-class people appearing in the British media over a relatively short period of time. There were also television programmes and newspaper articles which offered more positive images. This has raised questions for us about the kinds of representations which predominate, the social and political agendas set by them and their effects in determining attitudes about class. Dave Hill, for example, writing in the *Sunday Observer Life Magazine* (31 March 1996), noted that 'a recent Gallup Poll showed that 81 per cent of people believe there is a class struggle in this country compared with 66 per cent 15 years ago' (p. 26). This finding was borne out by a small survey of first degree students who responded to a questionnaire in a Women's Studies course (Zmroczek, forthcoming). In answer to the questions 'Does social class matter in today's Britain?' and 'Is everyone equal these days?', all but one of the forty students who responded were unambiguously of the view that class does matter and that people are not equal. The one remaining student proceeded to define three classes: 'the aristocracy, the middle-class majority and the underclass e.g. the homeless'. Some students expressed their distaste for class divisions in comments such as 'it *shouldn't* make a difference but it does' and others were clearly confused about the contradictions between their own experiences and the myths which bombard them. Some, possibly influenced by John Major's fantasy of a classless society, doubted whether they could still call themselves working-class now that they were (first-year) students. Perhaps there is some mileage in the claim that 'Class distinctions remain a red-hot British issue, partly because we're encouraged to believe they no longer exist' (Hill, 1996, p. 24).

As well as developing new perspectives on some more familiar themes, this volume raises issues which urgently need to be put on the agenda. Women write about retaining their working-class identities as a positive choice and of rejecting the common assumption that they strive to rise out of or escape from their working-class beginnings. This refusal to 'step up the ladder' has led us to question whether the ladder image is helpful at all in theorizing women's relationship to class. For all of us in this volume, class experience is deeply rooted, retained and carried through life rather than left behind (or below). In this sense it is more like a foot which carries us forward than a footprint which marks a past presence. How else should we understand the difficulties we experience within our families when we are perceived as 'getting above' our-selves? Why would we encounter such difficulty with the stereotypes of us if we had 'left it all behind'? And conversely, having absorbed elements of other class identities, why else would we experience so many contradictions in locating ourselves fully and clearly within our working-class communities? Such contradictions are particularly sharp for those with immigrant or refugee backgrounds and when combined with the experience of racism and nationalism, the workings of British society become transparent in all their ugliness.

Authors speak with pride and pain about their working-class origins, about the struggles of their parents, families and communities. They discuss the advantages of being working-class in relation to the development of what we would call good 'crap detectors' (for example, in the role of education in creating class difference and division) or of being in a position to obtain rich research data through a deeper understanding and connection with working-class interviewees. There are celebratory recognitions of group activities, of having deep connections to histories which are full of women's opposition, solidarity and struggle. They write too of the ability to 'cross' classes, to 'play' with accent, vocabulary and demeanour; of 'performance', 'masquerade' and 'passing' and the richness gained from seeing the world from different vantage points.

In contrast to this, authors write of their feelings of anger and guilt at being part of the academy, at the same time as being excited by intellectual work. Women who have gone through higher education often see themselves as being required to continue an ethic of service to others less 'lucky' than themselves. At the same time there are feelings of insecurity about positions attained but not 'deserved' and these are often expressed in the fear that one day the 'fraud' will be exposed. Overwork is of course frequently the solution to these feelings; as proof that we are worthy of our places in the academy and as fulfilment of the service ethic (especially since this often connects with wanting to decode the 'rules of the game' for those students in whom we see ourselves). This notion of 'being in service' has particular connotations for teachers (clustered at the lower ends of pay scales) and for researchers (on temporary or short-term contracts) from working-class backgrounds.

The difficulties of exploring class within feminism should not be under-estimated. Debates around class seem to sometimes provoke reactions of guilt, defensiveness or even hostility from middle-class colleagues and friends. This does not make it easy to develop new ways of understanding the diversity of women's lives nor to explore how we might act on social mechanisms which increasingly condemn large proportions of new generations to economic hardship, inadequate housing, ill-health and under-resourced schools and colleges. Our silences have needed to be broken so that by gaining confidence from each other we could explore new ideas and rework old topics from new perspectives. As can be seen from this volume, these new perspectives derive from diverse positions in which what it means to have a working-class background *is* different in each case. But it is not so different that we do not recognize each other and not so different that our connectedness (at least on this issue) disappears. As feminists we would also hope that women from other class positions will also begin to explore what class means for them and that this may lead to better understandings between women across class difference. This would be an important step in enabling all feminists to challenge oppressive and damaging class structures, mechanisms and institutions.

The period during which we have been thinking, discussing and writing about women and social class has seen the publication of new, relevant material from the USA (hooks, 1989; Tokarczyk and Fay, 1993; Penelope, 1994;

Zandy, 1995). It has been particularly exciting to find that the UK material also has relevance for women living in very diverse cultures and countries (Mahony and Zmroczek, 1994, 1996). New themes have emerged, we have learned of significant omissions in knowledge and understanding about class and the need for perspectives to broaden to include recognition of an international dimension to the debate on class. The result is that this book, which was to be the culmination of our work to date, has now become the first of a series.

It has been a privilege and a pleasure to work with the authors in this volume. Our hope is that our readers will feel similarly enriched in concluding – *class matters*.

References

BELL, D. and KLEIN, R. (Eds) (1996) *Radically Speaking: Feminism Reclaimed*, Melbourne, Spinifex, and London, Zed.

HILL, D. (1996) 'She Is . . . Are You?', *Sunday Observer Life Magazine*, 31 March, p. 24.

HOOKS, B. (1981) *Ain't I a Woman*, Boston, Mass., South End Press.

HOOKS, B. (1989) *Talking Back: Thinking Feminist, Thinking Black*, London, Sheba Press, and Boston, Mass., South End Press.

MAHONY, P. (1989) 'Sexual Violence and Mixed Schools', in JONES, C. and MAHONY, P. *Learning our Lines: Sexuality and Social Control in Education*, London, The Women's Press.

MAHONY, P. (1992) 'Which Way Forward? Equality and Schools in the '90s', *Women's Studies International Forum*, 15, pp. 293–303.

MAHONY, P. and ZMROCZEK, C. (1994) 'Invisible Boundaries', paper given at 6th International Feminist Book Fair, Melbourne, July.

MAHONY, P. and ZMROCZEK, C. (1996) 'Relating Radically', paper given at conference on The Politics of Radical Feminism, Melbourne, April.

MIES, M. and SHIVA, V. (1993) *Ecofeminism*, London, Zed.

PENELOPE, J. (Ed.) (1994) *Out of the Class Closet: Lesbians Speak*, Freedom, California: The Crossing Press.

STANLEY, J. (1995) 'Pain(t) for Healing: The Academic Conference and the Classed/Embodied Self', in MORLEY, L. and WALSH, V. (Eds) *Feminist Academics: Creative Agents for Change*, London, Taylor & Francis.

STEEDMAN, C. (1986) *Landscape for a Good Woman*, London, Virago.

TAKING LIBERTIES COLLECTIVE (1989) *Learning the Hard Way*, London, Macmillan.

TOKARCZYK, M. and FAY, E. (Eds) (1993) *Working Class Women in the Academy: Laborers in the Knowledge Factory*, Massachusetts, University of Massachusetts Press.

WALKERDINE, V. (1990) *Schoolgirl Fictions*, London, Verso.

ZANDY, J. (Ed.) (1995) *Liberating Memory: Our Work and Our Working-Class Consciousness*, New Brunswick, Rutgers University Press.

ZMROCZEK, C. (1992) 'Dirty Linen: Women, Class and Washing Machines 1920s–1960s', *Women's Studies International Forum*, 15, pp. 173–86.

ZMROCZEK, C. (1996) 'Common Interests: Women and Social Class', paper given at 6th International Congress on Women, Adelaide, April.

ZMROCZEK, C. (1996) 'Class in the Women's Studies Classroom', unpublished paper.

ZMROCZEK, C. and MAHONY, P. (1996a) 'Lives beyond the Text', in BELL, D. and KLEIN, R. (Eds) *Radically Speaking: Feminism Reclaimed*, Melbourne, Spinifex, and London, Zed, pp. 62–7.

ZMROCZEK, C. and MAHONY, P. (1996b) 'Women's Studies and Working Class Women', in ANG-LYGATE, M., CORRIN, C. and HENRY, M. (Eds) *Desperately Seeking Sisterhood: Still Challenging and Building*, London, Taylor & Francis.

Chapter 2

Class Matters, 'Race' Matters, Gender Matters

Tracey Reynolds

Introduction

Having being approached to provide a contribution for this book I stumbled at the first hurdle, when I commenced writing. When asked to describe myself I would immediately identify myself as a black working-class woman. But what exactly does this mean? I could not define what exactly constituted a 'black working-class woman' nor identify myself so strongly with what might be called an essentialist construction.

After giving it further thought I came to realize that in similar ways to discourses on black womanhood, discourse on social class is informed by stereotypical notions and common-sense ideology of what connotes an individual's social class. Often occupation type, level of education, speech and dialect, body language, manner of dress, spatial locality and even the type of housing someone resides in are used to judge a person's social class. Therefore, they act as important social class signifiers. Determining membership of a specific social class also has much to do with the labels attached to individuals by those in power, for example, white middle-class male elites, rather than how we recognize and identify ourselves. These labels, created by those in positions of power, are then internalized and employed in our definitions of self. I choose to define myself as a black working-class woman, but how relevant is the concept 'working-class' to my position as a black woman in Britain? By defining myself as working-class, does this mean that as a black woman I occupy the same social and structural position as a white working-class woman?

In this chapter I aim to address some of the above issues by examining the interactions between class, 'race' and gender and highlighting some of my personal experiences as a black[1] working-class woman growing up in Britain.

Identifying Differences in Constructions of Black and White Womanhood

Black women in Western societies including Britain have historically occupied a structurally powerless position regardless of whether one chooses to define oneself as working-class or middle-class. Often our experiences have been rendered invisible (hooks, 1989). Where they have been acknowledged, they are constructed in a negative manner which devalues our experiences. The black teenage lone mother 'scrounging' welfare benefits and the 'dysfunctional' family form popular constructions of black women and our families within the media, policy debates and common-sense discourse (see Reynolds, forthcoming). Over the last twenty years a number of black feminists in Britain, America, the Caribbean, Central and South America have begun to fight back, reclaiming our 'voices' in order to (re)define our experiences and challenge existing negative perceptions.[2] Where we have been denied opportunities in the 'traditional' routes of theory construction (e.g. academia), black feminist thought has been developed in 'alternative' arenas, such as fiction, poetry, oral history, art and photography, in order to articulate our experiences.[3] What has clearly emerged as a result of black feminist discourse is the fact that historical, cultural and 'race' differences ensure that black women occupy separate social positions and face differing social realities from white women irrespective of social class positioning. Consequently, our experiences as black women are different.

For black women this dichotomous divide of the gendered public and private sphere remains a complex issue. They have been simultaneously situated in both spheres. Existing power structures in society have ensured that black women, unlike men, have not enjoyed systems of privilege that derive from occupying a dominant position in the public sphere despite being situated there. Black women's role in slavery (Beckles, 1995), indentured migration of Indo-Caribbeans (Shepherd, 1995) and migration policies of the 1960s targeted towards Caribbean people (Bryan *et al.*, 1985) are clear examples of the way in which black women have been constructed as workers. Today 76 per cent of black women are economically active, engaged in full-time employment (*Employment Gazette*, 1993); 49 per cent of African-Caribbean families are headed by a lone mother, who assumes primary or sole responsibility for economic provision (OPCS, 1991).

These factors suggest that 'traditional' feminist discourse, with its emphasis on women's role within the domestic sphere, does not accurately reflect the lives of many black women. These debates also disguise the fact that a significant number of white middle-class women have benefited from black women's role as workers. It has freed them to some extent from domestic responsibilities, providing the opportunity for these women to pursue a professional career. Separate studies by Segura and Chang point to the current practice in America among professional middle-class families of illegally employing women from Central and South America as a source of cheap labour (Chang, 1994; Segura, 1994). In Britain, too, this practice occurs with the employment of women from the Far East, Indo-China and parts of Africa (Bhavnani, 1994).

(Re)contextualizing Social Class, 'Race' and Gender

Many black women in Britain identify 'race' as the starting point of any self-definition (Mama, 1995). A shared history of racial oppression, imperialism and colonialism, experienced by both black men and women, ensure that these women position class and gender as of secondary importance in the determination of their structural and social position. Whilst I would fully support the idea that issues of 'race' forge a common bond amongst all black people, I believe that it is too simplistic to focus on 'race' to the exclusion of gender and class. Just as black people share a common history, there exist many differences and great diversity between us. The complex interactions between 'race', gender and class contribute to the structuring of these differences both between black men and women and amongst black women ourselves.

The fact that black people are often looked upon by white people as a homogeneous group prevents class differences from emerging. Racism is endemic to British society and informs even my own perceptions of how white society perceives me. In situations where I have felt discriminated against I have immediately attributed it to my skin colour combined with my gender as opposed to my social class. I cannot recall an incident where class discrimination has come to the forefront of my thoughts.

Although I recognize that difference and diversity exists amongst black people, I am aware that in wider society we all appear to be the same. That common adage, 'you all look the same to me', prevails in some white people's perceptions of individuals belonging to 'other' ethnic groups. Identifying black people as a homogeneous unit also occurs in more subtle forms. For example, within feminist discourse, I note that in many books, articles, journals and conference papers, separate categories exist for white working-class and white middle-class women, but black women are rarely divided into different social class positions.

More often than not, where our class positionings are acknowledged, the terms 'black' and 'working-class' are used simultaneously, as if being a black person automatically equates with occupying a working-class position. This assumption is being challenged by a wealth of emerging literature in America which acknowledges the black middle class and the different position they occupy in relation to the working class and the poor (see McAdoo, 1988). My family background, upbringing, income and socio-economic group label me and enable me to recognize myself as working-class. However, it is important to note that there are many black people in Britain whose background and socio-economic group place them in the middle-class category. Black feminist thought in Britain needs to assume responsibility for developing and highlighting issues concerning difference amongst black women as little literature exists here which examines this subject matter.

(Mis)representations of Black Womanhood

As a black woman living in a white society, I am constantly being constructed and 'named' by others. bell hooks describes this as having our identity constructed by the 'power of the gaze' and 'power of recognition' of dominant groups (e.g. white male elites) (hooks, 1990). As I said earlier, images such as 'breeders', 'welfare scroungers', 'matriarchs' and the 'superwoman' inform popular conceptions of black womanhood. There exists a social class context to the way these images are constructed. In debates examining the experiences of the black professional middle-class woman, the image of the 'superwoman' comes to the fore:

> [B]lack women are out-performing them [black men], educationally and in the job market. These women acquire senior status at work, become part of a different culture and they move onto a world where they have few black male equals. (*Guardian*, 2 July 1994, p. 11)

Alternatively, the uneducated teenage mother, dependent on welfare benefits and living in an inner-city council estate and producing deviant dysfunctional families dominate in representations of black working-class women. These images have been popularized by the press:

> Latest unpublished Government statistics – obtained by the *Sunday Express* – reveal that almost six in ten black mothers are bringing up children on their own, urged on by our benefit system. (*Sunday Express*, 13 August 1995, p. 2)

The resurgence of an American debate which has found support in Britain, and further contributes to the vilification of black people, revisits the idea that black women (black men also) genetically possess lower intelligence than the white population (Murray and Herrnstein, 1994). If one equates intelligence with educational achievement, as Murray and Herrnstein explicitly do, then statistical evidence illustrates that proportionally black women achieve greater educational success than white women across all social classes. Sixty-one per cent of black women possess higher education and other professional qualifications (*Employment Gazette*, February 1993).

Education has always been a strong cultural force in the Caribbean and is highly valued. The fact that a large proportion of black women are achieving in education is regarded as nothing exceptional or new there. Within many black families education is promoted as a vehicle for economic and social advancement. It is perceived as a means for 'getting on' and 'bettering yourself' in society (Mirza, 1992), a way of progressing and building on what was achieved by parents, grandparents and fore-parents. In Western societies, education has the added dimension of equipping black women with the training and skills to cope in inherently racist societies and to exceed societal boundaries and expectations of us.

For many black women who have adopted what is essentially a meritocratic ideal of education, attempting to achieve educational success has been an uphill struggle, fraught with difficulties and tensions. A large number of black women have had to take the 'long back door route' (Mirza, 1993). In her study of black female students, Mirza identified that a significant proportion of black women were denied the 'traditional' route into higher education (GCSE/'O' levels and 'A' levels, followed by university at 18 years old), due to failings within mainstream education. I know of many black women who, schooled in inner-city areas, recount similar experiences of explicit and implicit racism, poor teacher expectations of them and a general lack of material resources within schools. As a result these women have had no choice but to obtain an education after they had left mainstream school, returning as mature students. In what Mirza terms 'strategic rationalization' she highlights the way black women strategically move into higher education (Mirza, 1995). Black women have actively sought out occupations (for example social work, care work and education) that offer them further scope for training and ultimately the opportunity to advance to higher education in order to obtain a degree and/or professional qualification.

The personal rewards and satisfaction of obtaining a 'good' education are high. This is especially so in a society which automatically labels you a failure as a result of being black. However, the costs are also high. Returning to education at a later age means that many black women have to juggle employment, education and childcare/domestic/family responsibilities. Of the African-Caribbean mothers in my study of black mothering who are engaged in educational pursuits (six to date), all are single mothers who do not have a spouse/partner within their homes with whom to share some of the burden (Reynolds, unpublished). This leads to physical, psychological and emotional stress as a result of having to combine these multiple roles. The costs to these women are often overlooked in analyses or are valorized in the form of the 'black superwoman'. Implicit in this construction is the idea that black women possess 'natural' biological characteristics which predispose them to actively seek and cope well with overburden! (see Reynolds, forthcoming)

Reconciling My Educational Experiences and Social Class Position

Fortunately I was one of the 'lucky' ones in that I managed to obtain my education via the more traditional route of mainstream schooling. My schooling itself in the outer London suburbs was fairly happy and the schools I attended still provide me with fond memories. I do not consider my childhood and schooling experiences to be any more special or different from those of most working-class black women growing up in Britain during the 1970s. I am sure most black women who read this will testify to similar experiences and perceive nothing unique in what I am saying.

From a very young age I was made aware of differences from the white children. At times there were overt racist comments such as 'black bastard'. At other times an ignorant curiosity belied a more subtle form of racism and white supremacy: for example, 'do black people live in mud huts where you come from?', 'is your hair made of wool?', 'do you eat cat food?'. In retrospect I can reflect that my teachers primarily operated on this latter level. I recall that the black children were always channelled into areas of sports and music as these were stereotypically perceived as the only areas that we were good at. Covert racism also informed interpretations of behaviour amongst black and white children which were also construed differently. The boisterous, naughty behaviour considered normal in white children took on a different meaning when black children behaved the same way. It suddenly became deviant, wild and aggressive. My parents, aware of these differing constructions according to 'race', stressed the importance to me of not following the action of the white children in my classroom and of maintaining obedience and good behaviour at all times.

By the age of 22, I had obtained a first class honours degree from a well established college of the University of London. All the way through my educational life, I have lived with comments by some teachers/lecturers which have attributed each educational success to a factor of luck. I first heard this when I was placed in and maintained my position in the top stream at secondary school and it is still something I am hearing today as a research scholar. The fact that I have worked hard and possess some degree of ability is an issue that is often not considered or is not openly voiced. One conversation I had with a shocked lecturer when I passed my degree with a high grade particularly remains at the forefront of my mind. He said that I was 'obviously a very lucky girl' as I had 'managed to slip through the net'. Far too often this 'net' appears to be set up as a barrier to prevent black women from succeeding. The fact that increased numbers of black women are 'slipping through the net' is indicative of our active engagement in breaking down these barriers.

For black women, black men and women in general, barriers still exist in the field of academia. Essentially, academia is a white middle-class pursuit. Patricia Hill Collins (1991) highlights this problem for the development of black feminist epistemology. She argues that black feminists are faced with a dilemma. Whilst black feminists are attempting to create their own epistemology distinct from and challenging white feminist epistemology, they are inhibited by having to use white male middle-class 'tools'. Moreover, to gain credibility within the establishment, white male elite frames of reference are employed. She argues that neither of these can be used to adequately reflect the black female experience.

As a young black working-class women within the institution, I am unsure where I fit in. Certainly, I cannot foresee me defining myself as an academic, nor do I feel comfortable with having such a term applied to me. Perhaps this has more to do with the way I perceive 'an academic'. I see it as a person who is relatively mature, possessing 'expert' knowledge, who confines themselves to the academy and distances themselves from the 'real' world. In no sense do any of these constructions apply to how I identify myself.

bell hooks and Patricia Hill Collins highlight the need for more black women to enter academia and assume positions of power to ensure that a platform is given to black women's voices and that change in the make-up of the academy is effected. But, as noted earlier, for many black women obtaining degrees as mature women students, costs are involved. Collins argues that often black women have to decide how they will position themselves in academia. Does one change one's behaviour to adapt to white middle-class perceptions of 'credible' research, or remain on the 'margins' creating 'radical', innovative research which departs from eurocentric masculinist 'traditionalist' research but more accurately represents black women's experiences? A third alternative is to adopt the 'outsider/within' approach where you use your knowledge of both 'worlds' to shift between the two positions where it is most beneficial and to produce 'knowledge' that is accepted by both worlds (Collins, 1991).

Ironically, it is within academia when meeting my black female peers that, in relation to them, I become most strongly aware of my social class positioning. Feelings of insecurity as a result of my working-class family background and my relatively young age and inexperience come to the fore. Most appear to be experienced in their relevant fields of work and come from a middle-class background. In these conversations, unlike my discussions with other non-black groups in society, I feel exposed for I can no longer hide behind the fact that I am a black woman and as a result one can never really understand what it is to be black and female. There have been many times when I have asked myself 'what are you doing here?' and felt that this is not really my world. Yet, paradoxically, the fact that as black women they can relate to my experiences also provides me with a sense of comfort. I am not placed in the position of having to constantly defend my blackness and my femaleness as I often have to do outside of this circle.

Conclusion

'Race', class and gender interact to socially and structurally position black women differently to white women. Historical and cultural factors also contribute. Feminist analysis should therefore move away from approaches which seek to compare and contrast the experiences of black women and white women, because even where the same social class position are occupied, they will face different social realities. To be a black working-class woman in Britain is construed as meaning something entirely different to being a white working-class woman in Britain. In particular, the latter does not have attached to it so many negative connotations.

Without meaning to diminish the significant contribution of black British feminists towards developing an understanding of the lives of black women in Britain, it is imperative that future analysis focus on difference and diversity amongst back women. Only then can social class differences and the way in which they inform black women's social and structural positioning be observed and challenged.

Notes

1 Usage of the term 'black' in this instance primarily refers to African-Caribbean people, although many of my arguments can be applied to other ethnic groups who traditionally fall under this 'umbrella' term, for example, Africans, Indians, Pakistanis and Bangladeshis.
2 For example, from the USA, bell hooks, 1989; Patricia Hill Collins, 1991; Carol Boyce-Davies, 1994; from Britain, Heidi Mirza, 1992; Beverley Bryan *et al.*, 1985; Amina Mama, 1995; Hazel Carby, 1984; from the Caribbean, Doreen Powell, 1986; Christine Barrow, 1986; Janet Momsen, 1993; Filomena Steady, 1981.
3 Examples of key black female literary authors include Toni Morrison, Maya Angelou, Alice Walker, Jamaica Kincaid, Joan Riley and Velma Pollard.

References

BARROW, C. (1986) 'Finding the Strategies for Support', in MASSIAH, J. (Ed.) *Women in the Caribbean (Part 1)*, West Indies, Institute of Social and Economic Research, University of the West Indies.

BECKLES, H. (1995) 'Sex and Gender in the Historiography of Caribbean Slavery', in SHEPHERD, V., BRERETON, B. and BAILEY, B. (Eds) *Engendering History: Caribbean Women in Historical Perspective*, London, James Currey.

BHAVNANI, R. (1994) *Black Women in the Labour Market: A Research Review*, Equal Opportunities Commission.

BOYCE-DAVIES, C. (1994) *Black Women, Writing and Identity: Migrations of the Subject*, London, Routledge.

BRYAN, B., DADZIE, S. and SCAFE, S. (1985) *The Heart of the Race: Black Women's Lives in Britain*, London, Virago.

CARBY, H. (1984) 'White Women Listen! Black Feminism and the Boundaries of Sisterhood', in CENTRE FOR CULTURAL STUDIES STAFF *The Empire Strikes Back: Race and Racism in 70's Britain*, London, Hutchinson.

CHANG, G. (1994) 'Undocumented Latinas: The New 'Employable Mothers', in GLENN, E., CHANG, G. and FORCEY, L. (Eds) *Mothering: Ideology, Experience and Agency*, New York, Routledge.

COLLINS, P. H. (1991) *Black Feminist Thought*, New York, Routledge.

EMPLOYMENT GAZETTE (1993) 'Ethnic Origins and the Labour Market', London, Department of Employment HMSO, February.

HOOKS, B. (1989) *Talking Back: Thinking Feminist, Thinking Black*, Boston, South End Press.

HOOKS, B. (1990) *Yearning: Race, Gender, and Cultural Politics*, Boston, South End Press.

MAMA, A. (1995) *Beyond the Mask: Race, Gender and Subjectivity*, London, Routledge.

McADOO, H. (1988) *Black Families*, 2nd edn, California, Sage Publications.

MIRZA, H. (1992) *Young, Female and Black*, London, Routledge.

MIRZA, H. (1993) 'The Social Construction of Black Womanhood in British Educational Research: Towards a New Understanding', in ARNOT, M. and WEILER, K. (Eds) *Feminism and Social Justice in Education: International Perspectives*, London, Falmer Press.

MIRZA, H. (1995) 'Black Women in Higher Education: Defining a Space/ Finding a Place', in MORLEY, L. and WALSH, V. (Eds) *Feminist Academics: Creative Agents for Change*, London, Taylor & Francis.

MOMSEN, J. (1993) *Women and Change in the Caribbean*, London, James Currey.

MURRAY, C. and HERRNSTEIN, R. (1994) *The Bell Curve – Intelligence and Class Structure in American Life*, New York, The Free Press.

OPCS (1991) *Population Trends*, Number 65, Autumn 1991: *Trends in the Number of One-Parent Families in Great Britain*.

POWELL, D. (1986) 'Caribbean Women and their Response to Familial Experiences', in MASSIAH, J. (Ed.) *Women in the Caribbean (Part 1)*, West Indies, Institute of Social and Economic Research, University of the West Indies.

REYNOLDS, T. (forthcoming) '(Mis)representing the Black Superwoman', in MIRZA, H. (Ed.) *A Reader: Black British Feminism*, Routledge.

REYNOLDS, T. (unpublished) 'African-Caribbean Mothering: (Re)Constructing A "New" Identity'.

SEGURA, D. (1994) 'Working at Motherhood: Chicana and Mexican Immigrant Mothers and Employment', in GLENN, E., CHANG, G. and FORCEY, L. (Eds) *Mothering: Ideology, Experience and Agency*, New York, Routledge.

SHEPHERD, V. (1995) 'Gender, Migration and Settlement: The Indentureship and Post-Indentureship Experience of Indian Females in Jamaica, 1845–1943', in SHEPHERD, V., BRERETON, B. and BAILEY, B. (Eds) *Engendering*

History: Caribbean Women in Historical Perspective, London, James Currey.

STEADY, F. (Ed.) (1981) *The Black Women Cross-Culturally*, Cambridge, MA., Schenkman.

Chapter 3

The Double-Bind of the 'Working-Class' Feminist Academic: The Success of Failure or the Failure of Success?

Diane Reay

This chapter explores the difficulty of reconciling socialization into academic culture with a subjectivity that still draws powerfully on working-class identity. It looks at the ways in which the influences of the past and the present are interwoven but also the myriad ways in which they clash and collide. The article goes on to explore the paradox of a contemporary female identity which is rooted in working-class class consciousness. This historical class consciousness conflicts powerfully with a contemporary identity which consequently often feels both fictional and fraudulent. By drawing on autobiographical material, I illustrate the problems of authenticity which beset working-class women who have become middle-class through education. I also discuss the difficult issues of difference feminism needs to address, and the important contribution working-class perspectives can offer to feminist thinking.

Academia has rarely developed complex understandings of working-class people. Even celebrated studies like that of Willis (1977) can be read as an indictment of the working class; they are so stupid that they invest time and energy into ensuring their own oppression. However, the biggest oversight for feminist academics from working-class backgrounds is the primacy the vast majority of academic studies have given to male experience. From quantitative surveys of socio-economic categorization (Goldthorpe, 1980, 1983; Lockwood, 1986) to ethnographies like that of Willis, women are invisible. In my own writing about the working classes I want to recognize what is problematic about working-class communities. Although many individuals within them challenge and combat discrimination and prejudice, they are sexist; racism and homophobia are endemic and women have to negotiate narrow, constricting versions of femininity. That is not the same as asserting that middle-class groupings in society are more enlightened. Rather sexism, racism and homophobia are more hidden and denied among the middle classes, but equally prevalent (Reay, 1995a).

Currently, even mentioning social class in academia feels 'out-of-place', naively old-fashioned. The invidious influence of the 1990s academic preoccupation with postmodern identities has resulted in the relegation of social class to an intellectual backwater. Class may be mentioned on the dust-jacket in books on education but once inside the text the experiences of working-class pupils are often marginalized or subsumed within understandings of middle-class experience as normative (see, for example, Evans, 1991). The current ethos in which social class is no longer treated as a useful category (Pahl, 1989; Pakulski and Waters, 1995) leads a number of male academics who were once working-class to deny they are really any different now. Female academics, writing about their working-class background, are much more likely to focus on issues around pain and loss (Stanley, 1995). What is missing from both perspectives is the experience of people who are still working-class and any engagement with the academic's current position of relative privilege. The possibility of a complex social trajectory for people who remain working-class is often denied.

The early 1990s was a period when much of the media focus seemed to be on the middle classes. Either we were all middle-class now or else the middle classes were variously viewed as under siege, in crisis or losing their privileges (for example, see Gray, 1994; Phillips, 1995). The processes impacting on working-class life have been reduced either to declarations about the disappearance of 'the working class' or to continuing pathologizations which neither of the working-class academic perspectives attempt to address. Modifying, reworking, updating theoretical understandings of the 'working classes' to match changing realities is rarely on the academic agenda. Yet in a period when government policies are increasingly directed at aiding the middle classes in protecting their social privilege (Ball, 1994) we need an analysis which theorizes the complex but strong linkages between class and inequality. My doctoral research uncovered a wealth of different activities middle-class mothers engaged in to ensure their families' continuing social advantage through education (Reay, 1995b). Middle-class women were investing time, energy and resources in processes of social reproduction. However, the cost of their labour was frequently borne elsewhere; by working-class mothers and their children who were forced to compete in an educational game they had little chance of winning (Reay and Ball, 1997).

The female academic from a working-class background is the end product of very different processes to those of social reproduction. She is caught up in change and social transformation. However, the positive connotations invested in terms such as transformation and change mask an inherent negativity often overlooked in discussions of meritocracy. In a critique of equal opportunities policies Kathleen Lynch writes that

> Divisions between the successful and the unsuccessful, between the haves and the have nots are merely exaggerated in a system guided by the principle of equal opportunities as it is now assumed that those who get to the top 'deserve to'; they owe no debt to their inferiors. This is one of the most divisive features of meritocratic systems and of equal opportunities policies premised on such principles. (Lynch, 1995, p. 15)

The contradictory positioning of the once working-class female academic juxtapose radical potentialities with confirmation of revisionist policies. There is an inherent paradox. While we bring with us insider knowledge of class inequalities, at the same time the academic from a working-class background represents a justification of right-wing rhetoric. We are the tokenistic edge of elitist policies: 'the inner-city kid with the right parents, the right teachers and the right brain'. We stand for a triumph of individualism over community; proof that equal opportunities work. Or, as Peter Saunders concludes in his study of educational achievement, success depends on ability not social class. He asserts that when middle-class children do better than working-class children it is due to inherited talents and personal qualities (Saunders, 1995). In a period of increasing class inequality (Oppenheim and Harker, 1996), we stand for the 'success' of meritocracy and validation for findings such as those of Peter Saunders. It is not a comfortable place to be.

Why did we work so hard in the first place? It seems incontrovertible to me that the educationally successful working-class girl has to work very hard indeed; at learning a totally new language, at undoing the silences of her childhood (Bourdieu, 1984; Borkowski, 1992); at transforming key aspects around female embodiment. Janet Zandy writes about the physicality of class difference:

> Working-class people practise a language of the body that eludes theoretical textual studies. Working-class people do not have the quiet hands or the neutral faces of the privileged classes – especially when they are within their own communities. (Zandy, 1995, p. 5)

Survival in middle-class contexts for working-class women often requires developing a decorum and reserve that fits in with middle-class standards of acceptable female sexuality (Walkerdine, 1995). It also demands a voice to replace the one that has so often been silenced in educational contexts.

How do we understand the desires and fears that accompanied such a difficult transition out of one class and into another? Kelly and Nihlen (1982) point out the gap in theories of social and cultural reproduction; the inability to explain 'the ones who got away'. Educational theorists fail to even engage with the overt psychological processes entailed in upward social mobility, let alone look beneath at the more hidden layers of compromise and compromising. However, the white working-class girl who becomes middle-class is implicated in what often feels like a treacherous process; one of shedding at least part, if not all, of her earlier class identity (Lynch and O'Neill, 1994). We have utilized one system of meritocratic individualism, the school system, in order to attain a place within another, that of higher education. How then to reconcile the working-class culture we started out with? As Lynne Chisholm cogently points out,

To feel that one can take one's fate into one's own hands is personally emancipatory, but it is not necessarily socially emancipatory. This is the contradiction and paradox at the heart of contemporary individualization processes from which girls and women may well benefit, but which are nonetheless ideological motifs whose decoding is a more complex affair than ever. Taking one's fate into one's own hands in this individualized way also entails high risks because not only success, but also failure rests with oneself. Partial autonomies are therefore always purchased at some cost. (Chisholm, 1995, p. 47)

A continuing sense of disloyalty and dislocation is another cost.

I suggest the female academic from a working-class background is unlikely ever to feel at home in academia. For many, socialization, at least within the family, was into collective and community-based understandings of the social world, not the competitive individualism we now face in which social networks are about instrumentalism, not connection. However, this is not to valorize working-class pasts. In a preoccupation with social change (we need something new to write about in the race to build academic careers) continuities are overlooked. Juxtaposing new fragmented, multiple, individualized identities against the certainties and secure homogenization of 1950s and 1960s communities weaves fictions of the past with the present. It was never certain and secure, any more than society is totally fragmented now.

Inherently 'intangible dreamscapes' (Raven, 1995), communities are more the products of desire and nostalgia; creatures of wish-fulfilment rather than of reality. Even I, growing up on a council estate housing coal-mining families, the archetypal working-class community, have to recognize retrospectively that there was no real community for us to belong to. Instead there were complex and competing groupings often based on extended families, but also on religion, politics, workplace and degrees of relative deprivation.

Conceptualizations of the working class and social mobility need to be understood in terms of the very different constituencies that make up the working class. Both Halsey *et al.*'s and Jackson and Marsden's educationally successful working-class boys nearly all came from a very particular section of the working class; aspirant, home-owning, predominantly Conservative-voting families with few children (Halsey *et al.*, 1980; Jackson and Marsden, 1963). Such families occupy the borderlands of social class. However, my working-class identity sprang from a militant working-class culture located on a sprawling council estate that housed coal-mining families, a sizeable minority of whom had six or more children. The culture combined tenuous educational aspirations with oppositional discourses of 'them' and 'us' in which the middle classes were uncomplicatedly homogenized as 'other'. This was unsurprising as most of the residents' relationships with the middle classes were either as employees or as pupils, never as friends or colleagues. Educational success was discursively constructed as the outcome of fighting 'them' to claim an entitlement which was withheld by a hostile system. Yet that apparently homogeneous community was characterized by internal differentiation and division.

It is important to place alongside the many simplifications of the working classes our own complex understandings, to demonstrate that just as there are many different middle-class groupings in society, there are myriad different ways of growing up and being working-class. I want to use my own working-class history to illustrate my point about working-class hetereogeneity but also to explain the legacy of working-class consciousness that I still struggle with as an academic. My father was an outsider; a cockney who married into a coal-mining family and never really belonged in spite of becoming a miner himself. In place of acceptance my father constructed his own community, his own iconography of working-class solidarity, a *weltanschauung* of them and us, the workers versus the bosses and their lackeys; a half-true construction in which only he stood strong refusing co-option, always arguing, disagreeing with management, refusing promotion. Out of this curious, confusing concoction of not being good enough while simultaneously being better came his children's drive for credentialism. We worked so hard at school not primarily to be acceptable to the middle classes, who were always the enemy, but to redeem our parents, to prove our family was 'just as good'. And yet when I see any documentary about miners I am overwhelmed, suffused with powerful feelings of belonging, along with a sense of outrage about their treatment. The irony is now there is no real community of coal-miners, however internally divided, to belong to. There is a further irony for me as a feminist academic in that I can see his hand guiding my conceptions of community. It is all about his version and very little about my mother's. In spite of my aim of painting an ambivalent, tentative picture highlighting complexities of interpretation and motivation, he is the hero of my fantasy of community; this man who never really belonged to the community he valorized.

Community is about the need to belong. My mother did not have a community to belong to either. She did have a large extended family. There is not the same sense of nobility and dignity in identifying with my female antecedents; both paternal and maternal grandmothers were maids or cleaners. Cleaning the toilets of the privileged does not have the same romantic resonance as working down the pit. Other siblings talk of my mother's ambition for her children. What I saw was her shame. She was ashamed: of the inevitable squalor from squeezing a family of ten into two bedrooms and a boxroom; of never having enough money; of being seen as profligate. Both parents felt inferior because that is what lies at the heart of working-class shame; a deeply felt sense of working-class inferiority which comes from seeing ourselves through middle-class eyes. Although I do not wish to generalize, and I recognize that some working-class people escape the sense of shame my family felt, in my doctoral work much later very similar feelings of shame and inferiority intermingled with anger and frustration were expressed by many of the working-class women that I interviewed. However, I was lucky because there was also rage and a powerful sense of the unfairness of things. While my parents' rage propelled me through the educational system, dealing with it subsequently in middle-class contexts has proved problematic. I regularly get angry about middle-class privilege and then guilty because I am now implicated in it. However, I have come to see that sense of unfairness as one of the most valuable things I possess.

If you have grown up working-class you know that the solution to class inequalities does not lie in making the working classes middle-class but in working at dismantling and sharing out the economic, social and cultural capital which go with middle-class status. I would suggest that the permeation of new middle-class values within the working classes has been disastrous. Collectivist understandings of self and social group have been increasingly displaced by individualistic notions premised on the self as consumer. The prevailing culture of individualism and competitiveness has given free rein to an end-of-millennium capitalism which seems increasingly out of control and unaccountable. The social groups who have had to pay the highest price for these developments are the traditional and the new working classes – the poor, manual workers, the unemployed, the low-paid in the service sectors and lone-mother families. Competition and individualism are all about hierarchy and pecking order in which the individual rather than her circumstances are judged. The working classes are no longer entitled to a sense of unfairness because everything from their financial situation and the state of their health to their children's schooling has been repackaged under late capitalism as the responsibility of the individual alone.

The answer is not to further empower ourselves within academic hierarchies but to listen to, and learn from, the still working-class woman so that there is an erosion of status hierarchies based on educational qualifications and/or wealth. Only through work which centres class injustice, as well as the injustices of 'race' and gender, can we keep at bay 'the alienation of advantage' (Hennessy, 1993). However, therein lies the double-bind. We know that taken-for-granted middle-class superiority is a sham but we learn this just as we are growing into a sense of our own importance. The struggle is to continue questioning academic culture and values while acknowledging the extent to which we are caught up in them.

As Ladwig and Gore assert, any discussion of social privilege and power needs to pay attention to 'questions of *academic* privilege, and power, competition, and contestation' (Ladwig and Gore, 1994, p. 236; authors' emphasis). I am now in a position of inevitable complicity. Any success in promoting issues which centre social justice has become inextricably entangled with self-promotion and struggles for power within academic fields. Daphne Patai remarks that what she entitles 'tiresome self-reflexivity' would be inconceivable 'in a setting in which material want was an incontrovertible fact of life' (Patai, 1994, p. 66). We academics, despite our incessant moaning about overwork and intolerable conditions, are in a luxurious situation compared to the growing ranks of the poor (Hutton, 1995). Inevitably, my rage has been diluted with guilt. I try to see myself through my mother's eyes because then I can see just how privileged I have become.

> The fact is that those of us whose medium is words do occupy privileged positions, and we hardly give up those positions when we engage in endless self-scrutiny and anxious self-identification. (Patai, 1994, p. 67)

Those are not all the facts. There are other things at issue for academics who were once working-class; questions around loyalty and disloyalty, belonging and not belonging. We have to live with the paradox that a defining part of our identity is turning into a chimera; our 'working-classness' is a fantasy that often we alone are still engaging in. My own experience of growing up working-class has left vivid memories of the heritage and history of my social origins imprinted on my consciousness. However, that consciousness, rooted in working-class affiliation, appears increasingly to be a misfit; a sense of self both out of place and out of time. Describing her complex social positionings as a working-class girl who became an academic and a poet, Maxine Scates writes of

> attempts to address contradictions of my own identity; an identity formed by what I now recognize as the working-class and existing in the middle-class. I have only just begun to realize the complexity of that identity, formed by denial of what one is or was, colonized and, through that colonization, then inevitably complicitous with what one is joining as that first identity is suppressed. (Scates, 1995, p. 191)

Kathleen Casey writes that for the black child to become educated is 'to contradict the whole system of racist signification' (Casey, 1993, p. 123). In the same way to become educated as a working-class person is to refute the whole system of class signification. However, as Scates asserts, it is a far more contradictory and compromising process. Casey writes that 'to succeed at studying "white" knowledge is to undo the system itself, to refute its (re)production of black inferiority materially and symbolically'. I would suggest a further version in which studying middle-class knowledge presents the individual from a working-class background with a dilemma. Far from undoing the system it can represent a collusion with it and act to reproduce rather than refute the (re)production of working-class inferiority. If we are the tokenistic proof of meritocracy then our academic success serves to underscore the unworthiness of those who fail. All too often when the pervading sense of inferiority which comes with growing up working-class meets a degree of academic success and recognition, we are seduced into seeing ourselves as special and more worthy, rather than more fortunate than those we left behind. Of course the middle classes, and here we are talking of the vast majority of academics, have a vested interest in overlooking the classed nature of society. To view the world through a class lens would be to focus on their position of relative privilege.

Prevailing academic discourses construct hierarchies of oppression which have nothing to do with the world outside but are all about vying for attention within academic circles. Middle-class, white feminists who focus on their oppression to the exclusion of their privilege, the eminent white, male academics who are still 'just working-class lads', just as much as middle-class male academics from public school backgrounds who are reinventing their schooling as a source of oppression, are buying into the narcissistic competitiveness of academia. A male academic suggested that I wrote about my working-class background because I wanted to compete in the academic game of being the most oppressed. However, it is not that straightforward. There is also a sense of impossibility; the psychic refusal of becoming middle-class. It is no longer an issue of not making a good enough job of passing because the process of completing three degrees has ensured that I do. Rather, it is the sense of treachery and accedence to institutionalized and socially endemic inequalities the middle-class label holds that I continue to struggle with, while needing to recognize that I am now seen as middle-class.

How can the academic feminist from a working-class background revitalize what is left of her working-class consciousness and utilize it positively? Certainly, in academia and other middle-class contexts there is a need for people who are prepared to strip away the denial and pretence, to unmask the dissimulation which we can see clearly because it was never part of our growing up. There is a culture of contempt, class contempt that is pervasive but rarely articulated. Experiencing both sides of that contempt can be used as a resource. I suggest that there can be a potentially radical role for academic women from working-class backgrounds. They have the possibility of subverting dominant discourses. Drawing on the extensive reflexivity of feminist theory and methodology, female academics from working-class backgrounds can not only theorize their complex social positioning as a complicated amalgam of current privilege interlaced with historical disadvantage, they can also highlight the intricate psycho-social processes of class experienced by the still working-class.

Commenting on the failure of academic theory to capture the richness of female, working-class experience, Roxanne Rimstead writes that

> It seems that the mundane and messy sphere of material struggle, class identification, complicity and the complexity of life in the concrete world have not been able to emerge through highly abstract language. (Rimstead, 1995, p. 211)

Although I am not suggesting that highly abstract language is always necessary, perhaps the once working-class, feminist academic can utilize her working-class experience as a resource in developing theorizations which recognize both the complicated emotional and psychological selfhood of working-class people and the material struggles that make up their everyday lives. Through such work she can show that class is much more than materiality; 'that it shapes values, attitudes, social relations and the biases that inform the way knowledge is given and received' (hooks, 1994, p. 178), while recognizing that poverty and inequality have material causes that need to be addressed. Such a theorization keeps firmly in the centre of the frame the people we really should be fighting for in a climate of increasing inequalities; not ourselves but the still working-class, black and white, male and female.

The experiences of the working classes get left out because they have no constituency in academia. This is not to be cynical but to acknowledge that academia is primarily a self-seeking culture premised on competition where class is often conscripted as a means to academic career promotion. As bell hooks points out,

> When those of us in the academy who are working-class or from working-class backgrounds share our perspectives, we subvert the tendency to focus only on the thoughts, attitudes and experiences of those who are materially privileged. (hooks, 1994, p. 185)

There have to be better ways of writing about class in academia. For too long it has been trapped in the male, Marxist mode where the focus on materiality neglects the elaborate psychological complexities of social class. Unsurprisingly, the excellent examples which exist are all feminist texts written by academics from working-class backgrounds (hooks,[1] 1984, 1989, 1994; Steedman, 1986; Walkerdine, 1990; Skeggs, 1996). Carolyn Steedman, writing about working-class childhoods, asserts:

> What case-studies of such childhood might reveal is a radicalised vision of society, of class-consciousness not only as a structure of feeling that arises from the relationship of people to other people within particular modes of production, but which is also an understanding of the world that can be conveyed to children; what might be called (as well as all the other names it is given) a proper envy of those who possess what one has been denied. And by allowing this envy entry into political understanding, the proper struggles of people in a state of dispossession to gain their inheritance might be seen not as sordid and mindless greed for the things of the market place, but attempts to alter a world that has produced in them states of unfulfilled desire. (Steedman, 1986, p. 123)

This is part of my effort to rework understandings of social class. I want to put the complexities of class inequalities on the academic agenda and have begun to try to theorize about the complicated interweavings of gender, class and 'race' in the experiences of working-class women (Reay, 1996a, 1996b). However, feminist academics from working-class backgrounds never escape those processes of compromise and compromising I described earlier. I realize that my own centring of class is part of a continuing project of reconciling what I have become with what I was, while simultaneously trying to carve out a self that I can feel at ease with.

Notes

I would like to thank Sharon Gewirtz for her very helpful and insightful comments on an early draft of this chapter.

1 Although bell hooks writes primarily from the perspective of a black feminist, in all her writings she draws extensively on her experience of growing up working-class.

References

BALL, STEPHEN J. (1994) *Education Reform: A Critical and Post-structural Approach*, Buckingham, Open University Press.

BORKOWSKI, B. (1992) 'Ausbruch und Aufbruch durch Bildung aus Milieu- und Geschlechtsrollen-Begrenzungen' ['Breaking out and up through education from milieu and gender constraints'], in SCHLUTER, A. (Ed.) *Arbeitertochter und ihr sozialer Aufstieg. Zum Verhaltnis von Klasse, Geschlecht und sozialer Mobilität* [*Upwardly socially mobile working-class girls. On the relationship between class, gender and social mobility*], Weinheim, Deutscher Studien Verlag.

BOURDIEU, PIERRE (1984) *Distinction*, London, Routledge and Kegan Paul Ltd.

CASEY, KATHLEEN (1993) *I Answer with My Life: Life Histories of Women Teachers Working for Social Change*, New York, Routledge.

CHISHOLM, LYNNE (1995) 'Cultural Semantics: Occupations and Gender Discourse', in ATKINSON, P., DAVIES, B. and DELAMONT, S. (Eds) *Discourse and Reproduction: Essays in Honour of Basil Bernstein*, Creskill, NJ, Hampton Press.

EVANS, MARY (1991) *A Good School: Life at a Girls' Grammar School in the 1950s*, London, The Women's Press.

GOLDTHORPE, J. H. (1980) *Social Mobility and Class Structure in Modern Britain*, Oxford, Clarendon.

GOLDTHORPE, J. H. (1983) 'Women and Class Analysis', *Sociology*, 17, 4, pp. 465–88.

GRAY, JOHN (1994) 'Into the Abyss?', *The Sunday Times*, 30 October.

HALSEY, A. H., HEATH, A. F. and RIDGE, J. M. (1980) *Origins and Destinations: Family, Class and Education in Modern Britain*, Oxford, Clarendon.

HENNESSY, ROSEMARY (1993) *Materialist Feminism and the Politics of Discourse*, New York, Routledge, Chapman & Hall.

HOOKS, BELL (1984) *Feminist Theory: From Margin to Centre*, Boston, South End Press.

HOOKS, BELL (1989) *Talking Back: Thinking Feminist – Thinking Black*, London, Sheba Feminist Pulishers.

HOOKS, BELL (1994) *Teaching to Transgress: Education as the Practice of Freedom*, London, Routledge.

HUTTON, WILL (1995) *The State We're In*, London, Cape.

JACKSON, BRIAN and MARSDEN, DENNIS (1963) *Education and the Working Class*, London, Routledge and Kegan Paul.

KELLY, G. P. and NIHLEN, A. S. (1982) 'Schooling and the Reproduction of Patriarchy: Unequal Workloads, Unequal Rewards', in APPLE, MICHAEL (Ed.) *Cultural and Economic Reproduction in Education*, London, Routledge and Kegan Paul.

LADWIG, JAMES G. and GORE, JENNIFER M. (1994) 'Extending Power and Specifying Method Within the Discourse of Activist Research', in GITLIN, ANDREW (Ed.) *Power and Method: Political Activism and Educational Research*, London, Routledge.

LOCKWOOD, D. (1986) 'Class, Status and Gender', in CROMPTON, R. and MANN, M. (Eds) *Gender and Stratification*, Cambridge, Polity.

LYNCH, KATHLEEN (1995) 'The Limits of Liberalism for the Promotion of Equality in Education', keynote address at the Association for Teacher Education in Europe 20th Annual Conference, Oslo, 3–8 September.

LYNCH, KATHLEEN and O'NEILL, CATHLEEN (1994) 'The Colonisation of Social Class in Education', *British Journal of Sociology of Education*, 15, 3, pp. 307–24.

OPPENHEIM, CAREY and HARKER, L. (1996) *Poverty: The Facts*, London, Child Poverty Action Group.

PAHL, R. E. (1989) 'Is the Emperor Naked? Some Comments on the Adequacy of Sociological Theory in Urban and Regional Research', *International Journal of Urban and Regional Research*, 13, pp. 709–20.

PAKULSKI, JAN and WATERS, MALCOLM (1995) *The Death of Class*, London, Sage.

PATAI, DAPHNE (1994) 'When Method Becomes Power', in GITLIN, ANDREW (Ed.) *Power and Method: Political Activism and Educational Research*, London, Routledge.

PHILLIPS, MELANIE (1995) 'Threatened, Lost, Self-Hating, Angry, Taxed, Envied and Insecure: Whatever Happened to the Middle-Classes?', *The Observer*, 2 July.

RAVEN, CHARLOTTE (1995) 'Tank Boys', *The Observer*, 30 July.

REAY, DIANE (1995a) '"They employ cleaners to do that": Habitus in the

Primary Classroom', *British Journal of Sociology of Education*, 16, 3, pp. 353–71.

REAY, DIANE (1995b) 'A Silent Majority: Mothers in Parental Involvement', in EDWARDS, R. and RIBBENS, J. (Eds) *Women in Families and Households: Qualitative Research, Women's Studies International Forum* Special issue.

REAY, DIANE (1996a) 'Insider Perspectives or Stealing the Words out of Women's Mouths: Interpretation in the Research Process', *Feminist Review*, 53: *Speaking Out: Researching and Representing Women*.

REAY, DIANE (1996b) 'Dealing with Difficult Differences: Reflexivity and Social Class in Feminist Research', in WALKERDINE, VALERIE (Ed.) *Feminism and Psychology: Special Issue on Social Class*.

REAY, DIANE and BALL, STEPHEN J. (1997), ' "Spoilt for Choice": The Working Classes and Educational Markets', *Oxford Review of Education*.

RIMSTEAD, ROXANNE (1995) 'Between Theories and Anti-Theories: Moving towards Marginal Women's Subjectivities', *Women's Studies Quarterly*, 1, 2, pp. 199–218.

SAUNDERS, PETER (1995) 'Social Mobility in Britain: An Empirical Evaluation of Two Competing Explanations', unpublished paper, University of Sussex.

SCATES, MAXINE (1995) 'Leaving it All Behind?', in ZANDY, JANET (Ed.) *Liberating Memory: Our Work and Our Working-Class Consciousness*, New Brunswick, Rutgers University Press.

SKEGGS, BEVERLEY (1996) *Becoming Respectable: An Ethnography of White Working-Class Women*, Cambridge, Polity.

STANLEY, JO (1995) 'Pain(t) for Healing: The Academic Conference and the Classed/Embodied Self', in MORLEY, LOUISE and WALSH, VAL (Eds) *Feminist Academics: Creative Agents for Change*, London, Taylor & Francis.

STEEDMAN, CAROLYN (1986) *Landscape for a Good Woman: A Story of Two Lives*, London, Virago.

WALKERDINE, VALERIE (1990) *Schoolgirl Fictions*, London, Verso.

WALKERDINE, VALERIE (1995) 'Subject to Change Without Notice: Psychology, Postmodernity and the Popular', in PILE, STEVE and THRIFT, NIGEL (Eds) *Mapping the Subject: Geographies of Cultural Transformation*, London, Routledge.

WILLIS, PAUL (1997) *Learning to Labour: How Working Class Kids Get Working Class Jobs*, Farnborough, Saxon House.

ZANDY, JANET (Ed.) (1995) *Liberating Memory: Our Work and Our Working-Class Consciousness*, New Brunswick: Rutgers University Press.

Chapter 4

Women, Education and Class: The Relationship Between Class Background and Research

Janet Parr

Introduction

This paper examines the influence of a working-class background on my early life, education, employment and subsequent return to learning as a mature student. This is then linked with my doctoral research on the experiences of mature women returners to further and higher education, using the women's own words to tell their stories.

Influences on My Own Education

Early Memories

One of the first remembered personal experiences of non-academic influences on my education was when I 'passed' the 11+ examination. I can clearly remember an aunt asking my mother 'will you let her go?' and being completely taken aback by this. It had not ever occurred to me that I wouldn't go – the last two years of primary education had been geared to 'passing the 11+'. The school had emphasized the selective nature of the 11+ and it was seen as an honour to go to the grammar school some ten miles away. Surely it had been decided on the basis of an examination that this was the right education for me, especially since I was the only girl out of the eleven pupils in my local primary school who had passed? I can remember holding my breath and waiting for an answer which was a 'yes, I think so' then keeping very quiet in case my mother changed her mind!

Another vivid memory concerns the end of my compulsory education. Attending a girls' grammar school, where I achieved eight 'O'-levels, it was generally assumed by my peers and the staff that able students would stay on into the sixth form and eventually go into higher education. For most of my friends at school, university or college was an automatic next step but there is no memory of this being a topic of conversation with my parents until I reached 16 when the topic was raised and it was made very clear to me that I was expected to leave school, get a job and contribute to the family income until such time as I married and set up a home of my own. I was, however, allowed to remain at school for a year providing I did a secretarial/accounts course which 'will always come in useful'. Although I made some attempt at changing my parents' mind, it was tentative and unsuccessful. I had had a fairly strict upbringing and was very much influenced by what they said.

It was only when studying sociology as a mature student that I began to put together the different pieces of a jigsaw to form a composite picture of the some of the major influences on my life at that time.

Extended Family and the Neighbourhood

I was born in the home of my maternal grandparents in a colliery-owned house in a mining village, almost in the shadow of the pit shaft. My paternal grandparents lived close by. My mother's father and her three brothers were miners and my father and his father were miners. My father left the pit shortly after the start of the Second World War to join the army and was killed in action when I was a few months old. My mother and I continued to live with my maternal grandparents for some years. Mum remarried when I was 4 but we did not move into a separate house, on the edge of the mining village, until after the birth of a half-brother when I was 8. The women in my immediate and my extended family either were not in paid employment or worked in manual or domestic occupations; the married ones fitted any work around the needs of the husband and any adult working sons, who generally worked a rota of three shifts over a three-week cycle. There was a clear and rigid division of labour – the women did all the domestic chores and childcare, often helping one another out, especially in times of illness. Mealtimes and household jobs were geared around the husband's shift work. The men worked at the pit, were generally responsible for the vegetable gardens, sometimes kept pigeons or ferrets and for social life mostly went to 'The Miners' Welfare' or 'The British Legion' perhaps accompanied on Saturday nights by their wives.

The infants' school was just down the road and was very much a neighbourhood school, attended by the majority of the local children. Because of the tied nature of the housing, there was at least one miner in each household in the village and all my friends' fathers 'worked at t'pit'. So the whole of my early socialization was very much influenced by one particular setting, and when as an adult student I read the Dennis, Henriques and Slaughter study *Coal is our Life* (1956) it was much like reading my own history.

Immediate Family Influences

Although my stepfather had a routine clerical job he was also from a background of manual occupations with a clear gendered division of labour within the home. He had first-hand experience of the poverty created by the economic depression and the unemployment of the mid 1930s in Liverpool where he was born and raised. From this background, any job was important and a good clerical job was better than a factory job and infinitely better than unemployment. My mother's education had been basic and she had worked in domestic and manual occupations until I was born, after which she did not work outside the home. In addition, none of my immediate or extended family, nor my stepfather's family, had experienced anything other than education within the compulsory system; they had all left school at the minimum leaving age, which for some of the older ones had been as young as 13. Only one other relative, my mother's sister, had gained a scholarship and gone to grammar school. However, she left at the minimum age of 14 and went into domestic service. University did not come within my family's experience and was never talked about.

Domestic Responsibilities

My mother had a serious accident shortly after becoming a widow and as well as being an amputee, which hampered her mobility, was prone to bouts of illness during the winter. From the age of 11, I had been running the household from time to time, doing the normal domestic chores which my mother would have done, sometimes being kept home from school. Although somewhat resentful of this, I never really questioned it – I had been raised in a culture where domestic chores were 'women's work'. Whether this was a question of class or a question of gender was not an issue at the time; it was simply what I was expected to do. However, I was very aware that friends at school, most of whom came from fairly affluent backgrounds, did not have this experience.

Many social factors then came together to influence my education underpinned by the environment in which I was raised.

Into Work

Bored at school, I left to work as a secretary/receptionist. I had a number of secretarial jobs both before and after marriage at the age of 20, none of them holding my interest for more than a few months. On getting married, I expected to do, and did, what was normal in my experience – work until children arrived, then stay at home as a full-time housewife.

However, a year after the birth of my first child, I was frustrated at home and returned to work part-time, with childcare provided by family and friends, but two more children limited work opportunities outside the home. Any subsequent work was generally casual and I can remember a feeling of restlessness.

Returning to Learning

A casual discussion with a graduate friend, whom I had met whilst running a playgroup, led to my enrolment for sociology at the local college. I was aware of a need to 'do something' and in hindsight, it is clear that I was not totally content with life as it was. I certainly had no long-term goals or 'grand plan' at this stage and had no intention of taking any examinations. Sociology was very interesting, although there were some anomalies for me. At this time, the discipline was very much in the functionalist/positivist mode and I had difficulty locating myself within this malestream structuralism. However, it did raise my awareness of the disproportionate allocation of constraints and opportunities in society.

The lecturer became a firm friend, and certainly a 'significant other', encouraging and supportive. When she suggested applying to university, I was very negative and could see many difficulties. What would my family do? How would I manage the housework? Would it affect my relationship with my husband? Anyway, university is for super-bright academics and I was not one of those. However, my lecturer friend was very persuasive and an application to a local university resulted in a request to attend for interview.

I approached the interview with trepidation, overawed by the whole setting – the building, the concept of university and that I was going to talk to university lecturers, with no idea what to expect. When the three male interviewers from three different departments were introduced, my heart sank – how on earth was I going to answer questions in all three areas? After a few general questions, though, the main concern seemed to be whether family commitments would interfere with studies and vice versa – legitimate questions as far as I could see at the time. When offered a place at the end of the interview, my feelings were ambivalent – a mixture of pleasure, pride and apprehension. These sentiments have been echoed time and time again by other women students I have met during lecturing and research.

The isolation felt in my first year at university was unforeseen. At 36, I was twice the age of most of the other students, or so it appeared, and although there were students who appeared to be close in age, no other mature student was doing the same combination of subjects. In addition, the majority of the students appeared to be from a background where university was a natural extension of their education; they seemed to be at home in the system and this made me very aware of the lack of the appropriate 'cultural capital' (Scott, 1991) in my own childhood.

My goals at university were fairly short-term – to get through the course and get a degree with little thought to a future career. Thinking about it, coping with a final year at university and a young family was probably as much as I could handle at one time. But again, the concept of 'career' was alien; providing for my own future was not something which I had seriously considered.

However, very shortly after I graduated, I was invited to talk to one or two mature women students at the local college at which I had done my 'A' levels and from this I was offered some part-time lecturing work.

A Growing Interest in Mature Student Issues

My lecturing was primarily with mature students, mostly female, many of whom talked to me about their problems. They talked, both formally in the classroom and informally at breaks, about their background, their early education, their families and current domestic situations. It seemed that women from all backgrounds were meeting a variety of barriers which might be grouped under the headings of practical, social and psychological issues. As a professional woman, a sociologist, with a growing leaning towards feminist explanations, and from a working-class background, my experiences as a mature student were seen as a valuable and appreciated resource. The students had a role model – I had done it – been to university in my mid-thirties with a husband, three children and a home to take care of, got a degree and was now in a respected profession. Many of these mature students were encouraged to go on to higher education and on becoming a part-time university lecturer, I continued with this informal support system, remembering the isolation I had felt during the first year as an adult learner studying at this level.

Back to Higher Education

Growing interest in the difficulties experienced by mature returners, and my interest in the education of adults generally, culminated in enrolment for a part-time Master's Degree in post-compulsory education and stimulated my current (doctoral) research into the experiences of mature women returners to further and higher education. This research is totally qualitative, using a grounded theory approach. Around forty-nine women, enrolled on a variety of courses in further and higher education at institutions in and around the Sheffield area, participated in the interviewing. The women come from a wide range of social situations – some women are married/partnered, some single, some divorced, and their current socio-economic positions vary, ranging from fairly affluent middle-class households to women living in a deprived area (Castle estate) which attracts development grants from the European Social Fund. However, regardless of their current position, most of them had originated from a manual working-class or routine white-collar background, and since this is my own background, I felt particularly advantaged in understanding the perspectives of the students with whom I spoke.

So in what ways have my experiences facilitated understanding in my research?

Links with the Research

With my background as a former mature student from working-class origins, it could be argued that considerable bias has been introduced into the research. However, I would go along with Sue Jones' argument that bias is not inherently bad and can be productively harnessed:

> The answer has to do with the way in which we understand and use the concept of bias, not as something to be avoided at all costs but as something to be used, creatively, contingently and self-consciously.
>
> We use our 'bias' as human beings creatively and contingently to develop particular relationships with particular people so they can tell us about their worlds and we can hear them. In doing this we use ourselves as research instruments to try and empathise with other human beings. No other research instrument can do this. (Jones, 1985, p. 48)

Jones' point here is that our backgrounds and experiences, not just as researchers but as people, are a vital contribution to good ethnographic research. The essential clause for me is '. . . and we can hear them'. Hearing implies understanding and I would argue that my background enabled an empathy and reciprocity with the interview participants and enabled the collection of much richer data than might otherwise have happened. Many feminist writers (see for example Brannen *et al.*, 1991; Reinharz and Davidman, 1992; Stanley and Wise, 1993) argue that woman-to-woman interaction enables women to be much more open about their experiences. Whilst this is largely true, Devault (1990) argues that this in itself may be insufficient and we need to take account of the differences between women:

> Women who are positioned differently learn to speak and hear quite different versions of 'woman talk', adapting to distinctive blends of power and oppression. Failures of understanding abound. (Devault, 1990, p. 98)

She goes on to discuss this issue in relation to skin colour, but there is no reason to suppose that it does not apply to class. This point was also taken up by Reissman (1987) when she argued that the cultural differences between a white Anglo middle-class interviewer and a black working-class Hispanic woman resulted in major misunderstandings by the interviewer. Mies also makes this point in rejecting the parameters of positivist methodology:

> The postulate of value free research, of neutrality and indifference towards the research objects, has to be replaced by conscious partiality, which is achieved through partial identification with the research objects. (Mies, 1993, p. 68)

Being a professional woman and a former mature student, concerned with education, but from a working-class background was an advantage in talking to the students in my research. There was a great deal of reciprocity in the interviews – students talked about themselves, but also asked questions of and about me. I told them something of my background and that my position as a lecturer and doctoral student in higher education had been arrived at by a somewhat circuitous route as a mature woman student from working-class origins. This was particularly useful when talking to the students in the neighbourhood centre on Castle estate, since my childhood had been circumscribed by some of the family and neighbourhood values about which they talked. This enabled an understanding of their ambivalent feelings about the conflicts between a desire for education and domestic responsibilities. For example, when I talked with Jenny, who lives on Castle estate, her description of neighbourhood influences sounded very familiar.

The Women's Stories

Jenny

Jenny is 37, married with three children. Her husband has been ill for the last thirteen years of their twenty-year marriage and she told me he is very resentful of her return to education. She has been studying at a neighbourhood centre for about three years, on a variety of courses which are free, supported by the European Social Fund because this is a designated deprived area. Jenny is aware of the social and cultural constraints on her life and is frustrated not only by private control, exerted within her family, but also public control, recognizing the neighbourhood norms which not only influence her husband's attitude but also serve to define her identity and lay some limitations on what she can do.

> We don't go out much 'cos of Trev's illness but I've noticed if we do go out the women sit down and have a drink when the male goes and fetches it . . . Trev's always kept me on a tight rein, never let me go out. I've never been to night clubs and things like this, but letting the man go for a drink, well he's a man, been working all day – it's acceptable. If you go in a pub, all eyes are on you. You're either two things – you're either on the game as they put it, or some bloody bloke's not got you in control . . . your husband's under t'thumb or he's a wimp or whatever they want to call them. And that's just because you go for a drink.
>
> This area that we're in now, Castle, it's still accepted that the man's the one that's the breadwinner. If the woman goes out then he's looked down on, er, so there's all that peer pressure to the males, 'What you doing letting her go out?' type of thing. It's high unem-

ployment round here, they just don't accept that there's a partnership. They were always brought up that the males went to work. My husband's one of six. I'm not saying they're uneducated but my mum-in-law's gone out cleaning, that's what was accepted. She were always in for the kids. In this area you'll find a lot of 'em's like that. They've always been there for the kids. They're not a good mother if they're not, you know? It don't matter whether they've laid on the floor, like I lay on the floor and do homework with my kids, but that don't make me a good mother. At the end of the day, if my kids have a hot meal, if they're clean when they go to school, if I'm there to pick them up, that makes you a good mother, that makes you accepted by society otherwise you're not accepted, you're like an outcast. Everybody, I don't care who they are, everybody has to conform to society in some ways, or life's made hard for you, really hard.

Even Jenny's return to education is tempered by what she sees as acceptable within the community in which she lives:

So rather than stay at home I went into education [but] I'm on call now for t'phone. In the last six months I bet I've been called out about twelve times – out of lessons, out of t'centre. It's a kind of draw – you've still got that string attached that you feel as though you're neglecting your family. It's what society puts on you, it's like a mental hold. The woman looks after the family and if you are not there for them you're neglecting them . . . But I am restricted to here. I'd love to do some type of research which I'd need to go to University or some type of higher education establishment, [but] I can't see a college being pleased if you get a phone call that says will you come out of college, t'little one's having an asthma attack! And I can't see him [her husband] letting me go on a campus life.

Education appears to be Jenny's lifeline. Remarks like these were scattered throughout the interview:

You need something like this. If it's only to keep your brain going, you know?

I've fought for what I've got. People don't realize how hard you have to fight.

It's the way that I escape the unfairness I suppose.

This student clearly feels the influence of neighbourhood norms. She talked to me freely, assuming my understanding. A childhood in a similar neighbourhood is helpful, but so, I am sure, was the fact that I am also a woman.

Jenny had moved into this neighbourhood when she married, pregnant at 16, and has been fighting the control since then. Dilys and Sheila, though, were faced with restrictive situations in their childhood, but again accepted this as normal, if unfair, at the time.

Dilys

Dilys is 34, married with two children aged 12 and 9. She is studying at a local college on the second year of a full-time secretarial course which is three days a week and a part-time social studies and humanities course which is one day a week. She also works four evenings a week. I asked her why she had not continued her education at 16.

> I never, ever got encouraged to go to school . . . my mam used to make me have time off school to clean the house . . . and so my friends – one came up to my house and another one came too and they said, 'we wondered why you weren't here', it was an exam or a mock exam or something and I was hanging washing up in the kitchen, it was raining, and I was nearly crying, I said, 'My mum wouldn't let me come to school, I've had to do the washing', and they couldn't believe it but to me it was, that was all I knew, you know. And I were cooking the tea and all this, that's how it was. . . .
>
> The deputy head advised me to go on a catering course at this college and I got on it and when they gave me the details, you'd got to pay something like £70 for a set of knives and I told my mum and my mum said, 'No chance, we're not buying them, get out of there and get a job' . . . so I told the teacher 'she wants me to get earning and get paying board', and so I got out there, got a job as a trainee manager and my mum just wanted that wage coming in . . . .

Dilys's return to education has been the culmination of many years of waiting, but what she told me reflected what many other students had said and reminded me very much of my own apprehension on returning to learning:

> I've always wanted to go back into education . . . it was reliving a childhood that I feel I lost . . . but when I came on the first day I was nervous as hell and I thought, 'God, what am I doing this for?' I was so scared, and I kept thinking, you're going to show yourself up, they're going to ask you all these things, they're going to talk about all these words that you don't know what they're talking about, and they're going to be all these posh people . . . .

Again, I could hear what Dilys was saying and feel her frustrations as a child, but we also had an empathy as mature women returners, with all the mixture of feelings that went with it.

Sheila

Sheila was born in a mining village as I was. She is in the third year of a four-year degree course with a social work qualification at a local university. Her story starts when she was quite young, at home, the youngest by eight years of five children. Her parents had made it clear that she would not be going to university when she passed her 11+, which was not the happy event she felt it should have been.

> I passed my 11+ to go to the grammar school . . . and then told not to get my hopes up because I wouldn't be able to go to university. In actual fact I think it was quite a worry to them that I was even going to grammar school for financial reasons.

> Everybody else's parents seemed to be celebrating this thing. The other people in my class at school got bikes and watches and things and you also got your name in the paper – your parents have to take your name and a letter, and that didn't happen for me. I was extremely unhappy . . . upset and angry. I felt lots and lots of mixed feelings. It's only looking back now that I also can see the worry that they had financially that I can handle all that, you know. I don't think there were any sort of thoughts at all about me achieving, I think that generally speaking my parents just thought I'd get married and that it wasn't important. But I have to say that I'm not sure how important it would have been if my brothers passed, because education didn't seem to be terribly important in any case.

Sheila felt that her education took second place to the domestic responsibilities which were expected of her as a young female. This appeared to cause considerable problems for her, particularly in school, but it reinforced the traditional gender role.

> I were very unhappy when I got to grammar school – lot of reasons, and one of them was that I always went to school with a sick feeling in my stomach when I hadn't done my homework and that were basically because at home I had jobs to do. My eldest sister by this time had just had her second child and was suffering post-natal depression, but we didn't know then it was post-natal depression . . . and I used to have to go home and look after the children. I was the youngest female and I had to go and look after the children and put them to bed after school and I had things I had to do at home.

> I didn't say anything because . . . right into finishing school I would have not had any sort of effect on my parents – my sister needed help

with the children. No, I didn't say anything because I thought it was pointless.

This is a very small part of Sheila's extremely painful story, illustrating some of the restrictions on her education. She went on to tell me that her return to education has been the fulfilment of a long-held, though maybe not always verbalized, ambition, and a redress of the unfairness she perceived as a child.

Heather

Heather was also raised in a manual working-class environment with a clear gendered division of labour. She is married with three small children and is enrolled on a full-time European Community funded course, Women into Management and Technology, at a local college.

> My dad worked in a steel works . . . my mum worked in a cutlery factory so hers were a manual job, so we used to all have us own jobs to do. Well, t'boys were older. We used to have to prepare for them. You know, we used to iron their shirts and make sure their trousers were pressed and their shoes were cleaned and all that . . . There were never any 'Ugh, why do I have to – ?'. There were none of that, 'cos it were just how you were brought up. There were no arguing, you'd got your job to do and you did it.

She told me that she had transferred this background into her marriage and whilst her partner is happy for her to do the course, he does little to help.

> He agreed I should do something I enjoyed doing, so yeah, he backed me up . . . but doesn't do anything practically to help. . . . He don't do anything in t' house . . . he wouldn't know where to start . . . he's terrible . . . but I suppose I've made him like it . . . I've carried on where 'is mother left off . . . .
>
> Me mam used to tell 'im to put t'kettle on if I were busy wi' kids, but he used to say 'that's what I pay'er for'. . . 'bloody pay her?' me mam used to say, 'you don't bloody pay'er for nothing' but he meant it really – he didn't think that were 'is job. So you've got to say well I'll leave t'ironing today and I'll do such and such today. But you can't, or I can't. I have to try, I mean, I stretch myself to such limits it's ridiculous – where I get so tired and I get ratty with kids.

Like the majority of the women with whom I talked, Heather felt totally responsible for the domestic chores and guilty if she could not fulfil her duties. From what she said, it was clear that she had been well socialized into this in her earlier years. I could empathize with her even though I had

had a supportive partner. Throughout all of my time in further education and university, I had the full support of my husband, who took on many of the roles which had automatically been mine prior to this time, for example giving the children their tea either because of late lectures or because of studying at home; bathing them; reading them a story and putting them to bed. He and the children grew much closer together, but my guilt feelings never really disappeared. Despite my increasing knowledge of sociology, my early socialization within a patriarchal working-class culture was still very influential.

Overview

Listening to the stories of many of the women I interviewed, of whom Jenny, Dilys, Sheila and Heather are a representative sample, was again like listening to my own history as a woman from a working-class background. I understood the neighbourhood pressures about which Jenny and others spoke because as a child I had lived in a similar environment and I still have contacts there. There was an empathy not only with Sheila and Dilys when they said things like 'I didn't say anything because I thought it was hopeless' and 'that's how it was', but also with the majority of women students who, like Heather, were trying to juggle domestic responsibilities and education. I was in there with them, feeling their experiences – as a woman, as a mature student and as someone who had working-class origins. And that is the difficulty – it is very difficult to untangle these influences, they clearly overlap and interlock.

Marxist feminists (see for example Bruegel, 1979; Barrett, 1988) would argue that class is paramount, and there is certainly evidence of class factors. As a female in a working-class culture, were attitudes towards my education any different from attitudes towards the education of males? Everyone in my own family had been expected to leave school and go out to work, whether they were male or female. Sheila also makes the point: 'I'm not sure how important it would have been if my brothers passed, because education didn't seem to be terribly important in any case.' So it would seem that class was a factor, but can this be separated from gender?

Radical feminists from Kate Millett (1970) to Delphy and Leonard (1992) argue from a variety of stances that it is the patriarchal structure of society which is the major influence, and again there is evidence to support this. Sheila talked of a very gendered upbringing and education, as did most of the mature students in the research. Heather's story is a lovely example of the gendered cultural influences on a woman's role. She reflects many other stories of students trying to juggle the demands of two greedy institutions – education and home – often fitting their education around their domestic responsibilities, and again this was something with which I could empathize. However, this was not restricted to women from working-class origins – women from quite affluent positions were telling me not dissimilar stories. For example, Rhona lives in a prestigious part of Sheffield and her husband is a company director on a high salary, but she still organizes her college work around cooking, cleaning and so on. Nola lives in the same area and although her partner cooks the evening meal, she has the other domestic responsibilities and feels particularly responsible for the childcare. She pays for this and her college course out of her Child Benefit because she doesn't feel it should come out of the family budget. Clearly, what women see as their responsibility cuts across class boundaries.

Conclusion

So to what extent has my working-class background helped in my research into the experiences of mature women returners to further and higher education? I have been able to use only small sections of a limited number of the women's stories. However, much of what all students said reflected my own life as a woman with working-class origins. I am sure that my own experiences facilitated a deeper understanding and an empathy with the women with whom I talked. However, I cannot extricate class background from my gender – both were influential on my life and beneficial in the research, as was my experience as a mature woman returner to education.

References

BARRETT, M. (1988) *Women's Oppression Today: Problems in Marxist Feminist Analysis*, London, Verso.

BRANNEN, J., DODD, K. and OAKLEY, A. (1991) *Getting Involved: The Effects of Research on Participants*, BSA Conference Paper.

BRUEGEL, I. (1979) 'Women as a Reserve Army of Labour: A Note on Recent British Experience'. *Feminist Review*, 3, pp. 12–32.

DELPHY, C. and LEONARD, D. (1992) *Familiar Exploitation*, Cambridge, Polity.

DENNIS, N., HENRIQUES, F. and SLAUGHTER, C. (1956) *Coal is Our Life*, London, Eyre & Spottiswood.

DEVAULT, M. L. (1990) 'Talking and Listening from Women's Standpoint: Feminist Strategies for Interviewing and Analysis', *Social Problems*, 37, 1, p. 98.

EDWARDS, R. (1993) *Mature Women Students*, London, Taylor & Francis.

JONES, S. (1985) 'The Analysis of Depth Interviews', in WALKER, R. (Ed.) *Applied Qualitative Research*, Aldershot, Gower.

MIES, M. (1993) 'Towards a Methodology for Feminist Research', in HAMMERSLEY, M. (Ed.) *Social Research: Philosophy, Politics and Practice*, London, Sage.

MILLETT, K. (1970) *Sexual Politics*, New York: Doubleday.

REINHARZ, S. and DAVIDMAN, L. (1992) *Feminist Methods in Social Research*, Oxford, Oxford University Press.

REISSMAN, C. K. (1987) 'When Gender is Not Enough: Women Interviewing Women', *Gender and Society*, 1, 2, pp. 172–207.

SCOTT, J. (1991) *Who Rules Britain?*, Cambridge, Polity.

STANLEY, L. and WISE, S. (1993) *Breaking Out Again: Feminist Ontology and Epistemology*, London, Routledge.

Chapter 5

Academic as Anarchist: Working-Class Lives into Middle-Class Culture

Kim Clancy

> It is in the end, the saving of lives that we writers are about . . . We do it because we care . . . We care because we know this: the life we save is our own. (Walker, 1984, p. 14)

> Write yourself: your body must make itself heard. (Cixous and Clément, 1987, p. 97)

Picture the scene. Three women are sitting round a table after supper.[1] The conversation moves onto issues of life and death, the meaning of life. One turns to another and asks: 'If you only had six months left to live – would you finish your PhD?' Absurd as this may seem, such a question has serious relevance in lives that are dominated by chapter deadlines and visions of the academic carrots that the prefix 'Dr' might bring. What startled me, though, was the immediacy and venom of my response. No! No! and No! again. Waste the last six months of my life writing this poxy PhD? You must be joking! 'So what *would* you do?' was the next question. Instantaneously an unexpected and extremely agreeable image flashed into my mind: It is dead of night on the university campus. My darkened figure steals from the shadows, spray-gun in hand. As I frenziedly spray graffiti all over the library walls, the bright bold letters spell out, unequivocally, my feelings towards the institution!

The conversation became increasingly merry as we explored the possibilities of penning a New Age bestseller entitled 'Freeing the Anarchist Within'. However, what it demonstrated to me was my continuing ambivalence towards the cultural and educational institutions of middle-class, middle England, those hallowed seats of learning that have kindly bid me enter – but only so far, mind! – an ambivalence which is rooted, I believe, as much in my class position as in issues of sex/gender. If, given only six months left to live, I would devote my dying days to defacing the walls of my university, what does this suggest about the nature of my relationship to academia, to books, to learning?

This chapter will explore how writers and writing, literature and reading, enabled me to leave my working-class roots and seek new identities in the alien, middle-class meccas of education, academia and the arts. 'Everyone knows that to go somewhere else there are routes, signs, "maps" . . . That's what books are' (Cixous and Clément, 1987, p. 72). I will ask: what was lost, exchanged, bartered in this journey from one class to another?

Books

Books have been my friends. Without books I would not be here. But books can also be used as barricades. It is true that words have helped me escape. I can pick up a pen and write my way out of poverty – literally. But language is an unreliable ally, evasive, suspicious, slippery. At what cost have I bought these words, exchanging one voice for another, slipping accents and identities on and off like second-hand coats until nothing in my wardrobe seems to fit?

To begin with, I used books to construct literary photofits of self. Two examples come to mind, the first from my late teens. On the morning of my English 'A' level, I rose before dawn, and stole out of the quiet house, copies of Wordsworth and Keats in hand. I headed for Ashworth Valley, the point at which the cobbled streets and terraced houses of the Lancashire mill town in which I lived reverted once more to countryside. This was real literature, this was what writers did! As I 'perched aloft' a rocky crag, red-gold sky above, tumbling waterfall below, I imagined that on that auspicious morning I too could join the elite: a good pass at 'A' level would ensure that I went to university. At that point, for me, university and literature meant the romantics – Keats, Shelley, Coleridge, Wordsworth – together with other mainstays of the English canon. That women were so underrepresented as to be more or less invisible, or that none of these male writers appeared to emerge from class backgrounds remotely similar to mine, did not pose a problem. It simply stood to reason that a 'writer' was not female or working-class, and that (miraculously) I would transcend these two states in order to join this elite crew.

In similar vein, it is interesting to read Maureen Duffy's introduction to the Virago re-issue of her first novel, *That's How It Was* (1983). She reflects upon the role of poetry in her own working-class girlhood, and the clash of class/culture which occurred when she went to grammar school. She unproblematically associates herself with Keats, her own marginalization as a working-class girl appearing not to impinge upon her ability to identity with this nineteenth-century, male poet:

> A great deal of my time was lived in a dream of verse writing, reading and learning. Much of it was spent in impersonating John Keats and imitating his odes. (Duffy, 1983, p. ix)

By the end of my first degree, the realization that my tutor thought me worthy of an MA (. . . er, what exactly is that, by the way?) filled me with joy and anticipation. English was the *only* option, and it was twentieth-century literature I was after. Also, as I tried to explain to the amiable man interviewing me for a university place, I had developed a particular penchant for a certain kind of narrative: It was always raining. The streets were wet, cold, and bleak. The landscape was grey and empty, or, alternatively, inhabited by figures whose *faces* were grey and empty. There was a central character, his (sic) worldview one of despair and alienation – an angst-ridden figure on the margins of society!

One might expect that the interviewer would have shown this manic-depressive the door! Instead he seemed to understand the points that I was trying to make: 'Oh, you mean existentialism,' he said. Did I? It sounded pretty impressive, so I nodded compliantly, as so many of we students from working-class backgrounds tend to do when confronted with an unfamiliar word or phrase. I had read Sartre and Camus while still in the sixth form but cannot recall making the connection. I wonder at this disjunction. Is it that the mind is not yet sufficiently confident (or perhaps merely not yet sufficiently trained?) to accumulate and regurgitate such terms, instead, simply sliding over anything it does not quite understand?

A further year of study. I was ripe for feminist theory. And yet, it seemed to pass me by. How? When I walk across that same campus today, see the noticeboards, the library shelves, it seems like some minor miracle. How much more fruitful and meaningful my work would have been. I was groping for feminist theories in order to make sense of, structure, simply HOLD the ideas struggling in my head. If my recollection is right, it simply was not on the agenda. My MA was written and taught by men. I do not recall feminism – or even women writers – being discussed at all. I may, of course, be mistaken in this recollection. I am sure that other MA students at the university were engaging with feminist theory. Somehow we simply did not connect. And I ask myself: how much might this have to do with class?

From the perspective of class, the problem is clear. Without the language to formulate the right questions, I could not see that what was glaringly necessary for my work to progress was feminist theory. Therefore I was not able to approach my tutors and ask to be pointed in the right direction. It is like being lost, without realizing that one is lost, and therefore not asking for directions. For me, this is such a class thing. I did not simply lack the cultural capital to challenge the syllabus or the tutors, I did not even realize there was a case to be made for such a challenge to take place. Accustomed to placing others on an intellectual pedestal, the very possibility of questioning the structure that the institution offered was alien to me.

And so I struggled on, choosing to study Nietzsche, Beckett, Kafka, Sartre and Camus, writers hardly guaranteed to lift my spirits from the abyss of self-doubt and alienation into which they had sunk! Which brings me to my second example of the working-class girl constructing and inhabiting a literary photofit.

I recall one bleak winter evening, sitting in my tiny seafront bedsit and grimly reading yet another existential tract, while the waves crashed onto the beach outside. Friends persuaded me to get my glad rags on and join the 'happy' throng at a night club, but I slunk out of the writhing, sweaty joint just around midnight. I began to walk home along the edge of the dark, blustery sea. What was the point of it all? I asked myself. Student angst indeed, but no less painful for that. The dark, crashing sea appeared very inviting – the openness, the expansiveness, in contrast to my poky bedsit, with gloomy Samuel Beckett huddled on the bed awaiting my return. Ignoring velvet dress and leather shoes, I walked into the freezing water, and continued to wade in until the dark salty waves were swirling around my waist. There was something so attractive about just letting go of it all – the turmoil, uncertainty and doubt that I was experiencing in relation to my studies, in relation to my self.

The sea had become very still. My body no longer felt cold, and there was a sense that I could simply carry on walking into its darkness, and that somehow that darkness would hold me, take care of me. Perhaps replace the books, which, it seemed, were beginning to let me down. I don't know what made me stop walking into the darkness of the sea. Perhaps a seagull crying out. Somebody shouting on the seafront. A sudden thought or memory. I only remember that my body turned, and I began to struggle out of the water, a somewhat difficult task as the tide was pulling me back and the loose, pebbly sand shifted and crumbled beneath my feet.

Back on the beach I walked quickly away from the sea and up onto the promenade. I was cold and soaking wet, clothes and shoes ruined. I got back to my room and locked the door. I lay down on the bed in my wet clothes and continued to lie there until the grey light of Sunday morning began to filter slowly into the room.

Both scenarios – the romantic and the existential – reveal how susceptible one can be to literalizing, actually becoming, the selves that one perceives to be more authentic or 'real'. I was a woman from one class attempting to enter another, and, without awareness, I took on board a particular romanticization of that state to which I aspired, a vision of self heavily invested in the literature I was reading. So the mind suffused with the nature imagery of Keats and Wordsworth constructed a tableau of herself as the solitary romantic, perched aloft a hilltop at dawn; whereas the mind full of the existential angst of Beckett and Camus constructed a tableau of herself as isolated nihilist walking into the dark ocean at midnight. Such tableaux flag up the fictionalizing of self, the masquerade, that we all engage in as social beings, regardless of our cultural identities and histories. In my own case, the literalization of these mental states suggests a self that was particularly vunerable because it was so marginalized; the conjunction of femininity, of working-classness, of my personal history/narrative, created the conditions for a fairly radical questioning of self and identity to take place.

Finally, in my early twenties, feminism lit me and I ignited. Exchanging books with friends; browsing for hours in the 'women's section' of bookshops.

Reading, reading, reading! What bliss to be alive and to discover that my feelings, emotions, confusions were shared, and that there appeared to be a culprit for them all – patriarchy! The joy with which clarity and certainty flooded through me. Reading, reading, reading! Discovering women's bookshops; joining women's bookclubs; reading *Spare Rib* and *Women's Review*; attending conferences; joining women's groups; feeling part of a much greater whole. I had finally found the kind of books which did not require a major change of sex before I could find myself, in the writer, the characters and the stories they told.

Working for a Living

I recall – with some amazement – the energy and conviction with which I approached my first term's teaching in a large comprehensive school. Desdemona was a doormat, I pointed out to the subdued English department, an unrealistic heroine, placid, pathetic, and a negative role model for girls! Male members of the department hastened to put me right: I had simply not understood the complexity of the characterization, etc. etc. Undeterred, I sallied forth in the way that only a freshfaced feminist can, setting up a Women's Group, attending NUT assertiveness training, and writing new, more radical course syllabi.

From there to a more public and powerful role as education officer in a large arts centre. Programming a cinema, editing a magazine, organizing dayschools, conferences and festivals, I was able to put my fledgling feminist vision into practice, in my choice of subjects, speakers and writers. Yet, busy as I was, trying to singlehandedly change the world, it gradually occurred to me that maybe *I* had a problem: the nagging insecurity, the lack of confidence, the general sense of fraudulence that I felt in relation to my persona as black-clad, heavy-earringed career woman in the arts. There were other women around doing similar work. But they often seemed different, exhibiting an unspoken authority and composure that I did not feel I possessed: the set of the facial muscles, the polish of the accent, the ability to make charming – if superficial and meaningless – conversation, to manage difficult situations with supercilious contempt. Was this really the state to which I aspired? I began to sense that it was less a gender thing than a class thing and attended a weekend for working-class women at the Women's Therapy Centre in London. The weekend blew me away. It was my first encounter with therapy and it turned me totally inside out. More pieces of that jigsaw masquerade, which calls itself *the* self, began to fall apart.

I began to see how my own story was shared by others; to see the way in which for many working-class daughters it is implicitly clear that in 'bettering' ourselves through education, we are simultaneously 'betraying' our roots, our culture. On a general level, by moving out of one's class one is implicitly criticizing it: this is good enough for you, but not for me. But I feel there is a specific cost to the working-class/middle-class daughter, a particularly painful struggle between middle-class daughter and working-class mother. Such a painful conflict is powerfully articulated by Carolyn Steedman in her book *Landscape for a Good Woman* (1986).

As I had already discovered in my first term at university, fitting into a new culture involves learning a new vocabulary, a new language; acquiring a shiny new accent, that heart centre of despair. I recall the discomfort of realizing that 'dinner' for my new chums meant the evening rather than midday meal; that the 'a' in 'bath' and 'path' was not pronounced in the same way as the 'a' in 'bat' or 'pat'. The implicit recognition – nobody suggested it openly – was that one way of speaking had to be unlearned and another way developed. And then – going home, to be accused of talking 'posh'.

For me, this cross-cultural clash is a bodily thing, it is physical. It is about inhabiting a body, a self, wherein the marks, traces, scars of eighteen years, are suddenly no longer good enough and must be denied. The denial of this language, this body, this self, is one cost to the working-class woman of entering the middle-class world. She becomes a Judas in the Garden of Gethsemene, exchanging her class heritage for ten pieces of silver.

And so, away from the arts, and back to academia, this time with a far greater understanding of the subtlety and complexity of the interconnections between language, subjectivity and identity. In my own research I have chosen to revisit those first ten years of my working-class childhood, to explore the shifts in cultural constructions of female sexuality in the 1960s. In my reading of the bodies of women such as Christine Keeler, Twiggy, or Rita Tushingham, I am seeking working-class heroines, those women who, like myself, like my mother, were yearning to escape. In my role as tutor I consciously try to use my position to expose the operations of power which situate myself as the expert, the authority, and my students as those who do not know.

My position is part-time and precarious, but, in many ways, I welcome this marginal status. Painful as it can sometimes be, it is also liberating, and I have chosen to perpetuate it. I do rejoice when those from less privileged backgrounds culturally 're-locate'. But I tried the career route in two institutions, and, for me at least, the further up the ladder I got, the less the place it led to seemed to offer real relevance. Is this really the meaning of life? A desk, an office, some personal power to wield, a busy day that maintains the illusion of purpose and identity?

I do, of course, believe that education can be about inner and outer transformation, about creativity and power. Why else would I be engaged in such work? But I also see how any institution perpetuates injustice, discrimination, compromise, in its hierarchies and its power struggles; how the institution can cultivate feelings of fear, insecurity and doubt, rather than engender a sense of freedom, trust and empathy. bell hooks has made this point well in her comments on career feminism (hooks, 1982, p. 191).

On the other hand, perhaps this is just sour grapes, and, indeed, who can say? Or maybe it is yet another example of a working-class woman sabotaging her chances, shooting herself in the foot, continuing to perpetuate her lack of institutional power and economic status. Is the margin the place where we working-class women feel most comfortable, because, after all, we know it so well? And yet . . . ? And yet, it doesn't really feel like that. I want alternative models of meaning to those that middle-class culture has so far offered me. I want the opportunity to redefine and reinvent myself, and help others to engage in similar transformations too. Where do I look for new roles, new possibilities of being?

Writing the Working-Class Heroine

I turn again to books. I have found my heroines in a number of locations. Many of them are writers, not all of them working-class; but most are speaking up and out from some sort of marginal position. This is how I recognize myself in their words. This is why their words mean so much to me.

The writers who have inspired me are many, but I owe perhaps the greatest debt to Hélène Cixous, to bell hooks, to Alice Walker and to Tillie Olsen. These women have been there. In their different ways they know about the struggle to define oneself rather than be defined, find community, forge alliances across differences, speak up for oneself. They put that knowing into language and their words are received by others.

Their work, together with that of other feminists, has challenged the boundaries, not only between text and reader, but also between academic disciplines, and between categories of writing, such as fiction, autobiography and criticism. It has created the spaces within which women 'silenced' in traditional arenas of cultural production – I am thinking in particular of working-class, black and/or lesbian women – can reconstruct themselves as active, creative producers of meaning.

I read Walker:

> I have not labelled myself yet. I would like to call myself revolution-ary, for I am always changing, and growing, it is hoped for the good of more black people. I do call myself black when it seems necessary to call myself anything . . . (1984, p. 133)

Or Olsen:

> As for myself, who did not publish a book until I was fifty . . . (1985, p. 38)

Or Cixous and Clément:

So I am three or four years old and the first thing I see in the street is that the world is divided in half, organized hierarchically, and that it maintains this distribution through violence. (1987, p. 70)

Or hooks:

I have been working to change the way I speak and write, to incorporate in the manner of telling a sense of place, of not just who I am in the present but where I am coming from, the multiple voices within me. (1989, p. 16)

To foreground the autobiographical is not to assume a fixed speaking subject, rather, it is to acknowledge that the self/multiple selves are constructed in the moment of writing, in the moment of reading. In this sense the working-class woman, writing these words or reading these words, now, right at this very moment, is disempowering those selves that, historically, have sought to entrap her, to silence her.

I am sobered when I read Olsen's description of the social and economic conditions which produce silence in the lives of working-class women. She compares the material circumstances of previous eras with those of the present day:

We have access to areas of work and of life experience previously denied; higher education; longer, stronger lives; for the first time in human history, freedom from compulsory childbearing; freer bodies and attitudes toward sexuality; a beginning of technological easing of household tasks; and – of the greatest importance to those like myself who come from generations of illiterate women – increasing literacy, and higher degrees of it. (1985, pp. 23–4)

It is even more sobering to read this with the awareness that the 'we' that Olsen invokes actually represents – in global terms – only a tiny proportion of women. What are the responsibilities of the handful of women – primarily Western, educated, white, middle-class – who do have access to the conditions which make 'speech' possible? Perhaps, at the very least, an awareness of the extreme privilege of our positions.

Conclusion

So where do I locate myself if I want to both celebrate a connection with my roots, and yet feel creatively alive – if not completely comfortable – in a different cultural environment? Where else but on the edges of these interconnecting worlds? As hooks (1994) has argued, the discomfort of being located 'in the margins' is ultimately worthwhile. Experiencing two worlds, but fully belonging in neither, can bring the pain of displacement and alienation. But the exile can become the outlaw: exploding the myths which accumulate around all social and cultural identities, myths which limit and constrain all women, whatever their class.

Note

1 Thank you to Sara and Margaretta for wonderful food and wise conversation!

References

Cixous, Hélène (1993) *Three Steps on the Ladder of Writing*, New York, Columbia University Press.

Cixous, Hélène and Clément, Catherine (1987) *The Newly Born Woman*, Manchester, Manchester University Press.

Duffy, Maureen (1983) *That's How It Was*, London, Virago.

hooks, bell (1982) *Ain't I A Woman: Black Women and Feminism*, London, Pluto.

hooks, bell (1989) 'Choosing the Margin as a Space of Radical Openness', *Framework*, 36, pp. 15–23.

hooks, bell (1994) *Outlaw Culture: Resisting Representations*, London: Routledge.

Olsen, Tillie (1985) *Silences*, London, Virago.

Steedman, Carolyn (1986) *Landscape for a Good Woman: A Story of Two Lives*, London, Virago.

Walker, Alice (1984) *In Search of Our Mother's Gardens*, London, The Women's Press.

Chapter 6

Something Vaguely Heretical: Communicating across Difference in the Country

Karen Sayer and Gail Fisher

Introduction

Gail and Karen first met at nursery school when they were around 3 years old, and, with one or two gaps, have known each other ever since. The key differences – re social class – in our lives today probably emerged at around the age of 15, and began as that strange mix of decision and drift which seems to steer so many of us onto one path or another in the end.

Gail decided, for her own reasons, to get pregnant at 16, then to marry; Karen decided to do 'A' levels, then to go on into higher education.

Since this 'parting of the ways', though, we have pretty much kept in touch. This has usually been by correspondence and the content of these letters has always been more reflective than 'newsy'. It therefore seemed obvious to Karen to include Gail, and to use the form of letters, when setting out to write this chapter.

In the two letters which follow, we have addressed who we are and where we are now, in relation to our class backgrounds. In the conclusion we have explored, together, the issues for feminism in what we have discussed. Since the letters were originally written we have worked on the overall piece quite extensively. However, it is still a dialogue between two working-class women who have had very different experiences of social class, and who have remained very close friends.

Karen's Letter

Dear Gail,

I've been asked to write a chapter for a book which focuses on working-class women's experiences of social class, from a feminist perspective. In order to do this I must reflect upon my own experiences; I must think about my own class identity, for example, also whether or not this is important to me, how it has changed, my relationships to others, and so on. It is about this last point that I am writing to you, as I feel that my friendship with you has been, and still is, something that is more important to me than my class identity, but that it is a relationship which may have been, or now is, shaped by class.

In fact, the only way in which I could write the chapter was to write to you. All of the academic forms of expression and writing that I have learned in higher education seemed unsuited to the process of personal reflection, even though theorized reflection. So, I have chosen this intimate or personal form of writing about my experiences, in preference to any of the usual, public forms 'more appropriate' to an academic book. It will be interesting to see if it can meet the normative standard of 'rigour' that is usually required of learned papers!

The difficulties women find in writing at all, and writing about themselves in particular, are well charted within feminist research. Feminist theorists have told women to write in, and therefore to find, their own way, their own voice. Many have addressed the question of language itself, have shown that it is far from transparent, that it helps construct reality, that it does not, in any way, simply reflect it. Other feminist writers have also stressed that the difficulty women find in writing, in making your/their presence felt as a woman, corresponds to women's wider invisibility – exclusion, pseudo-inclusion and alienation – within mainstream/malestream, traditional theories, such as those used in reference to social class.

The first time I encountered the idea of 'class' I was in the set 4 humanities group of my local, 600-pupil, comprehensive school. I don't know if you ever tackled this question in school, as we were at different schools, but it was an odd moment for me. I must have been about 12 or 13 (in 1979/80), and at that point in my school-life history and geography – possibly religious studies as well, I don't quite remember – were taught as one subject.

One day, the teacher asked us what 'class' we thought we belonged to, working, middle or upper. There was some confusion about how we could define ourselves according to these terms; we were unsure about how to classify ourselves. So, the teacher said that people whose parents did paid work of some kind, as farm labourers, or in a factory, for example, were working-class; those whose parents were teachers, or in a profession of some kind, were middle-class – the upper class was dismissed as an unlikely prospect for anyone in our set, which is quite telling in itself, I think. We then had to put our hands up when he asked 'who thinks they are working-class?', 'who thinks they are middle-class?' I remember being sure that it was better to be middle than working-class and that I was the only one to put my hand up for this 'option', as if I had a real choice.

My selection was based on my father being a driving instructor, which was a kind of teacher, it seemed to me. However, I also remember that neither I nor my teacher were completely sure about this, when I sought clarification. My very first intellectual encounter with the theory of social class therefore threw up one of its starkest problems: that it is very difficult to apply it to concrete, everyday life.

Which class do you think you belong to? Is this clear to you? And, has it changed? Would you want it to change?

My original decision that I was middle-class was, of course, equally based on the eerie sense that there was something at stake. Something which I would now call 'social status'. When I was taught about class at Portsmouth Polytechnic some years later (in 1985 to '88), the word 'status' was constantly in use. For example, in one seminar we discussed Weber's idea of class, based on that 'plurality of statuses between which an interchange of individuals on a personal basis or in the course of generations is readily possible . . . observable'.[1] At Portsmouth I was finally taught how to define class as an 'expert', but to some extent, I was still haunted by the sense that I should claim a class, that there was still something at stake.

In the relatively left-wing atmosphere of the Department of Social and Historical Studies it became obvious to me that it was 'good' to be working-class, not middle-class as I had once thought. There were also new, academic, questions raised about the usefulness of social class in pre-capitalist, non-industrial societies, which began to raise some doubts about the model for me – simply because I, like you, had come from a rural, non-industrial background. And, occasionally, once we had settled on Marx's theory as the preferred model for the duration, someone would add the cautionary addendum to their lecture that Marx – even 'complex' Marxism – was of course 'sex/gender-blind'.

Of course, as you know, I now describe myself as a feminist – whereas you, I think, are reluctant to do this? This was not the case when I went to Portsmouth. In fact, I had just got engaged and had been shocked at the suggestion that I did not have to change my last name when I married, if I did not want to. My fiancé was the son of a solicitor – quite a 'catch' – and I clung to this achievement as defining my identity in the strange new world of higher education. Phil was also important in terms of encouraging me to go into higher education; I had never thought of this as a *real* possibility until I had begun to mix with his male middle-class friends who all *assumed* they would be doing this. These friends unsettled my original sense of who I was, where I should be going, what I should try to achieve. But they never caused me to question my position in relation to gender .

I therefore came to feminist action through education, rather than the reverse. Before going to Portsmouth, I had been unable to think about my position as a woman beyond claiming the authority and status given to married/sexually mature women in our society. Higher education offered me a way of seeing myself as both subject and object in intellectual terms – i.e. it enabled me to engage in reflective activity, using feminist theory, for the first time.[2]

But why, in what way, was it now better to be working-class – in the 1980s radical academic context – rather than middle-class as I had at first thought? And what problems did the issue of the usefulness of class raise for me with my village background?

Well, just looking at my letter to you so far, I can see that I am already slipping into using a specific kind of language that is part of academic 'discourse' – the institutions, publications, etc. of higher education – and that this is clearly not a 'working-class' language. If I look at my manners, my dress, income, lifestyle, even my accent and self-confidence, I could now clearly be described as a member of the educated middle class. To use Weber again, I, as with all academics, have acquired status through the prestige of my occupation. But if I, or other lecturers, want to be radical in Marxist terms, I and they need to be, or to have been, working-class, according to the Marxist or socialist model.

I am grossly oversimplifying the experience of my tutors here, not to say my own, but there was an undeniable romance for the left in being working-class, as providing a uniquely communal identity, solidarity and therefore platform for action in the Thatcher years.

The dominant image of the working-class community at the time I remember as rather 'Hovis'-like. It consisted of cobbled streets, factories, chimneys, pubs, flat-caps and whippets. It was, on the one hand, a very male image, and, on the other, undeniably *urban*. This suited the largely male socialist and Marxist historians who taught me, who originally came from urban working-class backgrounds, but I was unable to lay claim to it. As a rural woman of class unknown – my feminist activity *and* my rural origins overrode my class identity – I was at a considerable distance from the 'Hovis' myth. Where socialist men were able to own it, and therefore provide themselves with a moral thinking based on it, in a world which seemed increasingly morally bankrupt (at least as far as the left were concerned), I had to find an alternative moral framework that was closer to my conception of myself.

This takes me back to the key question, for me, of the applicability of 'social class' to non-industrial contexts, and to our childhood in the countryside. The feeling that the worker 'had to be boiled in the factory pot' before *he* would revolt accords with the widespread view that country people are innately conservative. The male peasant is a generic kind of 'Hodge',[3] the female a buxom wench, the countryside a site of leisure, not 'work'.

Now, much of my research has looked at the formation of exactly these kinds of images, and the way they impacted upon the lives of nineteenth-century working-class women in the countryside. I finally published on it in 1995 as *Women of the Fields: Representations of Rural Women in the Nineteenth Century* with Manchester University Press.[4] And I am continuing to pursue the subject in my current research on the country cottage, which you helped me formulate.

This dogged attachment to one area of inquiry comes from my own, unacademic, gut-feeling that these images are both unfair – immoral even – and remote from my experience of country life; that they are produced by the marginalization of rural issues, concerns and experiences. This marginalization has happened because of the hegemony of the city, in my view. The process of industrialization, the development of capitalism in the country is rarely admitted. In the country industrialization is seen as a kind of fall from grace, whereas in the city it is considered to be a form of progress. Culture – the City – is superior to, and always divided from Nature – the Country – the one being defined against the other.

There has been a lot of work done by feminist theorists on the way in which paired opposites like this characterize Western, patriarchal thought. As a 'theory of society' class itself is characterized by oppositions like middle-class/working-class; or, in everyday language, haves/have-nots, and so on.

Where is this taking me? So far: firstly to the realization that it is very hard to apply an urban-defined social model to the countryside, where it will automatically become ambiguous, opaque and unstable. Secondly to the recognition that class has also been defined in such a way as to marginalize women, so that theories of class have had little or nothing to do with working-class women's experiences, even when/if they are applicable to working-class men. Thirdly to the conclusion that, in the light of these points, it is not surprising I have remained unable to fix my class position. In fact, I tend to prioritize identities rooted in 'friendship', 'family', 'feminism' and the country when talking about myself, as the basis for action, as my moral framework. In fact I remember playing a game with you where you have to fold up a piece of paper into a kind of star which you then stick on your fingers. Your friend asks a question and the star is opened and closed in sequence until it reveals an answer – written on the inside. All the answers I put in my star centred on being a 'country-girl' and hating the town. This sense of opposition to the city on my part has stayed with me.

Of course, it is much easier to decide what somebody else's class is than to pick out your own! When I asked Mum about my class she was quite clear that I am working-class, while my friend and colleague Ruth felt able to say, exactly, 'upper-working-class, bordering on lower-middle-class'. My class only becomes 'visible' to me when I experience a vague sense of annoyance with the kind of people I would describe as 'snobs', 'pretentious', 'bourgeois', 'stuck up', etc. It is also apparent at odd times when I feel the need to prove that 'I have not changed', that 'I'm no different to you really' with people I grew up with. Otherwise, my class becomes a resource for me, which helps me to relate to and mentor my students. In other words, it is a fluid relationship.

It is almost impossible to stop and think at any point in time 'what class do I belong to now?' because of this fluidity. It is only possible to think about it, if at all, in terms of my lived relationships with others. It also seems that there is a lag between the class that I was born into and the one I have 'achieved'. My status has shifted a little, enough to make me feel uncomfortable with both the haves and the have-nots. This is revealed to me either when I feel self-conscious about the wages I earn, or, when I, like many other educated, originally working-class women, feel uncomfortable with some of the 'rules' of the academy.[5] I am in a sense both working-class and middle-class. This is due to the effect of my education, but I should also say that I have always had this kind of split, as Mum and Dad have also experienced this 'lag'.

Mum and Dad were always keen that I should 'get on', be successful in whatever I did. Sometimes they talked about this in terms of education, but mostly they were just supportive whenever I had an idea about what I fancied doing. Once they suggested I set up a bed and breakfast business, but I didn't fancy the cooking. I grew up in a pretty large house (an ex-pub), and, of course, Dad was a driving instructor who owned his own business, while Mum looked after the petrol station attached to the house and did the housework. We went on holidays abroad – off-season, when Dad had a slack period.

When I go back over my childhood in these terms I can see that it was not 'typically' working-class, it was very different to yours, but setting the material points aside, I can also remember that Dad thought I wouldn't want to know them once I had gone to Portsmouth, and that both of them were impressed when they met someone who had a degree – a little fearful even. Mum was concerned that there would be a difference in station between me and my solicitor's-son boyfriend (I was in fact very confused by his family's codes and rules at first), both Mum and Dad used phrases such as 'the likes of us', and both of them always expressed respect for the local landowners, wealthier farmers and professionals who lived in the area.

Mum and Dad left school at 14 and went to work, Mum as a secretary in a print factory, Dad as a mechanic in a boat-yard. The house was bought with the help of a council mortgage when the pub closed – Dad's dad was the landlord, Mum's parents ran the village shop. The furniture is largely inherited; they never throw anything out – it might come in useful. Mum keeps the books for both businesses – as in most working-class families, where the wife looks after the household budget – and they generally 'muddle through'. They dress to be practical, not fashionable. I grew up in second-hand clothes (except for my school uniform), which were well suited to all the tree-climbing you and I did in our youth. Mum still does all the cooking, with the main meal – dinner – in the middle of the day, and tea at around 5 p.m. They don't have dinner-parties, and everyone eats off their laps watching TV – except for the odd birthday tea, and Sunday lunches. They live in the house as a working as well as domestic site; people come in and out of the kitchen all the time and use the back door. None of this is quite middle-class is it?

The village we grew up in, of course, hardly provided an arena in which to make our own way. It can best be described as a parish in which about fifty-five women, men and children live, scattered through various farms – now mostly owned by large companies, managed by external representatives – with small clusters of labourers' houses and the odd manor house, now owned by professionals who have come in search of the rural idyll. It hardly provides scope in which to make a living. The only work available in the village is on the farms – now greatly reduced by mechanization and generally part-time or casual – everyone else must leave to find employment, or commute. When I asked Mum about this she and I worked out that most of the people of my age had left – except your brother who is a pigman and possibly a couple of those who grew up on farms, who now help their parents – and that only three people of her generation who had grown up in the village still live there. The country community is far from static or stable.

Mum and I noticed that those who live in the village are also all white. This probably includes my family, but this was not particularly clear to either me or mum when we discussed it. My mum's dad was born of a white man – who managed a tea plantation in Darjeeling – and an Asian woman – who was the daughter of the landowner. This couple had married at the cost of being disinherited by both of their families. My granddad had been one of seven sons and four daughters, and had left India to be a Rhodes scholar. The First World War had intervened and he eventually ended up working as a casual labourer in East Anglia. He finally married my grandmother, who was a housekeeper in Stockton, and his family then helped them set up the village shop. My mum had always told me this story, and I have always laid claim to this part of myself and our family history – it formed a magical, romantic story for me in my childhood. But I have still always been able to lead the privileged life of a white woman. There was only one black girl in my comprehensive school – a couple of years below me – otherwise I only met people of colour abroad. This has made 'race', not just class, a complex, hidden and uncomfortable issue for me, especially when I left home, even though – or partly because – I was aware that I must not be 'prejudiced'.

What is striking to me throughout this brief description of my family, of my upbringing and childhood surroundings, is that it is clearly not urban. I was always, and still am, as thrown by urban working-class, fashion, manners, 'streetwise'ness, body-language, and 'house-proud'ness, as by urban middle-class etiquette. 'Race' only became a problematic relationship, rather than a romantic story, for me when I entered the city. In the end, my education was an escape from the countryside, rather than an escape from my class. I had no ambition, as such, when I was 15/16, I just needed a way of making a living, and a way of leaving a place that held no real opportunities for me.

I hope this makes some kind of sense to you, I'm groping around in the dark here to find a way of saying that I often feel we have more in common, as countrywomen, than we might with women from the city, regardless of the different paths we have taken, our different status, because of our shared moral values and experience based in a rural identity. That social class can never totally accommodate all of the experiences we, as *rural* women, have. Write back soon and tell me what you think.

Karen

Gail's Letter

Dear Karen,
There seems something vaguely heretical in using the written word in connection with working-class women, when the main method of communication

between us would normally be verbal, informal and subjective. It makes your concern over the use of notes peculiarly apt, and the use of them oddly appropriate.

I don't remember the subject of social class being raised at any of the schools I attended, certainly not in an educational context. So my knowledge of class is entirely in the realms of life experience. From that point of view the main and most noticeable 'differences' are purely practical, and relate to the rural background we share.

When you first asked me to consider what belonging to a class meant to me, my first reaction was that the 'working class' is the only social class that people do not aspire to! It is considered somewhere you work yourself up from. 'A nice place to visit, but you'd not want to live there!'

Which seems to suggest a level of shame in staying put. Not something I feel. Of course it's not as simple as that, we have this urge, a drive to compete, to succeed, and moving up the social ladder gives people a concrete way to measure their personal worth within the framework of the society in which they live. But a definitive description? I don't see how one is really possible when so much of our 'selves' is invested in the experience of living within whatever group we find ourselves in that the notion of description itself is highly subjective. Which brings me to my reluctance to describe myself as a feminist. I may wholeheartedly agree with the principles involved, but that isn't the issue for me. I have acute problems with the way *descriptions* are used as labels. Too much is assumed when someone else calls us by a label. Our politics, religion, hopes, dreams and aspirations, how we live, where we live, who we actually are as individuals is brought down to a common denominator and a label slapped on, and the actual individual submerged beneath that 'assumption'. My reluctance to call myself a feminist is a part of my awareness of who I am set apart from any of the roles I am expected to play. Like my description of myself to my children when they call me 'Mum'. 'Mother is what I do, Gail is who I am.'

My views are shaped by my environment and the assumptions others automatically make on learning I am from the countryside. My accent, the way I dress, my background give people enough reason to dismiss me because of the assumptions they make about who I am and my areas of interest, as it is, without my voluntarily assuming any description which may only address one aspect of who I am.

My family has not greatly affected my way of viewing myself as working-class; however, they and that social class have imposed interlinking restrictions. My father's insistence that I work rather than go on to further education, my mother's notion that it wasn't worthwhile pursuing my interest in art, because it was 'inappropriate'. This was tied up in the idea of the course my life was supposed to take, because of the social class I was born into. My parents concentrated on the practical and the immediate, which does seem to be a trait linked with being working-class. I suppose if living day-to-day is hard enough, looking forward becomes impractical, the focus has to be on immediate needs. Further education would have meant I was a continuing drain on the low wage my father earned as a farm labourer. There was the attitude that my brothers could continue in education, if they wished, but then it was expected to be in the line of vocational training.

The general practical problems with further education for me personally were with public transport, in other words, it was, and still is, practically non-existent in the countryside.

The immediate and practical for me, now, can be given a rough description by the following.

Living where we do now it's a mile to the nearest phone box, post box and road wide enough for two cars to pass. Being working-class usually means living near, at or under the poverty line. So we do not have a phone, we have a car. Not particularly because we can afford one, but because it's necessary. Because we cannot really afford it, we maintain and repair it ourselves, outside, in whatever the weather throws at us.

Likewise, we have an open fire, and the odd job or two we might be able to do for our neighbour, a farmer, may be paid for in wood. Dead trees, standing often in the middle of fields, accessible only when weather and growing season permit. Coal is a luxury, wood is damned hard work! If more people tried standing in the open, splitting logs with a wind chill factor of $-10°C$, were only able to afford enough fuel to heat one room, had to get up to ice 'ferns' on the inside of the bedroom window, they would have a greater understanding of 'there's nothing like a real fire'.

This, and other rose-tinted notions of what life is like, or rather what life *should* be like, in the countryside mean a growing rural population of the 'middle classes', who are so attached to their notion of the rural myth that they believe they have more right to implement that myth than the working-class rural person has to live and work in the countryside.

As you know, for some reason people have this inability to see the countryside for what it largely is, an industrial landscape. Green fields are little more than a very, very slow-moving production line. The lambs in the field are someone's Sunday lunch. The apples are 'fresh' (perhaps being stored chilled for months before being offered for sale). The grass is supposed to always be green and sweet-smelling, the sky is supposed to always be blue. It is always 'quiet', 'peaceful'. This doesn't take into account lorries, tractors, harvesting machinery, travelling very slowly along roads barely one car wide! It ignores the fact that harvesting has to happen when the crops are ripe, the weather fine, so that the noise of working machinery can go on very late into the night, and, of course, the eternal 'problem' with smell! This isn't a very 'pretty' picture, I know, but then, reality isn't often equated with aesthetics is it? You know it is difficult for people to accept that the myth is just that, a myth. If closing down one of the few employers in the area means less work for those born into the working class in that area, and the prices they as 'middle/upper-middle-class' professional people can afford to pay for houses is so far above what the average working-class person can hope to match, it is nothing to 'do' with them, not something they are willing to listen to, and certainly not something they want to do anything about.

If you look at the type of housing being built in rural areas it is patently obvious that the working classes are not the target buyers, and that we are being slowly pushed from the country into the towns; those coming into rural areas do not view this as their problem, they have paid for their piece of the myth, and want what they believe the countryside should be like.

Finding employment in the countryside is not easy, and as time goes by, the opportunities are becoming rarer, especially for women who have traditionally been involved in field work. Mechanization in agriculture is largely, but not solely, to blame; like any 'change' there are many 'causes'. The rural working-class woman has little in common with the new arrivals in the countryside, and is often considered subtly inferior. Old assumptions about the lifestyle, intelligence, even cleanliness, of the working-class woman as housekeeper haven't gone away. Like sexism, they've just gone underground! As newcomers increase, the working-class woman is invariably pushed into the background. Playgroups which were originally run by the working-class women as a way of meeting, sharing experiences and advice, have become the concern of the middle-class newcomers, and there is little common ground to work from. When we are outnumbered the immediate concerns such as the nearness of these 'meeting places' is outweighed by the 'facilities' which may be offered in the next village hall along. This is little problem for someone who has two cars to a household, but it is a real barrier for those who do not.

Increasingly, the rural working-class woman who has made the decision to have a family is finding herself isolated in an environment which offers little hope of a future in the area she was brought up in and would prefer to stay in, given a choice.

These, for me, are some of the 'practicalities' of being a rural working-class woman. Coping with these, and other problems, is how I measure my independence from the restrictions brought about by being who I am, where I am.

What is more important, more immediate, but intrinsically interwoven with the notion of social status and class, is the notion of integration between the classes. I believe the nature of friendship is based in shared experience, and our background has influenced and will continue to influence our lives. Class is another label, at the end of the day I have to look at life from the point of view that 'I am myself, you are yourself, equal but different', and the differences provide me with as much of a key to understanding myself and others as the similarities.

Gail

Conclusion

The two letters we have written clearly show the differences in our current circumstances and class positions, but also that we still have a lot in common, can still share experiences and cross gaps between us that might seem unbridgeable. In other words Karen can talk with Gail about the practicalities of country life, while Gail can equally talk with Karen about the intricacies of class theory. We can do this because, to some extent, we share an interest in rejecting conventions and because of our commonality of background, in other words, because we are both unconventional countrywomen.

From our letters it also becomes apparent that feminism means different things to each of us, but that in some senses our experience of it is similar.

To Gail it is obvious that the differences between women are as important as the commonalities. The concepts of feminism are not usually discussed or decided by working-class women, let alone by those that remain in the country. New moves in feminism don't reach out or down, far enough or fast enough. This needs to be addressed.

For Karen, the differences in the experience of learning about feminism, and in being able to take on this 'label', are significant and need to be tackled if feminism is going to attract younger women in the future.

Both of these concerns seem to be about the same thing, communicating across difference. One of the reasons that working-class women generally have little interest in learning about feminism, however, is the language – phrases like 'communicating across difference' do not help!

Notes

1 Now, here I come to a difficulty in writing. If this is to become an academic paper, I must place a reference or a note here – to show where the quote I have just used comes from. In fact, many scholars, feminists included, now see notes as a site for the expression of marginal ideas, where they can add extra comments, provide leads and say occasionally outlandish things. But, can a note be used in a letter? Given these points, I will use notes here only in order to add odd points of information, or comments, and will not reference any academic texts. Strangely enough, I have no idea where this particular quote comes from – though presumably it is by Weber – as I found it in my first-year lecture notes, not exactly a 'legitimate' or rigorous source!

2 I believe that this form of 'consciousness-raising' has now become increasingly important for younger, working-class, women, who were not and could never have been part of the rise of second-wave, often middle-class, feminism in the 1970s. Elements of the feminist argument are so much part of our culture now – e.g. having the right to vote, access to higher education and the professions, the existence of the Equal Pay Act and the Sex Dis-

crimination Act – that the ways in which women now come to recognize their social position as women have changed dramatically. Sexism has become very subtle since 1975. Hence, I often hear my women students – who are mostly working-class, by virtue of the university they have come to – explain that they do not need to be, or are not, feminists, because women have equality now and they themselves have never been oppressed. This changes as they work their way through the institution; partly through experience, but mostly due to being offered new ways of seeing.

3 'Hodge' being the familiar name given to country *men* from the mid nineteenth century.

4 Incidentally, my education has obviously affected my class position, but it has not had as great an effect as it might have, as the path I have taken has been a kind of 'Cinderella' route. This has been shaped by education policies which have been directed towards greater access to education – in some cases aimed at opening doors specifically for the working classes. I went from a comprehensive school to a sixth-form college – bussed to both by free coaches – to a polytechnic (on a full maintenance grant – one of the last) – into a new (1960s) university, and then to work in a new (1990s) university. This change in the extent and availability of education has undoubtedly changed its prestige, so that the status I might have gained from my current occupation is not a great as it once was.

5 I often feel inarticulate and clumsy in this supposedly elite environment – as if I were a country 'hick'. This is probably partly due to issues of gender, and to do with the 'rules' of speech, i.e. spoken language, to do with my 'country' identity, but is also clearly connected with class as I have heard originally urban working-class men say a similar thing in this case. There is an *Educating Rita* aspect to this, though it is not an issue for me in terms of my friendship with you and my family.

Chapter 7

'You're not with your common friends now': Race and Class Evasion in 1960s London

Shani D'Cruze

My academic, historian's frame of mind persuades me that class consciousness means experiencing a set of shared interests; a location of self as participating in certain cultures; an appropriation of particular narratives of people, society and history as components of self-identity. If this is the case, class conscious-ness is something which my own social identity has never managed to get exactly right. This chapter represents a personal effort at making some sense of such things. This isn't academic writing, though it leans on an historian's intellectual training. It draws on fragments of recuperated memory, on family papers and photos and on long phone conversations with my mother. It ad-dresses the issues around my own on-going sense of personal oddity, of cul-tural outsiderness, of not quite belonging. For me, as an historian, one of the places to look to explain such discontinuities might be in the historically located ways that class intersects with gender, age and race. I'll begin with one particular recollection.

This memory is of the day Dad and I went to Safeways. It wasn't a regular occurrence. I was somewhere between 9 and 12 years old. The memory has a weekday feel about it, because Dad was wearing his going-to-the-office over-coat. We didn't have a trolley. Perhaps we had been sent out late in the day for something forgotten in the weekly shop. Anyway, for a household on a tight budget, sending Dad to the shops for more than a couple of items was always a risky business. He could leave home with a ten-shilling note (50p) and a list that said 'Bread, Milk, Stork, Toilet Paper' (total cost then, around 2 to 3 shillings / 10 to 15p) and come home three hours later with threepence (1.5p) change, a huge tin of pineapple chunks (very expensive), milk chocolates for Mum (she likes plain) and a tortoise.[1]

Safeways was the first proper supermarket in Sydenham (London SE26). Before Safeways there was only Sainsbury's with its decorated tiles and the wooden counters round the shop where you had to queue separately for cheese, eggs, or dry goods. I remember its smell, the serving assistants in white overalls, being left to mind the pram containing younger siblings, or being sent to stand (embarrassed) in one queue whilst Mum was in another. Safeways did a lot to change our diet – the frozen chicken; Angel Delight; olive oil for salad dressing (as well as the treatment of children's earache); bean sprouts; the occasional mango; the okra which Mum boiled up in the English style, producing a rather bitter and glutinous mess. Not, mind you, that we had been unaware of exotic eatables before that. We had two sources of supply and knowledge. Firstly, Mum's father had run a greengrocery business, so she was used to interesting fruit and veg. I'll return to this side of the family later. Secondly, my dad worked as an accounts clerk in a firm of fruiterers in Covent Garden. Bruised or back-of-the-lorry peaches, strawberries, asparagus, tangerines and mushrooms came to our table in the 1950s and early 1960s even though they were far too expensive at the local greengrocer, if they showed up there at all. At the same time we were eating our way through lamb curry, not served *à l'anglaise* with pudding rice, boiled potatoes and frozen peas, but with patna rice and hot lime pickle. Later on, when Safeways arrived, there were pappadums, too. The hot lime pickle came from an acquaintance who sang in the same church choir as my parents. The culinary expertise (the okra incident was far from typical) was Mum's. This was a skill acquired in defiance of her mother-in-law, who thought Mum's cooking was not adequate for her son's dietary requirements. For the D'Cruzes are an Anglo-Indian family. My paternal grandfather was (in 1930) an Assistant in the prestigious firm of Jardine Skinner & Co. Dad spent his childhood in Calcutta. He had a public school education at La Martiniere College. La Martiniere was a high-status establishment founded in 1836 chiefly for European and Anglo-Indian children (Abel, 1988, p. 57). Dad left La Martiniere in 1930. He worked in the Civil Service and, like his father, in a commercial firm. He left Calcutta for the 'Mother country' in the spring of 1948, eight months after Indian Independence (14th August, 1947). He met my Mum not long after through the evangelical church they both attended.

What a wealth of cultural and historical signification there was in the remembered family kitchen table of my own London childhood. Lamb curry and rice, brinjal pickle followed by a one-fifth share of a rather flavourless mango. Sunday lunch of roast frozen battery chicken, bitter where its gall bladder had burst (we children would fight over whose turn it was to eat the leg) and a pudding of those tinned pineapple chunks served with Butterscotch Angel Delight. There are narratives here about material consumption and mass marketing, about imperial pasts touching at once my own family life and the world market for mangos and pappadums. There is an insight about the boon of convenience foods to working mothers in the post-war labour market engaged in a perpetual, invidious balancing act between scarce time and scant income ('Mum, why don't you make us chocolate cake any more, we don't like Heinz steamed puddings?'). Our family diet also reflected aspirations of social mobility (we ate 'pudding', you notice, not 'sweet' or 'afters'). It reflects ideals of betterment through education, of a liberal curiosity about the world and an appreciation that 'different' didn't necessarily mean 'worse' (plain boiled okra excepted) and certainly always meant 'interesting'. I certainly knew no one else at my all-white primary school who ate like that. I was the only kid in my class with an Urdu first name and a complicated surname. I was also the only one who knew how many pice there were in an anna and how many annas to a rupee. I knew about Mahatma Gandhi and Jawaharlal Nehru. Nehru in particular seemed very glamorous, great and good by comparison with Macmillan, Douglas-Home or Wilson. Nehru's successor Lal Bahadur Shastri didn't come up to the mark at all in my adolescent judgment. Indira Gandhi was a great improvement and became a model of What Women Can Do. Luckily for my own development it was not until much later that I began to understand that there was also a downside to her political techniques. In many ways the India-thing was a compensation for the trials of being adolescent, too clever for my own good, pushy, gauche, with frizzy red hair, glasses and a funny name. I wanted to be a pretty blonde and to be called Jayne or Linda. But then didn't we all? I would have died for a satin party dress with a sticky-out petticoat (which we couldn't afford), but the only sticky-out thing about me in those days was my teeth.

I was aware from an early stage that there was something different about my father and his family. They spoke differently. They said 'put it by' instead of 'put it away'. He taught me to lay out my long division sums in a different way to that taught at school (which raised some comment). I still do it his way. While most English adult women I knew wore their hair short and 'permed' my paternal grandmother had long white hair which hid in a bun at the nape of her neck by day but spent the night in a long, long, long plait down to her waist fastened with pale blue ribbon. It didn't look quite grown up somehow, particularly since she was a tiny person. She nevertheless had a habit of command. We fetched and carried for her when she came to stay – mostly, I have to admit, with the ill grace of childhood. ('But Granny, I want to watch *Top of the Pops*'). She was not inclined to bustle. Alone indoors she would watch the almost dry washing get draggled in the rain then remark to my mother with some asperity that she should have brought it indoors before leaving for work. My mother, who had learned with a jolt when first married the amount of deference and servicing that her mother-in-law expected, attributed it to Granny's earlier life surrounded by SERVANTS. Both Granny and Dad managed to convey something of the inferiority of SERVANTS. Dad in many ways was a kind and tolerant father – so tolerant that it was another of my mother's frustrations that all the telling off was left to her. But one of the things that regularly made him screw up his face in disapproval was when we walked around the house in bare feet. To him this was the mark of low caste. We were acting like 'the sweeper's children'. For some years our downstairs neighbours were a Pakistani family. To Granny these people were 'Hill Indians', or 'Bengalis', which explained both their uncivilized ways and their unattractive appearance. Indeed, our downstairs neighbours *were* rather short and square of build, but then, so are the D'Cruzes.

I can find an explanatory framework for some of this in the history of the Anglo-Indian community in British India. There had been people of mixed European and Indian blood in the sub-continent since the Portuguese settlements from 1498, but the advent of the men of the British East India Company from the seventeenth century rapidly expanded the mixed-race population, who were useful to the British in subordinate positions in the administration and the military. Calcutta, founded by the East India Company in 1698, came to be a prosperous trading city and the home of a large Anglo-Indian community into the twentieth century. Anglo-Indians retained their strong identification with the British throughout the nineteenth century, dying alongside them in the Indian Mutiny (1857). The British remained somewhat ambivalent about the Anglo-Indians, however, perceiving them as more Indian than British and certainly racially and culturally inferior to themselves. Nevertheless, post-mutiny suspicions of the native population secured the Anglo-Indians reserved white-collar occupations in the subordinate (Uncovenanted) ranks of the Civil Service and in public works, in particular the mail and telegraph service and the railways. Thus in class terms, notwithstanding a few high-flying exceptions, Anglo-Indians formed an occupationally distinctive part of the lower middle class. They were mostly urban dwellers in an overwhelmingly rural, peasant-based economy. Their economic and political dependence on the British Raj reinforced their social and cultural identification with the British. Secure, if often low-paid, salaried occupations left them a capital-poor community and proved a disincentive to their diversifying into other skills and occupations. They formed a recognizable interest group which became increasingly politicized after the First World War. They formed associations and shared leisure activities often based on the local Railway Institute, or institutions like the Rangers Club in Calcutta (formed 1879) or around Christian religious groups who were also key in organizing schools delivering European education. They wore Western dress, spoke English, and married either other Anglo-Indians or lower-class British (often soldiers).[2]

Thus Anglo-Indians weren't quite a class. Abel defines their consciousness as that of a 'community'. There were Indians in equivalent occupational positions and not all Anglo-Indians were on the white-collar boundary between middle and working class. They might identify with a British administrative elite, but they certainly were not part of it. Furthermore, in distancing themselves from Indian culture, Anglo-Indians would have perceived themselves as outside the caste system. I do, however, think that there were ways in which the cultures of caste *and* class may have helped shaped the consciousness of Anglo-Indians. The relationships between class and caste in early-twentieth-century India is a topic far too complex to properly explain in a chapter of this type, even were I qualified to do so. Nevertheless, my limited studies have raised some points that have made me ponder. The four broad groupings (*varnas*) established in Sanskrit texts of Brahmins (priests), Kshatriyas (warriors), Vaishyas (merchants) and Shudras (servants) were too generalized to form a basis for action (Moorhouse, 1983, p. 102). It was the myriad subdivisions or *jatis*, all of them local and 'united by a varying degree of occupational identity, common rites and customs, and taboos on marriages or eating outside the group' (Sarkar, 1989, p. 158) that had immediate social, and increasingly (as the independence movement and mass electoral politics developed) political effect. The compositions and status of *jatis* was not fixed and unchanging, but actively negotiated, particularly after the 1901 census when the British attempted to classify them according to their 'social precedence' (Sarkar, 1989, p. 55). Moorhouse (p. 102) compares the 'very fine distinctions' of class protocol of British India to the caste system and Sarkar (p. 158) refers to modern historians who have argued that, at least in some cases, caste conflict could provide a vehicle for class conflict. Nevertheless, the institutionalized and ritualized complexities of caste, its marriage prohibitions and most importantly its use of pollution beliefs, seem to mark a far more nuanced and acute expression of status difference than existed, for example, amongst the English working and lower middle classes in the early twentieth century. Sarkar (p. 158) notes that in some regions 'the lower castes were supposed to pollute not only by touch but by sight'. Mary Douglas' (1991) social anthropological work on pollution beliefs indicates that they are used to establish boundaries where things are changing or unclear. Anglo-Indians aspired to the mores of British India's middle-class and upper-class cultures, yet manifestly this was an aspiration incapable of realization, and they were subject to both structural and informal exclusionary practices. They were also living within a caste society which operated formalized pollution rituals to mark boundaries of social status. Their own social position was marginal and liminal, positioned between the Indian and the British. Undercurrents of prejudice concerning mixed blood – 'miscegenation' – recurred periodically from both sides. Things were unclear. From the point of view of Anglo-Indians, attempts to distance themselves from Indian culture and society can to an extent be read as an attempt to protect from pollution, to preserve 'caste'. Perhaps attempts to model their culture, occupations and social relations on the British can be interpreted in terms of an (unsuccessful and probably wrongheaded) attempt to identify by 'class'.

British rule in India depended on the compliance of Indian elites, some of whom were left to rule substantial territories unmolested by colonial administration. British and Indian upper classes mixed socially in India, creating a shared cultural arena based on hunting, sport and socializing, though of course this begs questions about the differential experience of Indian women, English women and men of both races. From the later nineteenth century and increasingly after the First World War, political pressures for 'Indianization' had led to the opening up of career paths for elite or talented Indians into the upper echelons of civil and public service, often with degrees from Indian universities. From the point of view of Anglo-Indians, however, 'Indianization' meant increasing competition for jobs with no compensating opportunities for career development. The European education, to which they clung as an entry into white-collar work and as a mark of their cultural association with the British, led to Cambridge University Entrance Examinations (exactly those which my father sat at La Martiniere in the 1920s). Few Anglo-Indians had the wealth to make their way into European universities, and Cambridge examinations did not prepare them for Indian universities. Anyway, their entry into white-collar jobs under the Raj had hitherto been so secure they paid little attention to higher education.

The movement for Indian self-determination, developing from the first Indian National Congress (1885) and far more assertively after 1918, effectively left the Anglo-Indians high and dry. Their historical and robust alliance with the British predisposed them to stand aloof from independence movements, until by the 1930s they became sufficiently organized and politicized to argue their corner as a 'minority group' and finally secured for themselves certain safeguards for employment and education after Independence. Nevertheless in the political ferment of the 1940s independence struggle their interests preoccupied the British far less than the much more dangerous problems of Hindu-Muslim conflict. A good deal of the historical, economic and cultural rationale of the Anglo-Indian community left India along with the British and those that remained did so with their vestigial privileges held essentially at the grace and favour of Nehru's state. As Moorhouse (p. 144) says, in the end the Anglo-Indians 'felt that history in some puzzling way delivered to them far less than it had promised; that the patrons in whom they had placed such trust had sold them short'.

As Abel (1988, p. 29) argues, if the Anglo-Indians had long formed a distinctive community, historically they increasingly became one marked by marginality. Their cultural position was defensive and their economic situation was dependent. Little wonder, then, that such a community should seek to establish clear boundaries between itself and native cultures and society. I wonder if this marginality can do something to account for the rather contradictory messages that my father's origins brought to my growing up. Firstly, I learned that his Indianness was different and interesting. There were stories about his school, his home, his comfortable life. To the extent that I participated in that it made me a bit special. India was a fantastic and glamorous place where one could be rich and have servants in contrast to our own 'hard-up' childhood. (Of course, although the D'Cruzes were quite comfortable, many Anglo-Indian families were not at all rich.) India was the origin of wonderful fruits, sunshine and spicy and delicious food. On the other hand 'servants' – that is to say Indians in general – were inferior. This was a notion that Mum's liberal humanitarianism forbad us to apply to people of other races. ('Why is that man black, Mummy?' – 'Don't stare like that, it's bad manners'). It certainly did not compromise my hero-worship of Nehru, but to me he was almost entirely a personal discovery. I made scrapbooks and collected pictures and newspaper cuttings. And, now I come to think of it, my perceptions must have been shaped by the comparatively benign BBC view of him that was current in the 1960s.

At home, nobody talked to me about politics or Partition. Bengal, in north-eastern India, had a substantial Muslim population. My father lived there, in Calcutta, throughout the decades of civil disobedience and the Quit India movement. Between 10th and 17th August, 1942, Calcutta saw massive strikes (*hartals*) in support of the Quit India camapign. Many violent labour disturbances and riots followed over the next few years. In 1943 the Bengal famine devastated the region, exacerbated in part by inefficient and slow-moving British attempts at relief, and more than 1.5 million died. I knew nothing of all this, until I was preparing for some postgraduate part-time teaching. I do remember one of my father's memories of sitting on a high wall, watching a religious riot in the street below. But the reasons for it were never discussed, and I took away from the conversation mostly a feeling of the naughtiness of the Indians for rioting and the cleverness of Dad for climbing the wall. This may well refer to the events between 16th and 19th August, 1946, when communal riots were triggered by a Direct Action Day called by the League Against Imperialism. Muslim rioting was countered by Hindu and Sikh forces intent on killing. Four thousand people died and, as reported to the Viceroy, 'the removal of the very large number of decomposed bodies' caused the administration a large problem (Sarkar, 1989, pp. 394, 406, 432).

Perhaps in terms of his own consciousness and certainly in terms of what he told his children, this must amount to a major denial on the part of my father. My mum recalls talking him to see the film *Gandhi*. He didn't want to go and emerged from the cinema boiling with rage. The film, he said, was all lies. None of it was true. He and his family 'weren't interested' in the independence movement. They 'didn't take any notice of him [Gandhi] – he was a native'. A native. Not interested. These days I interpret the racism of this mixed-race family as being due to their ambivalent position in British India, when whiteness was so manifestly privileged, and also to their own mounting insecurity as Independence loomed. After all, they, like so many other Anglo-Indians, left in 1948 presumably because they felt there was nothing for them in Nehru's India. Dad, in what seems to have been a deliberate ritual of closure, dumped his birth certificate, other official papers and a good deal of hot-weather clothing over the side of the ship that carried him from India to Britain.

The D'Cruzes insisted that they were both white and British. In fact Anglo-Indians' legal status under the Raj could be ambiguous. They were defined as 'statutory natives' as far as their employment in the Civil Service was concerned but treated as British subjects in terms of their education and in that they were eligible for military call-up (Abel, 1988, p. 129). Dad made his journey to London on an Indian Empire passport, issued on 8th September, 1947, just weeks after Independence. It's in front of me as I write, with its picture of a rather handsome 27-year-old; purposeful around the eyes but with revealingly slouching shoulders. The passport gives his status as a 'British subject by birth'. As became clear when package holidays had become cheap enough even for our household economy, being a British subject was not the same as being a British citizen. It was impossible for years to obtain a full British passport for my Dad. I'm using the passive voice because I am describing my mother's efforts. He would have nothing to do with it. He steadfastly refused to admit his lack of full British citizenship, and to fill in the necessary forms to apply for it. It was one of those things that did provoke him to rage. Until his death in 1985 he had no legal right of abode in Britain, only a right of 'readmission'. His 1980s passport has a visa for France from one holiday trip and a British Immigration Office stamp when he returned. The D'Cruzes were not quite white in British India (take a look at the snapshots). Dad's status in Britain remained legally a marginal one. Mum recalls them being paged over the tannoy at Heathrow as they were heading for a holiday in Spain in the early 1980s. Dad was terrified, seeing deportation looming. Actually he had lost his boarding pass and someone had handed it in. But that fear in a sixty-something-year-old man. Still not quite British. Not quite legal.

Their experience as immigrants in 1950s Britain can only have reinforced the D'Cruzes' emphasis on a non-black identity. This experience was one of the reverberant silences of my childhood. It was far from an empty silence, however, and as I look back I can interpret more and more of our life as a family within the context of English racism. Dad's commercial experience and qualifications were Indian, and so carried no weight in England. Perhaps it was a refusal to accept this that fuelled his lack of application in studying for English accountancy qualifications, despite the holes in the housekeeping made by the correspondence course fees. He never qualified. He spent his working life as a book-keeper, of considerably less status than being (as his 1947 passport states) an 'Assistant with Messrs Jessop & Co Ltd, Calcutta'. In England, he never had a prestigious job. His wages were always low. He stuck with a job for as long as he could. He was unemployed for a while when I was about 11. This was a disaster. It was not easy for him to get another job even in the full-employment 1960s. He was eventually taken on as a clerk by a mail-order firm – run by a Dutch family.

He never 'got on' in his working life mostly because, despite his meticulous (pedantic) book-keeping, he was always prickly with employers. He resented the loss of status that immigration had brought him. All this subliminally rubbed off on me. When asked at school, I remember (privately embarrassed by my own dishonesty) describing him as 'an accountant'. I seem to recall I was trying to get one up on a girl whose dad was a bus driver. I think it was something to do with the fact that she had new pointy-toe shoes with kitten heels and I had Tuf Go-Girls (heavy-duty things, saved up for and built to last). Being hard up in the 'you-never-had-it-so-good' 1950s and 1960s combined with a family narrative of a lost paradise where you had servants, affluence, high status and baby parrots as pets, served to reinforce my self-perception of awkwardness and outsiderness. It was writ large after all, in my funny name, on my not-pretty, not fashionably attired body, in my smarty-pants cleverness, which made my alienation a self-fulfilling prophecy. I was always the last to be picked as a partner in country-dancing.

I am the eldest in our family and my father's first child. When I was tiny we were very close. Dad was brilliant with babies and toddlers all his life. He could always silence a howling, fractious infant. It was when people became big enough to come back with snappy answers that he began to flounder – and usually strode off without answering. I don't really remember him having any close friends outside the family, though he maintained all kinds of jolly acquaintances with ladies who travelled on the same commuter bus as him. He was a gentle man. I remember him nursing us and mopping up after us, though all this was generally done inefficiently. He was an affectionate man, but he always had a trick of squeezing your hand a bit too hard. ('Oh Dad leave off' – 'don't talk like that, you're not with your common friends now'). He was not a drinker, though he liked an occasional Guinness. He never smoked. His hopelessness with money meant that Mum managed all the family finances. He was not given to sports, though he had done weight-lifting at school. All in all he was quite bad at the everyday ramifications of masculinity. In my teens, I remember his silhouette appearing behind the glass panel of the front door in the late evening while I was on the doorstep 'saying goodnight' to the latest ghastly boyfriend – though he never opened the door or put up a challenge. He explained what he was doing as 'worrying'. Usually we described this mood as 'sulking'. Depression was a major and recurrent component of his character, exacerbated in old age by diabetes. Before he was diagnosed he would eat half-jars of jam from the cupboard with a spoon, explaining he was 'tidying-up'.

The mode of 'worrying' was central to his role in the family. He saw it almost as the job that he did to keep us all well. In many ways it also seemed in his eyes to exonerate him from all kinds of other jobs – like tackling the landlord over the condemned gas heater in the bathroom, for example. (We heated our washing water in kettles for more than a year.) It also compensated for the fact that he was not able to provide the large income, houses, servants, comfort that he had grown up expecting to be there for his family. His worrying was a burden laid upon us. We wounded him by doing things that increased it – like getting a boyfriend in my case, or a music scholarship to public school in the case of my brother. Dad wanted all his chickens safe in the nest. And to a degree, of course, he was right. The world was hostile. He came from a community which according to its historian 'was despised by both the Indians and the British' over a long history, whose cultural experience was one of marginality and of having lost out (Abel, 1988, p. 30). He had experienced the disruption of emmigration amidst the political and social upheaval of Indian Independence. He had come to Britain perceiving himself as a middle-class, professional citizen and found hostility, racism and low-paid clerical work which would only buy damp, cold, crumbling, rented housing and no sticky-out petticoat for his darling daughter.

I began this piece with a memory of Dad and myself in Safeways. It is a story which has a denouement, which is why I remember it so clearly. I recall that particular supermarket trip as an enjoyable opportunity to be with Dad. He was in a good mood. I wonder if we were buying pineapple chunks and tortoises. It was in the checkout queue. A man pushed in ahead of us. The other side of Dad's character was to bristle with anger when he felt he was being shamed or put down. Can I interpret this as a potential loss of caste? The man in question seemed to be working-class, and I don't think we looked any posher, yet to us he was distinctly 'common'. Thus the ambiguities between class and caste recurred. A brief altercation ensued which ended when the man looked down on my five foot five father and said 'why don't you get out of this country and go back where you came from?' Silence. No answer. I was shocked and mute. Why didn't Dad say that he was white? And British. But it could not be said. Suddenly I realized for the first time that Dad's Indianness meant that in certain company, he was BLACK. And if he was, so was I.

It was that experience that pretty soon led me to reinterpret a good deal of what I had been hearing (or half hearing) from my mother's family for all my life, about the degeneracy of the 'sambos' and 'niggers' who had come to live in their part of south London. As I grew older, their criticisms of my father explained through his 'otherness' became more comprehensible. Their back tracking and half apologies – 'of course he isn't black like THAT' (in their neighbourhood 'THAT' meant Afro-Caribbean) – were a measure of their inept attempts to negotiate the competing discourses of class, race and family. I should say, also, that my mother's cousin had married an Italian and my mother's brother had emigrated to France and eventually married a French wife. The gradations of their prejudices emerged, though the Frogs and the Eyeties took some flak at times. Though this family, the Cracknells, seem superficially far better rooted in community and culture than the immigrant D'Cruzes, they too were a hotbed of tensions and contradictions located in this case principally around class. This was their echoing silence.

You can hear it, of course, in what I say about my own childhood. The competing narrative to my father's tale of Worry was one of Betterment through Education. This was my mother's refrain – still is. Social mobility and personal development were for her progressive and positive things. And she won, of course. My brother conducts orchestras, my sister and her husband run a data comunications consultancy and I lecture in one of our New Universities. Mum also made a professional career for herself, against the odds and later in life. She made unsuccessful starts in both teaching and nursing as a young woman. Later she went back to work, driven by financial need, in the 1960s and by dint of much hard graft, some imaginative job changes and training in counselling ended as a College Welfare Officer. At first sight this would not seeem too odd for the descendants of a lower-middle-class family in trade. My great-grandfather Cracknell ran a greengrocery business, and this passed to his son, Leslie. My mum, June, is Leslie's eldest daughter. Her school reports from Lucas Vale Primary are glowing. In 1940 she won a grammar school scholarship and spent the war dodging the doodlebugs to attend Prendergast Grammar School.

However, this is only a superficial account. It took the forceful intervention of Grandma Cracknell to ensure that June was allowed to take up her grammar school place. According to June's parents this would mean 'Getting Above Her Station'. There were tensions and contradictions around class identity in my mother's childhood household. Her mother was from a working-class family, the Browns. Grandad Brown had been an engineer.

Grandma Brown remained a stalwart and admirable example of self-helping working-class culture, almost for her full 100-year life. She was active in the Co-operative Party and became a Labour Councillor. I remember her council flat. No children's books or toys. Just orderly ranks of *The National Geographic* bulging with Knowledge, card games with Rules and the necessity to eat up one's bread and butter before any cake came on the scene.

My mother's mother, Edith (née Brown), had been in service before her marriage. She would wave her duster from an upstairs window to signal to Leslie when he came by on the grocery cart. She and her mother did not get on. Actually they did not talk for years. Edith's rebellion rejected betterment and education. She was as anti-intellectual as anyone I have ever met; a long-term devotee of Patience Strong poetry and Woolworth's make-up counter. She was also a histrionic domestic tyrant who had refined emotional blackmail to an art form. Her husband, Leslie, was a generally good-humoured man who, unlike my own father, scored quite well in the attributes of working-class masculinity. I remember his bicycle clips, and his Saturday afternoon smell of beer and roll-ups, his after-lunch snooze under the newspaper. He was also a lousy businessman, and his career as a business proprietor was comparatively short-lived. He earned a blue-collar wage for most of his life. His reflex when met by domestic frustrations was often a violent one. In this kind of household, clever eldest daughters with grammar school ambitions had a hard time. My mother went to grammar school until matriculation exams and the sixth form. Then, without telling her, her parents arranged with the school that she would leave after two terms in the sixth form. She came home one day and was told she was never going back. Even when she had left home her parents put a halt to her professional aspirations (girls are only fit for Woolworths, they said). Mum secured a teacher training place at Homerton College, but the entry form needed her parents' signature in consent. And they refused to sign.

So where does all this locate my childhood? In terms of income we were generally worse off than many working-class families. Mum saved up to have our shoes mended. We were rarely told off for evading domestic chores and being found with our noses in a book, but were berated for breaking or spoiling things that were too expensive to replace ('Shani, you're so thoughtless'). Our poverty was a contradiction and an embarrassment. We lacked the access to Grandma Brown's culture of working-class autodidacticism. For us, betterment could only mean class mobility, but we were too hard up to make the grade. Early on, Dad had talked about taking Mum back to India. To sunshine, a professional life and servants. Of course it never happened. It was a fictitious paradise, but it was one we had definitely lost. And it remained to haunt us, because it never ceased to haunt my father.

As a child and a teenager, I lived between the Scylla of Worry and the Charybdis of Betterment through Education. With my funny name, peculiar diet and too-clever-for-my-own-good-ness, it meant my social identity was fractured and disorientating. When I was 20 I married a skilled working man, a printer. ('Shani, you're just like your mother.') I worked in an office. I recall getting on better with the Asian accounts clerks than with the white women bought-ledger clerks. I was certainly too clever for my own good in that situation, and only after I extricated myself from it did I find university, history, feminism, an academic job. Thus my own personal history has skidded across class without really coming to rest. How middle-class is it to be a new university lecturer now that the groves of academia have become more than a little trampled by the consequences of mass higher education? The job that I do isn't the same as that done by the people who inspired me as an undergraduate. I've inherited my maternal grandmother's histrionics and love of cheap make-up and my paternal grandmother's dislike for subservience and housework. It's such a relief on Mediterranean holidays to be in a culture where other (older) women's body language can be as voluble as my own. And yet that's not my culture either.

If I retain that marginality, I think that I have managed to make it a source of inspiration and celebration rather than anxiety. When you're not on the inside you can move, and see, and speak. If you're lucky you can also see what the bastards are up to. My politics is a feminist one, though when teaching post-Thatcherite undergraduates who think it means dead-end, man-hating, narrow-minded polemic I sometimes wish I could think of another word for it. And feminism itself puts you in the academic, intellectual and creative spaces between disciplines, epistemologies and discourses. Along with the sceptical outsiderness of marginality, I also retain difference in its poststructuralist sense. It lets you make connections without swallowing things whole. I like the subversiveness of poststructuralism and dislike the (potential) nihilism of postmodernism.[3]

And when it comes down to it, feminism also prompts me to find my politics in my life as well as my work. So these days, if I remain not quite comfortable being English, or either middle-class or working-class, at this stage in my life, these are creative if not entirely comfortable cultural spaces. I Worry, though it does not paralyse me as it did my father. I'm still sold on Education but first and foremost not for Betterment but as a means to enable people to see power at work and argue back. Education, feminism and outsiderness enable an element of negotiation and play in one's social and cultural identity. When you're forty-something (God, when did that happen) an unusual name and spicy cookery are positive advantages. And smart-alec cleverness can evolve into something more utile. I've moved on. Dad would be proud of me. In those days, I just wanted to be blonde, pretty and called Jayne – and to have a dress with a sticky-out petticoat. Now, I wear my frocks as fancy as I like.

Notes

My thanks to Christine Zmroczek and Pat Mahony for constructive and supportive criticisms; to June D'Cruze for everything she has contributed to the making of this chapter – and its author.

1 The tortoise proved to be an escapologist cucumber-junky who could climb two-foot-high wire mesh fences and made a break for the hills a year or so later. Other creatures who found their way to our house in Dad's pocket or tucked under his coat included a puppy who bit my mother, a kitten called James who got into fights and developed infected abscesses, miscellaneous mice, hamsters, goldfish, rabbits and a couple of 'male' guinea pigs (who produced numerous offspring).

2 In my discussion of the historical background of the Anglo-Indian community I have drawn on Abel's detailed social history, Moorhouse's popular history of British India and Sarkar's more academic study.

3 Chris Weedon's (1987) *Feminist Practice and Poststructuralist Theory* offers a clear and sensible introduction.

References

ABEL, E. (1988) *The Anglo-Indian Community: Survival in India*, Delhi, Chanakya Publications.

DOUGLAS, M. (1991) *Purity and Danger*, London, Routledge.

MOORHOUSE, C. (1983) *India Britannica*, London, Granada.

SARKAR, S. (1989) *Modern India, 1885–1947*, 2nd edn, London, Macmillan.

WEEDON, C. (1987) *Feminist Practice and Poststructuralist Theory*, Oxford, Blackwell.

Chapter 8

Contested Categorizations:
Auto/Biography, Narrativity and Class

Bogusia Temple

Introduction

In 1985 Sue Webb argued that the re-formulation of the social class debate which had then resurfaced in the journal *Sociology* was primarily for and about male sociologists (Webb, 1985). In 1995 the debate in *Sociology* continues: the 'problem' of women and class is discussed, for example, by Richard Breen and Christopher Whelan (1995) and Stephen Roberts and Gordon Marshall (1995). I believe, however, that there are more fruitful ways to analyse people's lives which do not involve a classification of the lives of one half of the world's population from the perspective of a small part of the other half. I argue here for an approach which centres people as active participants in the construction of categories such as 'women' or 'class' and which makes their experiences important tools for analysis.

Recent literature on auto/biography and narrativity has been valuable in informing my views in this area. As these writers show, we all build narrative accounts of our lives in which we portray ourselves for an audience. These accounts or stories may be contradictory. The content of the categories people use to define their lives changes as does the salience of the categories to the account given. Calling these accounts 'stories' or narratives does not imply they are trivial or false. Margaret Somers (1994) asserts that they are the bricks with which we build our 'identity'. I am concerned here with the ways in which *researchers* use the concept of class but many of the points I make apply equally to lay conceptualizations.

Lack of Fit?

The way in which I, and indeed all researchers, approach a subject such as class, is via my own 'intellectual auto/biography' (Stanley, 1990). This is

> an analytic (not just descriptive) concern with the specifics of how we
> come to understand what we do, by locating acts of understanding in

an explication of the grounded contexts these are located in and arise from. (Stanley, 1990, p. 62)

Researchers' intellectual autobiographies influence their interpretation of their experiences as well as those of others. The linkages between autobiography and biography have been described by Stanley (1992) using the notion of 'the auto/biographical I'. The connection between autobiography and biography are described by the term 'auto/biography' and the 'I' denotes a process of knowledge construction in which the researcher is an active agent. All researchers pick out the slices of other people's lives which are of interest to them. They select what is important and what is to be left out and arrange the results from their own perspective. The information presented to them by those involved in the research is in itself selected. When looking at how others such as Breen and Whelan (1995) and Roberts and Marshall (1995) have constructed their accounts of class, for example, I use my own experiences to ask: what does this say about my own life? That is, what how good is 'the fit' between this analysis and my own life? Does it make sense of my own life? If not, as Holton and Turner (1994) argue, there are other ways of constructing the concept.

This does not mean that all experiences and definitions arising from them should uncritically be accepted. Diana Fuss (1989) asserts that experience is a window on the world of ideology, not a direct access to 'truth'. It is impossible to put forward a definition other than from one's own locatedness in the social and material world, and that definition will not be accepted by everyone. This acknowledgment of the active participation of people in the construction of accounts of their own experiences involves accepting differences between accounts as not necessarily wrong but as built for different purposes and with different audiences in mind.

Recent developments in the study of narrativity provide valuable tools with which to look at the ways in which researchers and those they research develop as well as analyse concepts such as class. For example, Somers (1994) argues that one way to avoid making aspects of identity (such as class) too rigid is to incorporate into the notion of identity itself the 'categorically destabilizing dimensions' (Somers, 1994, p. 606) of space, time and relationality. She does this by reframing narrativity by shifting the focus from representations to ontological narrativity. In other words, rather than attempting to do the impossible, that is, 'capture' the social world on paper, she looks at how people tell others about themselves and their world. Social life, she asserts, is always itself storied and narrative is an ontological condition of social life (1994, p. 614). Ontological narratives make identity and self something that one becomes (1994, p. 618). Looking at the concept of 'working class' she goes on to say that different people in similar 'class' situations may have different degrees of power. It is thus more appropriate to look at 'group embeddedness and cultural representations' than class attributes when considering social action. As a result we would be 'considerably less concerned with "deviation"and more fascinated by variation' (Somers, 1994, p. 632). In my view this kind of approach avoids an analysis which is constantly aiming to fit women in (or to leave them out). People are involved in a variety of narratives and relationships:

> From this angle of relational membership, identities are not derived from attributes imputed from a stage of societal development . . . , or by 'experience' imputed from a social category . . . but by actors' places in the multiple (often competing) symbolic and material narratives in which they are embedded or with which they identified. (Somers and Gibson, 1994, p. 76)

These ideas from auto/biography and narrativity can be used to discuss the process of producing categories such as class and the elusive nature of such productions.

Pedigree and Audience

Having said that researchers' social positions are relevant to how they see 'class' it is important to say something about my background and approach to research. My 'story' inevitably influences how I see 'class'. I am the eldest daughter of three born in England to parents from Poland who had settled in a town in the Midlands after the Second World War. The issue of class had a particular salience in our lives because of what my parents considered was the mismatch between the term others used to describe their class and their own reality. Both my parents had manual jobs and were on low incomes. However, they hotly denied they were 'working-class'. My mother had (English) qualifications. Her father had been a professional in Poland and her mother had not gone out to work. They had been respected in their community in Poland. My father, a manual worker, was an important figure in the local Polish community. It was fate in the form of the war which prevented him from getting a better job. Also, our family did not lead a lifestyle they considered to be 'working-class'. They realized the importance of education, they didn't spend their evenings in a pub, and they owned their own home. We were respectable and middle-class. Class for them was as much about attitude and lifestyle as occupation. The mismatch between my parents' views on class and the more traditional view based on the occupation of 'the head of the household' was evident when we went to school. This was a school run by Catholic nuns which had a very good academic reputation. Those who failed the 11+ could pay to send their children there. The children who went there were predominantly those of professional parents. Only a very few went from our local school and as a pupil there I felt the differences between 'them' and 'us'. We couldn't afford expensive games equipment or holidays abroad, we hadn't been to private primary schools, and our lifestyles were very different. We also spoke differently. However, I found it difficult to place this difference as I was unsure whether it was due to my being Polish or being considered working-class. I felt confused: my parents were right: in some ways we were different from 'working-class' people, but they were also wrong in that at times at school I did not feel we lived the same kinds of lives as 'the middle classes'. For example, we spoke differently and I never felt comfortable in the speech lessons where it was obvious that the 'posher' you sounded the better. I feel now that part of my confusion lay in trying to separate out which parts of my sense of difference were due to my 'Polishness' and which to my class or gender. I have now come to realize that although I may focus on one or the other of these they are in effect inseparably linked, and not necessarily in a confirmatory way.

At home we discussed concepts of class with occupation often central. The difference between my parents' views and my own centred around the fact that for them occupation was never the key point of any discussion around class, while for me it sometimes was. My experiences at school showed this very clearly. Other factors were more important for my parents. They developed narratives around what was salient to them: class (defined in their own terms as status not arising out of occupation) and inseparable from ethnicity. Gender was assumed to be unproblematic. They argued that their status (which to them was what class was about) in the community came from my father's organizational and leadership skills. Also, many of their friends in manual occupations earned more than those in professions, and this enabled them to lead a life that was not typical of those normally defined as working-class. It couldn't be a case of just occupation or income.

Affirming my class position, then and now, in any once-and-for-all way is problematic for me. My parents never considered they were working-class. Whether I say I am from a working-class background or not varies. When I registered for my PhD I was still trying to decide whether being a second-generation Pole was relevant to my life at all. This coincided with an unease with academic life which I perceived as an environment stratified according to gender and 'class', in terms of background as well as occupation. Someone who had remained a researcher for as long as I had was assumed to be a failed lecturer: the 'couldn't you get a lecturing job?' question I began to dread. Oxford or Cambridge college names had a value and status of their own. I still found these feelings of unease difficult to verbalize. My understanding grew as I began to read feminist work in all its diversity and finally I began to call myself a feminist. The kind of feminism I am interested in gives me a perspective from which I can describe my contradictory/interweaving experiences of ethnicity, gender and class without having to establish a core to any of them. I also discovered the literature on sexuality, something I had very much taken for granted.

My writing to date has been largely around the ways in which people have tried to label me as Polish, or alternatively denied me that label (see, for example, Temple, 1994). The similarities between the debates over class and ethnicity strike me as of relevance here (as are those of gender and sexuality). I have argued that attributing any exclusive label such as 'Polish' to me is to missname my experiences. There is no core or essence to this category or to my 'self' which can be matched up together. For example, being able to speak the language is not an indicator for inclusion since in my research I found people who could not speak Polish but who were considered active members of the community, whilst fluent speakers were often excluded or excluded themselves. Acceptance or rejection of the label was occasioned and had as much to do with who was ascribing it as to any characteristic of the person involved. Choosing to do my research in a Polish community in England highlights the connections between my life and my work. However, these connections are present in all research, whether acknowledged or not.

My experience with the label 'working-class' is much the same. I am from a working-class background, or not, according to circumstance. In the Polish community I grew up in I am mostly not. Even there, however, I sometimes insist that I am. Similarly in academic circles I sometimes own the label, sometimes not. To some extent it depends on the purposes for which it is being used.

The work of Fuss (1989) is again of value here in unravelling the tensions around wanting to use categorizations such as class but not wanting to attribute any unchangeable essence or importance to them. She asserts that 'essentialism' and 'constructionalism' are not mutually exclusive. It is possible to define class with a core or essence, such as occupation, always at the centre of the definition, an 'essentialist/foundationalist view' – that is, using a perspective that argues for one recoverable reality that is the same for all. Equally, it is possible to deny that any particular characteristic is always at the centre of a definition using a 'social constructionist' position. This approach sees the social world as jointly fashioned by subjects in their interactions. Arguing that there is no 'essence' to such categories as 'woman' or 'class' is in effect arguing that 'in essence' they are socially constructed labels. As Fuss states, constructionalism operates as a more sophisticated form of essentialism, anti-essentialists still preserve the category of essence. She goes on to argue that no categorization is itself progressive or otherwise, that is, a social constructionist position is in itself inherently no more valuable for women who want to look at the social world than an essentialist one. What is important is why the category – 'woman' or 'class' – is used in the way it is. Identity is a political construction, and in Fuss's terms, it is possible to have a commitment to a linguistic essentialism and not to an ontological one (Fuss, 1989, p. 5). I can use the term 'class' without implying that I have a fixed definition of what it is.

As political constructions the extent to which concepts contain and describe each other varies. Two occasions on which I am called working-class may therefore 'feel' very different depending on circumstances, particularly on who is speaking. For example, affirming I am from a working-class background with other academics who appear to have a positive evaluation of the term makes it more comfortable to include myself.

The lack of fit between my experiences and much academic writing is due, I believe, to the concentration of much of such debate on one characteristic of my life at one point in time defined in a narrow way. The interconnections between class, gender, ethnicity and sexuality, for example, are rarely discussed. Looking *within* a category, what it means to belong to a category such as 'women' has been contested, for example, by Fuss (1989), Alcoff (1988), and hooks (1982). The writing of black and lesbian feminists (for example hooks, 1982; Rich, 1983; Allen, 1990; Collins, 1990), auto/biographical writing (for example Steedman, 1986; Brodzki and Schenck, 1988; Stein, 1988; Stanley, 1992), as well as historical/philosophical research (see here Lerner, 1979; Riley, 1988; and Hall, 1992), provide many sites of 'difference' within a category, here 'women'.

Looking *across* categories feminist debate is addressing the problem of how to take diversity seriously without establishing hierarchies or denying oppression. For example, the collection of papers edited by Haleh Afshar and Mary Maynard (1994) discuss the interrelationship between age, class, disability, 'race' and sexuality. I have only recently begun to consider feminist contributions to debates on age and disability (see for example Lloyd, 1992; Rich, 1992) as a result of working on projects related to the services provided for older people and for disabled people. My life history and my intellectual auto/biography are valuable in discussing why I have chosen to focus on some aspects of identity, such as class and gender, whilst staying away from others such as disability until others have used their life stories to draw out such influences. Future research is needed into the ways in which the different narratives of identity we construct coalesce with those of others. However, the epistemological significance for debates on class of the interconnections, contradictions and confirmations of categories needs to be more fully explored. Constructs such as class and gender can be used to confine, contain and sustain each other. Alternative definitions can be used to contradict and subvert such definitions.

My views on my class position are due in part to my past experiences as well as my present circumstances. It would be possible to say little about my life without connecting it to my past and my present. The lifestyles of others in my household are relevant. For example, although neither of my parents had well-paid jobs, by restricting personal spending they accumulated savings which they used to enable their children to do the things they were unable to, for example, to buy new clothes and go on trips abroad with school. Moreover, without looking at their attitudes to life and at how money was distributed within the household we can learn only a limited amount about the use of resources and power. Money for personal spending was restricted, but not in the same way for my mother and father, and less so for the children. It is the use of resources and its distribution my parents were talking about when they pointed to the importance of attitude and lifestyle. Defining class relationally and flexibly with other categories avoids the kind of analysis which limits research to particular fixed and unchanging characteristics and defines out of existence one of the most interesting ways of stratifying without essentializing. Focusing on the status of one member of the household *a priori* limits the possibilities of looking at how categories are used differently on different occasions by different people.

In sum, my class position is a result of my life history as well as those closest to me. It involves the interweaving of life stories and choices. Picking out small details of my life such as the occupation of my partner may build one definition of our 'class' but picking out other slices of our individual and overlapping lives may give an entirely different picture. Sometimes, I refuse to name my experiences as 'class'-based because of the way the concept has been defined in others' narrative accounts of themselves. Sometimes it is so tangled up in my other narratives that I can't define it separately at all. And maybe I wouldn't want to.

Discussion

Describing my intellectual auto/biography and calling myself feminist encourages me to locate my writing in a particular tradition that increasingly is drawn to discussions of difference as well as similarity in the experience of different kinds of oppression. The move to include those who were previously 'other' (for example black and lesbian women) is welcome by those who consider that an undifferentiated concept of 'gender' may be unable to describe experiences sufficiently. But raising these differences can also raise problems. For example, I mentioned previously that I felt my experience of academic life was as it was because I am a women. Maybe however there are other ways to name my experiences, or maybe, as I am increasingly drawn to believe, it is impossible to unproblematically separate my experiences into neat categories (see here the work of Joanna Bourke (1993) for a similar view). I can illustrate the problem by describing something that happened to me in my first job. A senior male academic, on being told my name, replied: 'I can't remember that. I'll call you Barbara.' Did he feel able to do this because I was his junior, because I was a woman, or because I was foreign? I feel it was probably all of them. But like everyone telling a tale I sometimes use it to illustrate either sexism, racism or power relationships between tenured academics and researchers. The challenge for feminism now is to discuss social inclusion and exclusion in ways which are not mutually exclusive of the different ways in which life is stratified. Possibilities exist for increasing our understandings of the ways in which different people tell about themselves. Within this feminists need to explicate the ways in which categories are experienced (for examples of such work to date see Floya Anthias and Nira Yuval-Davis (1993), Joanna Bourke (1993), and Haleh Afshar and Mary Maynard (1994)). We need to do this, moreover, without specifying any of the categories that lives can be classified by as in essence different from the others. For example, selecting sex as a biological construct but race as a social one, as Fiona Willams (1989, p. xv) does, provides a problematic basis for analysing the connections between them since one category is separated out as different in kind from the outset.

If, as I argue above, we have more than one narrative of self within which concepts such as class and gender can be differently constituted, then the challenge lies in explicating the circumstances in which concepts and narratives are developed. No category would be developed merely as a temporary expedient tacked on to overcome problems in other people's work. Rather each category would be constructed as temporally and spatially located in subjects' narrative accounts. The researcher could then discuss these using her sometimes overlapping, sometimes contradictory experiences.

References

AFSHAR, H. and MAYNARD, M. (1994) *The Dynamics of 'Race' and Gender: Some Feminist Interventions*, London, Taylor & Francis.

ALCOFF, L. (1988) 'Cultural Feminism Versus Post-Structuralism: The Identity Crisis in Feminist Theory', *Signs*, 13, pp. 405–36.

ALLEN, J. (Ed.) (1990) *Lesbian Philosophies and Cultures*, Albany, State University of New York Press.

ANTHIAS, F. and YUVAL-DAVIS, N. (1993) *Racialized Boundaries: Race, Nation, Gender, Colour and Class in the Anti-Racist Struggle*, London, Routledge.

BOURKE, J. (1993) *Working Class Cultures in Britain, 1890–1960: Gender, Class and Ethnicity*, London, Routledge.

BREEN, R. and WHELAN, C. (1995) 'Gender and Class Mobility: Evidence from the Republic of Ireland', *Sociology*, 29, pp. 1–22.

BRODZKI, B. and SCHENCK, C. (Eds) (1988) *Life Lines: Theorizing Women's Autobiography*, Ithaca, Cornell University Press.

COLLINS, P. H. (1990) *Black Feminist Thought: Knowledge, Consciousness, and the Politics of Empowerment*, London, Unwin Hyman.

FUSS, D. (1989) *Essentially Speaking*, London, Routledge.

HALL, C. (1992) *White, Male and Middle Class: Explorations in Feminism and History*, Cambridge, Polity.

HOLTON, R. and TURNER, B. (1994) 'Debate and Pseudo-Debate in Class Analysis: Some Unpromising Aspects of Goldthorpe and Marshall's Defence', *Sociology*, 28, pp. 799–804.

HOOKS, B. (1982) *Ain't I a Woman: Black Women and Feminism*, London, Pluto.

LERNER, G. (1979) *Placing Women in History*, London, Oxford University Press.

LLOYD, M. (1992) 'Does She Boil Eggs? Towards a Feminist Model of Disability', *Disability, Handicap and Society*, 7, pp. 207–21.

RICH, A. (1983) 'Compulsory Heterosexuality and Lesbian Existence', in ABEL, E. and ABEL, E. (Eds) *The Signs Reader: Women, Gender and Scholarship*, Chicago, University of Chicago Press, pp. 139–68.

RICH, C. (1992) 'Ageing, Ageism and Feminist Avoidance', in CROWLEY, H. and HIMMELWEIT, S. (Eds) *Knowing Women: Feminism and Knowledge*, Cambridge, Polity, pp. 55–7.

RILEY, D. (1988) *'Am I That Name?': Feminism and the Category of 'Women' in History*, London, Macmillan.

ROBERTS, S. and MARSHALL, G. (1995) 'Intergenerational Class Processes and the Asymmetry Hypothesis', *Sociology*, 29, pp. 43–58.

SOMERS, M. (1994) 'The Narrative Constitution of Identity: A Relational and Network Approach', *Theory and Society*, 23, pp. 605–49.

SOMERS, M. and GIBSON, G. (1994) 'Reclaiming the Epistemological 'Other': Narrative and the Social Constitution of Identity', in CALHOUN, C. (Ed.) *Social Theory and the Politics of Identity*, Oxford, Blackwell, pp. 37–99.

STANLEY, L. (1990) 'Moments of Writing: Is there a Feminist Auto/biography?', *Gender and History*, 2, pp. 58–67.

STANLEY, L. (1992) *The Auto/biographical I: The Theory and Practice of Feminist Auto/biography*, Manchester, Manchester University Press.

STEEDMAN, C. (1986) *Landscape for a Good Woman: A Story of Two Lives*, London, Virago.

STEIN, G. (1988) *Lectures in America*, London, Virago Press.

TEMPLE, B. (1994) 'Constructing Polishness, Researching Polish Women's Lives: Feminist Auto/Biographical Accounts', *Women's Studies International Forum*, 17, pp. 47–55.

WEBB, S. (1985) 'Counter Arguments: An Ethnographic Look at "Women and Class"', Studies in Sexual Politics, 5, Sociology Department, University of Manchester.

WILLIAMS, F. (1989) *Social Policy: A Critical Introduction: Issues of Race, Gender and Class*, Cambridge, Polity.

Chapter 9

Missing Links: Working-Class Women of Irish Descent

Meg Maguire

This chapter considers three main issues. Firstly I am intrigued by the manner in which class operates as an unstable category in relation to the lives of women of a working-class background who work in the academy. Secondly I want to account for the relative invisibility of women of Irish descent. In particular I want to argue that class, culture and faith (frequently a silenced aspect of culture), operate in various complex ways and at different moments in time to shape the social world of working-class women of Irish descent in higher education. Finally I want to problematize 'the academy', its unevenness and internal contradictions. In order to address these issues I will draw on some aspects of my biography.

Difficult Questions – Different Selves

I was born in London in 1949, the first daughter and first child of an unskilled manual labourer and a nurse both of whom had come from Southern Ireland in search of jobs, freedom from small village life and any other opportunities which were to be had. I went to a Catholic primary school where I passed the 11+ and moved on to a girls' Catholic grammar school. I trained as a primary school teacher in a non-denominational college. After more than a decade of teaching in urban schools I moved into higher education as a teacher trainer in a Catholic training college. Currently I work at King's College, London with intending secondary school teachers and on a Master's course in Urban Education.

This brief account of my life raises some complex questions for me about my class and my cultural background. If I define class historically, in relation to my socio-economic origins, then I am working class. If I define class culturally in relation to my current occupational status then I am middle-class. However, if I define class politically in relation to the fact that I sell my labour in exchange for a wage, that I have relatively little say over my pay and conditions of work, that I work in a setting of high insecurity and instability, then I may well define my class differently again. In a period where 'society is dividing before our eyes, opening up new social fissures in the working population' (Hutton, 1996, p. 106), where labour is being restructured and fragmented in an unprecedented manner, it may be that the 'old' stable categories of class will no longer do. What all this means is that I have a range of ways through which to 'explain' and 'theorize' my unstable/stable classed self. Although my status is undoubedly middle-class, part of my self-identity remains located in my past and in my particular formation of working-class life. But this experience is particular and specific in other ways.

The fact that I am first-generation Irish in Britain and have been brought up as a Catholic speaks to issues of difference which raise questions in my exploration of self-identity and culture, questions which have only recently been addressed in literature (Lennon *et al.*, 1988). Am I Irish or British or am I Irish and British? Or am I Irish in Britain? Am I British when I am in Ireland? There are other related issues of difference, specifically the question of religion/faith. What are the differences between Catholics and members of other faith communities in Ireland? In the case of culture too, there are ranges of ways through which 'being of Irish descent' can be constructed; some ways are situation-specific, such as when visiting my family in Ireland, where I am decidedly unambiguously Irish, or when attending Irish Catholic funerals. Other ways are more political, such as choosing to participate in particular political demonstrations or in other matters of self-identity where I relate to those whom I regard as 'people like me'.

I want to question here what is it to be of working-class Irish Catholic descent and work in higher education. What cultural habitus has positioned and (re)produced me? What dilemmas and paradoxes are involved? And of what use is an exploration of these contradictions to women in the academy? In what follows I shall 'try out' some ideas about identity and difference for women in the academy using parts of my own biography as a touchstone. However, there are some critical matters which I want to underscore before I start the main task. Currently there is a concern to move beyond any limiting essentialist construction of 'women'. There is rightly a concern with issues of difference. But there are some conditions of our lives which bind us together as women in the academy. Overwhelmingly women are marginalized, positioned as 'other' and rendered invisible in the academy. As elsewhere, women are systematically discriminated against in relation to pay and promotion. There is a further issue involved in all this which is important and frequently sidelined. Any attempts to interpret the social and material world need to recognize the specificities of time and place. Time and space work together to construct a unique 'framework for experience' (Harvey, 1989, p. 214).

> Modernization entails, after all, the perpetual disruption of temporal and spacial rhythms, and modernization takes as one of its missions the production of new meanings for space and time in a world of ephemerality and fragmentation. (Harvey, 1989, p. 216)

My experiences of growing up as a working-class girl/woman of Irish Catholic descent are rooted in a specific historical moment and a particular locale – south London. Growing up and being schooled in the 1950s and 1960s in a deeply devout Catholic Irish family has a uniqueness and a specificity which have to be recognized and which are as yet undocumented. Differently aged women from different places but from similar but shifting cultural backgrounds will have different stories to tell. My particular experience of a Catholic education in London is shaped and framed by a specific ethos which has now been displaced or at least partly eroded in many schools. My biography is constructed from within the 'iron cage' of a particular place and a particular moment in time. It is important to recognize the limitations of a partial and fleeting insight into an experience of schooling which may not now be as commonplace as it once undoubtedly was; nevertheless I hope that giving some expression to this particular herstory will contribute to our knowledge about women. As Magda Gere Lewis (1993, p. 17) says,

> The voices of my social difference will be heard in this text. However, this is not a theoretical liability. Rather it is the basis for political action. I believe that achieving solidarity across our differences – however these may be marked in gender, class, race, ethnicity, desires of the body, body proficiency, and presentation, or any other socially divisive category of our human be/ing – is the challenge of feminist practice.

Women: Outsiders Still in the Academy

While it is important to celebrate the fact that women have been moving into the academy in increasing numbers as students, and now make up more than half of the undergraduate cohort in the UK as elsewhere (Lewis, 1993), women who work in higher education are still outsiders in the academy. Women academics are in the minority in higher education and they are more frequently positioned in the lower ranks. They are concentrated in subordinate positions within an occupation which is organized and managed by dominant male workers from the same occupational class and educational background. For example, in 1989 in the UK university sector as a whole there were 3,852 male professors and only 113 female professors (UFC, 1990). Currently, women who work in higher education are increasingly subjected to forms of 'casualization'.

> The number of university staff – mainly researchers, but increasingly, teaching and other staff – now on short term contracts exceeds one quarter. No other profession in this country is in that position. And since more than 60 per cent of the total intake of women were

recruited onto short term contracts in both 1986 and 1987, it is clear that women are bearing the brunt of this pressure. (Aziz, 1990, p. 38)

There is a growing literature on women as teachers in higher education (Stiver Lie and O'Leary, 1990; Kelly and Slaughter, 1991, Stiver Lie *et al.*, 1994). There is also an appreciation of the contradictions involved: women who teach in the academy are generally qualified to postgraduate level and are relatively privileged – there are relative degrees of comfort and power available to these women (Bannerji *et al.*, 1991). At the same time these women take longer to progress in the academy when compared to male colleagues of similar standing and the 'minority at lower levels becomes a still smaller minority at higher levels' (Sutherland, 1994, p. 176). Lewis (1993, p. 55), writing about Canadian women in higher education, puts it like this: 'the reality for many academic women is that they do not hold full-time, fully funded academic positions, but are granted only a tenuous and underfunded existence'.

Acker has documented the way in which the 'male as norm' academy is constructed to position all women as 'other'. However, she argues that the differences which exist between those admittedly few women in the academy have not yet been recorded.

> We also lack figures on the class background and ethnic composition of the academic profession (and other workers in higher education); we have no easy way of assessing the combined effects of class, sex, 'race' and other characteristics such as sexual orientation (Kitzinger 1990) on subject specialities, promotion prospects, or any other aspect of being an academic. (Acker, 1994, p. 143)

For those who construct class in a relatively 'closed' manner, all women in the academy can only ever be middle-class. Those of us who inhabit a more messy, sometimes incoherent social world are at times situated in a place with no border. We are made aware that our classed knowledge does not 'count' in the academy, yet we know it exists and is sometimes the most 'real' way of knowing. We are aware that we pass into, between and across class divisions and boundaries; passing or voicing ourselves at specific times in particular moments and places. We are aware too, that our class positions have internal contradictions and differences. To be white and working-class from one locale is to be 'different' and yet the same as someone from another area (see Reay, in this volume). Those of us from working-class backgrounds in the academy are aware of our internal differences but sometimes need the power of solidarity to 'cope' with working in higher education. And the related sense of 'homelessness' differs between institutions of higher education. 'We need to recognise that this is a racist, classist and heterosexist society and that the university is structured to perpetuate those relations' (Bannerji *et al.*,

1991, p. 8). However, what I want to argue is that working-class women of Irish descent who work in higher education have experiences and particular sets of discourses to draw on which can reveal these uneven power relations.

The Cultural Habitus of Irish Catholicity – Home and School

Bourdieu (1990, p. 53) calls the historical routines and regimes which order and pattern our social contexts a cultural habitus: 'systems of durable, transposable dispositions, structured structures predisposed to function as structuring structures'. As a girl growing up in inner London in the 1950s I inhabited a particular habitus which spoke strongly and firmly to me about what was 'proper' and 'common-sense behaviour'. This was a rich and varied cultural experience drawing on a world of powerful dualisms – good/bad and right/wrong – from which there was no escape. Certain behaviours were either a sin or they were not. And even if you were not actually caught out in any mischief, the consequence was the same because the Catholic catechism which we all learned by rote at school told us that 'God knows and sees all things – even your most secret thoughts'. Our lives had a regular and unchanging pattern particularly at the weekend; fish or eggs every Friday for dinner (lunch), Saturday night baths in preparation for mass on Sunday and no breakfast that morning because we all went to Holy Communion in our best clothes which were put away after church.

We were brought up in a world peopled by angels – good, bad and guardian ones, saints for all occasions such as St Jude the saint for impossible things, a last resort, as well as great miracles and cures. It was possible to make special novenas in order to guarantee special consideration at the time of death. Each night before sleep, the catechism told us that the four last things ever to be remembered were 'Death, judgment, hell and heaven'. The happiest day of one's life was making first Holy Communion where the girls dressed up as brides. In some ways this can be seen as repressive, controlling and fearful which it undoubtedly was, but in other ways it opened up a rich inner world of powerful legend, myth and mystery. We sometimes went 'home' in the summer to Ireland where, after a dreadful journey on what we called the 'cattle boat' because the journey was so rough and the facilities so poor, we were freed to spend days wandering in the fields and playing in the hay and barns of neighbouring families (Lennon, *et al.*, 1988). At these times we 'knew' powerfully that we were Irish.

In London we were taught by our families and in school that Catholics had been oppressed and that many martyrs had died for their faith. We were the inheritors of a great legacy which had to be treasured and passed down to our children. It was critical to attend a Catholic school which would respect and nurture the 'Faith of our Fathers'. For my mother, delivering and collecting us from primary school presented an opportunity to join the mothers' club and spend time with other migrant Irish women. As with other migrant Irish women (Lennon *et al.*, 1988) the community in the church helped maintain connections with 'home' and provided a space for connecting with others in the diaspora. My father was very involved in the life of the parish and was wary of 'outsiders'. He strongly disapproved of any of us having non-Catholic friends as we grew up. Catholics had fought to maintain the faith; their story is a fight against repression and a source of consolation and support. For many this provides a strong unifying feeling. In Ireland, Catholicism was, partly, an act of resistance to the English oppressors. Thus the Catholic Church and the parish provided a strong central cultural habitus for my family.

Overall, the economics of growing up in a context of relative poverty of the sort experienced by many migrant communities set within a cultural/ religious context where suffering was to be welcomed as a test of faith and endurance frequently meant that class anger and rage were displaced into a form of acceptance, passivity and apolitical reaction. For many women of my mother's generation for whom birth control and divorce were non-starters, their religion provided a shelter from the storm. As Rossiter (1993, p. 193) says, 'religion is, on the one hand, the embodiment of ideological and institutional sexism, and on the other, a consolation and an inspiration'. For many families the facts of their working-class material circumstances were mediated through and by their faith. Thus, the experience I describe here is profoundly a working-class Catholic formation.

School was supposed to shore up the foundations of the 'good Catholic home'. In some ways this is what it did. In other ways, the English school system occupied a contradictory position in the lives of Irish Catholic working-class children which was not always appreciated by our parents who believed that their responsibility was to uphold the work of the school. Although the majority of the children in my primary school were of Irish descent, our teachers were not. We never learned about Ireland or our history and culture. Our accents were corrected as was our spelling, notably from Mammy to Mummy. Our parents filled in some of these gaps for us and there were Irish dancing lessons in a local community hall for those who could afford the classes as well as the costume. But we were being schooled to be British. At a prizegiving one year, the English National Anthem was played and I stayed sitting down – not a major act of resistance but one for which I was severely reprimanded. In my secondary school, where I did history at 'A' level, we studied events at Drogheda from an English perspective. The English nun who taught history mispronounced the place – which is the local town where my family lives – and when I said the name correctly, my pronunciation was corrected. Small examples, but instances of a long-term tactic – the 'denationalization' of the Irish in Britain (Hickman, 1993).

And what of class? At primary school we were all working-class although there were visible fractions depending on what street or block you lived in or your family circumstances. It is a frequently made mistake to think that working-class culture is not as variagated and internally differentiated as any other. We were all migrant families and as such were at the bottom of the list for council accommodation. In the post-war 1950s London we all lived in crowded rented accommodation and our parents dreamed of council flats. Many of us came from large families which compounded the housing problem. Our culture was working-class Irish but there were those of us who were 'rough' and those of us who were 'respectable' as well as those of us who teetered haphazardly between these positions. Degrees of economic hardship and relative poverty lay behind these internal class divisions but some of us could be saved and education was the passport.

Passing the 11+ opened up for me the world of the Catholic girls' grammar school where I learned quite quickly what class really meant. It meant that you had to be 'middle-class' and that any sort of 'working-class' formation was 'common' and to be avoided. From suitable words – 'ladies go to the lavatory not the toilet' – to suitable clothing, particularly a uniform which was clearly 'different' from those worn in secondary modern schools, it was evident that the ethos was middle-class and that we had better fit in and quickly. The working-class cultural capital of my childhood counted for nothing in this new setting. Evans (1991, pp. 26–7) has commented on her own experience in a girls' grammar school that

> The sheer cost of passing the eleven plus was identified, rightly, in the 1950s as a disincentive to working-class children and their parents. The emotional and social cost of being plunged into a middle-class world was doubtless considerable, but equally significant for many homes must have been the capital outlay necessary to take part in this new educational experience.

She is right. In my case my uncle in Ireland sent over the money for my uniform which was only obtainable at an expensive and exclusive London store which made my mother and myself feel very uncomfortable and unwelcome. Evans (1991, p. 27) also says of her school,

> Nevertheless, one or two working-class pupils did enter this select, and selected, world. Yet how they were expected to survive it, and not commit suicide in the playground, is a vivid, if retrospective question.

Perhaps if you had been taught to 'pass' on being Irish in England it was a little easier to 'pass' on class as well after a few early errors. After all, 'clever' girls learn fast if they have to! In some ways, the experience of attending a Catholic grammar school provided a direct continuity with my home; early morning mass, more saints and angels, special Catholic groups to join. In other ways it was a major disruption. Irishness and working-class culture had no place while Catholicity provided a unifying factor. The normalizing ssumption was of Catholicity – but a middle-class Anglo Catholicity.

Moving on very quickly from school – to college – to work – my 'choice' of career was not very surprising. For a working-class girl, becoming a teacher was a step up. It is part of a tradition of class mobility and dislocation stretching back to the early nineteenth century (Maguire, 1993). I was the first in my family to go on to a form of higher education – never mind that teacher training was a gendered choice or that my route was class-specific; teacher training and not university, for no one gave me any career advice and my parents were not aware of alternative possibilities. Indeed, for a 'good Catholic girl' teaching children was a 'nice' safe choice. In ' "Carry on Caring": The Work of Women Teachers', Acker (1995, p. 33) says that 'My view is that there are certain cultural scripts seen as suitable for women in a given place and time'. And for me, a working-class woman at a teacher training college in the late 1960s, the 'choice' of teaching was almost inevitable.

Girls and women have traditionally been (re)produced through discourses of femininity, maternity and caring. Thus teaching and nursing are 'common-sense fillers' between leaving school and starting a family. To an extent, this process has been differently constructed for middle-class girls – further and higher education are additional interrupters of the inevitable process, although middle-class women may 'return' to their career while working-class mothers look for a job. However, Irish Catholic working-class girls are exposed to additional discourses in schools which render their culture invisible and to a church which historically has constructed women through, by and for men. This is a powerful habitus which may have particular repercussions for working-class women of Irish descent who work in higher education. Although these women are 'middle-class' in status and occupation, for some, the legacy of passivity and deference to men, to father and 'priest as father', the invisibility of Irish culture coupled with the tactic of 'passing' on class/ 'race' may produce silenced women. Some of these women may lack the assertiveness or the sense of 'rightful place' which seems to be part of the cultural capital of middle-class women.

I wondered in school, in college and in teaching, where we stood and who we were, the Irish in Britain? Particularly when teaching in inner London throughout the 1970s and 1980s I was disconcerted not to see any mention of my community although we were and are the 'biggest' ethnic minority in the UK. Hickman (1993, p. 298) has written about the 'masking of Irishness both within official discourse and for the children of working class Irish immigrants' and the way in which 'the Irish are frequently ignored or marginalised in discussions about ethnic minorities in Britain' (p. 285). For example, when the government set up a national inquiry into the educational needs of ethnic minorities in the UK, no mention was made of the Irish in Britain (The Swann Report: DES, 1985). It was as if the community did not exist. This omission and silence has 'complex consequences' (Hickman, 1993, p. 298) for children of Irish descent even if they attend Catholic schools. Quite simply, if your culture has been discounted the consequences are clear.

Outside of the home, every state mechanism attempted to deny them their Irishness and encouraged them to assimilate – to become integrated. In order to be accepted into society they had to reject their Irish identity. (IBRG (Lambeth), 1988)

When this distortion is worked through a state educational system which represents middle-class culture and habitus as the 'best' and 'most desirable', then for working-class Irish people there is a double pressure to reject both their 'race' and class. For 'successful' girls in the traditional academic sense from these backgrounds, there are the inevitable further pressures of a gendered regime and the patriarchy. Within all this for women, teaching as a 'caring' job is rendered not only acceptable, but desirable. For some Catholics teaching has the added virtue of making a social and ethical contribution – of doing good to others. It follows from this, and it is no surprise, that women in the academy are traditionally located in areas such as teacher education, educational departments and nursing studies which may well not be regarded as 'properly academic' (Bagilhole, 1993). This vexed issue of subject/discipline/area where women are positioned in the academy needs further research.

So far, I want to suggest that some aspects of my cultural habitus were repressive, limiting and highly sexist, racist and classist. At the same time I believe that my habitus provides a particular cultural 'capital' (Bourdieu, 1984) on which I can draw at certain times. My background provides me with a strength and sense of historical solidarity. It also provides me with a way into different sets of meanings and ways of seeing the world as contradictory, inconsistent and ambivalent. While habitus plays a powerful role in the construction of self and identity, it is important to recognize the unevenness and incompleteness of this process. The construction of identities is not a predetermined linear process of (re)production. Identity is not predetermined or static but open, fluid and uncertain. At this point it is critical to recognize the specificity of locale and the power of place in shaping our social worlds. As a child, being of working-class Irish descent positioned me in a powerful and all-consuming discourse. It was all I knew. But growing up in the inner city, living and working in inner London in the late twentieth century, being exposed to a range of counter-hegemonic discourses from literature, the media and shifts in society, is inevitably bound to interrupt and disrupt, to render unstable the old settled cultures, the old settled stories.

A Working-Class Women of Irish Descent in the Academy

My first job in the academy was in a Catholic college of higher education where I was responsible for training teachers. In many ways my work and conditions of service were similar to the working world of the school teacher.

We started teaching at 9 a.m. We were in college five days a week. We had to teach to an agreed maximum which was fifteen contact hours. We then had to visit students in school to observe their work. We also had to do marking and a great deal of preparation. Additionally, we had pastoral responsibilities for a great many students as well as administrative tasks. If we taught in the evenings, this was constructed as a 'window of opportunity' into high-status work which could possibly enhance our careers. Most of my colleagues who were used to working a 100 per cent contact time in school, and who were not unionized, saw little wrong with these conditions. We were 'in the academy' but the reality was more like the school house than the university. There was little incentive to participate in conferences, do research or give papers. None of us published anything at all. Indeed the dominant culture was 'school-focused' and not 'academic'. In many ways we prided ourselves on our continuity with school teaching; this provided us with a degree of authenticity. We lacked the confidence to assert ourselves as academics. Our work was in the main vocational, not intellectual. Only one person in my department had a PhD and she encouraged me to register for one as quickly as possible.

I spent five years at this college and I know that many of my teacher-education colleagues in the academy 'enjoy' similar experiences today. It is not just a question of the other side of the binary line – it is about culture, history, custom and practice. It may also be about the nature of the discipline itself – feminized vocational work like nursing, teaching, community work, may be more susceptible to poorer conditions of service. The academy is not of a piece, is not the same for everyone. There are important class and gender divisions within the world of higher education. Women who teach teachers are disadvantaged and their subordination is often disguised, from themselves as well as others, through discourses of impartiality, neutrality and professionalism (Maguire, 1993).

In this college, as in other institutions of higher education, there was never any need to assert that it was a middle-class setting. It was all perfectly clear. No one other than the cleaners or gardeners spoke with an inner-city/working-class accent. The secretarial and administrative support workers were all well-dressed 'nice presentable ladies' who embodied a middle-class persona. Historically teacher training colleges were places which stressed gentrification. The class basis of the institution permeated all aspects of life and impinged upon the students as much as it did the tutors. This occurred through a displacement of class. Class and occupational status were coupled together so that attending or working at the college as a tutor was rendered middle-class. The same is still true today in many institutions and departments of teacher training. Class is displaced by countervailing discourses such as professionalism and individualism. In particular, the emphasis on the 'child' at the centre of teaching and learning, where the child is not conceptualized as classed, 'raced' or gendered, has always contributed to these displacements and to an omission of the discussion of structural and material constraints. The focus is on the individual who, it is alleged, can escape from the 'limits' of class inheritance. And this, of course, has been the secret promise of teaching and education for the children of the working classes in Britain. But the trade-off seems to be that class is not mentioned, it does not exist. However, in my experience social class plays a fundamental and comprehensive role in the life of the academy but one which is deeply laid down and does not need to be activated. It is a slow, silent but deep constant in the lives of all who work in the academy, whether in a college of higher education or a university.

However, the fact of working at the Catholic college of higher education, while limiting and restricting in some ways, was also liberating and empowering in other respects. In many ways, working in a Catholic environment with other Irish people was a form of 'coming home'. It was comfortable and familiar although sometimes aggravating. I could 'read' the culture in a way which I have not been able to do so well in other institutions. Many of the students came from the same background as mine – some were recruited directly from Ireland. And yet some of the stereotypical working-classed Catholic practices of my childhood were being challenged by feminist theologians and by some of the wonderfully transgressive women with whom I worked. However, working at this college was professionally another form of 'prisonhouse' (Steedman, 1987) where your heart and mind and body were devoured for the sakes of the students instead of primary school children. The institution was different; the discourse was identical.

> I never left them: they occupied all the night-times, all my dreams. I was very tired, bone-achingly tired all the time. I was unknowingly, covertly expected to become a mother, and I unknowingly became one, pausing only in the cracks of the dark night to ask: what is happening to me? (Steedman, 1987, p. 127)

I now work at one of the 'old' universities. I continue to teach teachers, both pre-service and in-service. But the expectations now of me are that I have an academic role to fulfil – publication and research are perhaps more important than teaching in this setting. Here there are different oppressions, opportunities, silences and voices. I recognize the way in which women are constructed as the 'other academics' (Acker, 1994) and frequently talk to women from other universities about issues of our lower profile in the academy. Yet rarely in these arenas is the talk of class, perhaps because many of my colleagues now come (or seem to come) from middle-class backgrounds – more so than when I worked in the training college. And when we talk of race relations' issues, anti-Irish racism is scarcely mentioned as a feature of contemporary life.

Speaking Ourselves: Women in the Academy

My childhood and education taught me many things. One was that what counted as knowledge was an ideological construction. My own different knowledge of class and culture was not valued at school or college and was rendered invisible. Any attempt to voice these was ignored or repressed. In order to 'succeed' I was expected to displace my own experience and 'take on' a different perspective – white, male and middle-class. However, this 'common-sense' hegemony of white male middle-class dominance of the academy is masked by a version of neutrality. Robertson (1992, p. 44) has written of the way in which some educational institutions have 'avoided or dismissed analyses and research which identify systematic bias' in their practices. She explains this avoidance as 'the utilization of the prerogative of every dominant class, which has been called "the right to not know"' (*ibid.*). Higher educational institutions may be resistant to recognizing their involvement with inequality. But no institution is immune from the cultural beliefs and values of society. They may eschew inegalitarian talk but they 'speak' inequality in and through their forms and practices.

Women in the academy share sets of gendered expectations and institutional factors which can work to limit and restrict our development. 'Women's emphasis on pastoral care and teaching is to the detriment of their careers . . . they may be convinced that they are not "proper" academics' (Bagilhole, 1993, p. 272) although clearly this emphasis is not the same for all women. At the same time the differences between women of the same occupational status are frequently overlooked and thus parts of our lives are rendered invisible. What I have started to do in this chapter is to focus on a hitherto neglected community: working-class Catholics of Irish descent. This is a first tentative step. The intention has been to reveal more of the differences between women in the academy, specifically those of social class. Until now, class issues (in higher education) have commonly been hidden behind the rhetoric of professionalism or buried beneath the mobility and status gained through formal education. But the fundamental intention behind all this is not just to contribute towards any further fragmenting and dissolving of women as a theoretical and analytical category. 'Transforming the terms of our difference towards the possibility for social equality is the potential achievement of feminist politics' (Lewis, 1993, p. 17).

References

ACKER, S. (1994) *Gendered Education*, Buckingham and Philadelphia, Open University Press.

ACKER, S. (1995) 'Carry on Caring: The Work of Women Teachers', *British Journal of Sociology of Education*, 16, 1, pp. 21–36.

AZIZ, A. (1990) 'Women in UK Universities – The Road to Casualization', in STIVER LIE, S. and O'LEARY, V. E. (Eds) *Storming the Tower: Women in the Academic World*, London, Kogan Page, pp. 33–46.

BAGILHOLE, B. (1993) 'How to Keep a Good Women Down: An Investigation of the Role of Institutional Factors in the Process of Discrimination against Women Academics', *British Journal of Sociology of Education*, 14, 3, pp. 261–74.

BANNERJI, H., CARTY, L., DEHLI, K., HEALD, S. and MCKENNA, K. (1991) *Unsettling Relations: The University as a Site of Feminist Struggle*, Toronto, Ontario, Canada, Women's Press.

BOURDIEU, P. (1984) *Distinction: A Social Critique of the Judgement of Taste*, London, Routledge and Kegan Paul.

BOURDIEU, P. (1990) *The Logic of Practice*, Cambridge, Polity.

DES (1985) *Education for All: The Report of the Committee of Inquiry into the Education of Children from Ethnic Minority Groups* (The Swann Report), London, HMSO Cmnd 9453.

EVANS, M. (1991) *A Good School: Life at a Girls' Grammar School in the 1950s*, London, The Women's Press.

HARVEY, D. (1989) *The Condition of Postmodernity*, Cambridge, Basil Blackwell.

HICKMAN, M. J. (1993) 'Integration or Segregation? The Education of the Irish in Britain in Roman Catholic Voluntary-Aided Schools', *British Journal of Sociology of Education*, 14, 3, pp. 285–300.

HUTTON, W. (1996) *The State We're In*, 2nd edn, London, Vintage.

IRISH IN BRITAIN REPRESENTATION GROUP (LAMBETH) (1988) *Racism and the Irish*, pamphlet.

KELLY, G. P. and SLAUGHTER, S. (Eds) (1991) *Women's Higher Education in Comparative Perspective*, Dordrecht, Boston and London, Kluwer Academic Publishers.

LENNON, M., MCADAM, M. and O'BRIEN, J. (1988) *Across the Water: Irish Women's Lives in Britain*, London, Virago.

LEWIS, M. G. (1993) *Without a Word: Teaching Beyond Women's Silence*, New York and London, Routledge.

MAGUIRE, M. (1993) 'Women Who Teach Teachers', *Gender and Education*, 5, 3, pp. 269–81.

ROBERTSON, H.-J. (1992) 'Teacher Development and Gender Equity', in HARGREAVES, A . and FULLAN, M. (Eds) *Understanding Teacher Development*, New York, Teachers College Press/London, Cassell, pp. 43–61.

ROSSITER, A. (1993) 'Bringing the Margins Into the Centre: A Review of Aspects of Irish Women's Emigration', in SMYTHE, A. (Ed.) *Irish Women's Studies Reader*, Dublin, Attic Press, pp. 177–203.

STEEDMAN, C. (1987) 'Prisonhouses', in LAWN, M. and GRACE, G. (Eds) *Teachers: The Culture and Politics of Work*, Lewes, Falmer Press, pp. 117–29.

STIVER LIE, S. and O'LEARY, V. E. (Eds) (1990) *Storming the Tower: Women in the Academic World*, London, Kogan Page.

STIVER LIE, S., MALIK, L. and HARRIS, D. (Eds) (1994) *The Gender Gap in Higher Education* (*World Yearbook of Education*), London and Philadelphia, Kogan Page.

SUTHERLAND, M. B. (1994) 'Two Steps Forward and On Step Back: Women in Higher Education in the United Kingdom', in STIVER LIE, S., MALIK, L. and HARRIS, D. (Eds) *The Gender Gap in Higher Education* (*World Yearbook of Education*), London and Philadelphia, Kogan Page, pp. 131–42.

UNIVERSITIES FUNDING COUNCIL (UFC) (1990) *University Statistics 1988–9, Vol. 1, Students and Staff*, Cheltenham, Universities Statistical Records.

Chapter 10

Switching Cultures

Monika Reinfelder

This chapter reflects on my journey as a German working-class woman through an English middle-class education and profession; my concern for class politics and my alienated encounter with middle-class, heterosexual feminism.

Recent feminist theory in this country has attempted to denormalize 'whiteness' and heterosexuality ((charles), 1992; Kitzinger and Wilkinson, 1993; Hickman and Walter, 1995), but has not extended this to middle-class culture (manner, accent, social rules, lifestyles, etc). As in all power relations only the oppressed is in a position of knowledge of both forms (e.g. lesbian/ heterosexual, black/white, working-class/middle-class, disabled/able-bodied), while the oppressors are impaired by their assumption of normality. Their power position permits a lack of reflection. This chapter therefore is a plea to non-working-class feminists to denormalize their class position.

There is nothing new in this. Middle-class feminists in the USA showed initial concerns to deconstruct class more than twenty years ago:

> [T]he more privileged white, middle and upper class women have not recognized how they and the movement are oppressive and have not taken effective action to eliminate or at least work against class, race, and heterosexual oppression. . . . The issue is how will we eliminate the cause of these divisions – classist behaviour, class power, and class privilege – not how to shut up those who are bringing the problems out of the closet. (Bunch and Myron, 1974, p. 10)

That this did not happen in this country is most curious as many middle-class feminists identified as 'socialist' rather than as radical, thereby wanting to indicate that class as well as gender is an important tool of analysis. However, this analysis remained at the level of abstract theory, or used working-class women as data, but did not deconstruct middle-classness. Attempts to integrate women into Marxist class analysis in the form of the 'domestic labour debate', to address 'dilemmas of sex and class' (Phillips, 1987), as well as to posit women as a class (e.g. Delphy, 1984; Hanmer *et al.*, 1977; Walby, 1986) pre-empted the problematization of class as a dividing factor in the Women's Liberation Movement. And many for whom class was a lived experience took it for granted that we were exploited on the basis of class and instead focused on our exploitation as women.

In my case, class exploitation was more recognizable at first than the exploitation of women. I had the misfortune of encountering feminism in the form of women who complained about marriage, housework and childcare. At the time it was beyond me why any woman would even consider such activities. For me they constituted unacceptable and unnecessary choices, while wage labour was a necessity that involved no choice. I considered myself a post-feminist before feminism and immersed myself in the analysis of capitalist value relations instead. I do not recall what exactly made me conscious of my feminism, but it was certainly one of the most liberating experiences in my life. However, our focus on women's oppression pushed class oppression aside. Even concerns around sexuality, 'race', ethnicity and disability often left our class differences unacknowledged.

The idea of this volume was not only to look at class from a theoretical perspective, but to ground further analysis in our own experiences as working-class women. Most of us met in workshops organized in an academic context. Although not all of us are academics, most of us have a shared experience of having to move in a middle-class environment. This affects some of us more than others, some to the point of leaving the profession we had previously aspired to, not least because we felt it might offer an escape from the claustrophobic intellectual environment we had sometimes come from. Little did we know that some of us would suffocate even further.

I was prompted to write this contribution when a colleague, whom I greatly respected, left her job. Heavy workloads had prevented us from discussing the issues that so upset her. This led to her isolation as a working-class woman in a very stuffy middle-class environment in which she had difficulties coping. She was less experienced than I in criss-crossing class boundaries, and I felt that my silence (as well as that of others) had contributed to her alienation. In order to survive in our work environment we assimilate middle-class behaviour and are not always recognizable to each other. It is hoped that this chapter as well as others in this collection will be a small contribution to the prevention of working-class women being undermined professionally because of their class background. As such it not only is an appeal to middle-class women to denaturalize their class position, but also requests working-class women in middle-class environments to be 'out of the class closet'.

I do not wish to idealize working-class culture. I came to this country wanting to improve my material position through education (i.e. to learn English). This was in 1970, well after the 'economic miracle' that seemed to have passed my family by. I also hoped to widen my mental outlook; I felt restricted by my background, though at the time I had not identified this as 'class'. There is less working-class pride in my native country than there is in England where I first heard the term 'working-class', mostly in a derogatory sense. When, at university, I was asked to identify my class position, I did not know what that meant. In Germany discussions about class politics were restricted to the organized left and the academic environment to which I had no access. German language otherwise avoids reference to class. The different terminology used for manual worker (worker) and office worker (employee) acts as a useful divide and rule tactic, giving white-collar workers the illusion of belonging to the *Mittelstand* (= middle estate). Given that my mother worked as a single parent and part-time office worker (employee) I concluded that I must be middle-class (in spite of every male relative being in manual work). Anecdotes about hunger, homelessness and unemployment were not identified as discussions about class in my family; and none of us ever ventured outside our community (except when we went to see our GP or dentist) and therefore we did not differentiate ourselves from another class. We were the 'class-in-itself', 'not for-itself'. The only exception was my grandmother who other relatives whispered about because she voted 'red'. I did not know what that meant, I don't think the others did either. This taken-for-grantedness is succinctly expressed by Wolfe:

> I'm beginning to sense that class may have been the central driving force shaping my thinking, my feelings, my relationships. In fact, the influence of class has been at once so pervasive, and so woven into my sensibilities and reactions, that I've never been able to isolate or analyse it before.
>
> At last, I think I'm finally starting to 'get' class. (Wolfe, 1994, p. 291)

When I came to this country I could not distinguish, at the outset, between middle-classness and Englishness. Again, this was not conscious. Typical of the German post-war generation (and insulting to Jewish people) I had erased 'nationality' from my mind. For me there were only people, nationality did not matter. It took me a while to recognize that I was out of step with the rest of the world. Initially, like many first-generation migrants, I tried to assimilate. I even felt complimented by the fact that people never guessed my nationality (and even less my class). It was only when a 'friend' told me that she didn't like Germans, but she liked me because I was almost English, that I learned that rejection of nationality is the privilege of those who are in a position to reject. As Rommelsbacher explains:

> What existential importance the nation has after all can only grasp those who have experienced the loss of national belonging, especially refugees and migrant workers. German Jews had to experience the robbing of their national belonging in an absolute existential way. Not only was their *Heimat* taken away, but their fundamental right to existence was denied. (Rommelsbacher, 1995, p. 194, my translation)

The intersection of class and nationality is complex and still leaves me dislocated when switching between English middle-class, English working-class,

German working-class and German middle-class cultures. The lack of theorization becomes more apparent when forced to switch cultures, and I am influenced by German feminists who at last have begun to theorize their political/cultural identity in the context of German (racist) history (e.g. Thuermer-Rohr, 1994; Rommelsbacher, 1995). This has led them at least to pose the question of an *historical* identity rather than assume a *natural* one. For me middle-class culture in the UK is inextricably tied to the dominant ethnic group. The specificity of middle-classness is linked to English colonial/imperial history which has contributed to the formation of the personalities of the English middle class (see Ware, 1992).

In my social, political and work environments I am constantly praised and criticized for being very upfront and direct by English women (not by women from other cultures, which leads me to think that I am just 'normal'). This causes ambivalence in some women who on the one hand approve of directness (after all feminism demands it) and on the other hand are threatened by it for reasons unknown to me. One even made a video of my 'directness' which subsequently made me feel like an exhibit (foreign species demonstrating culturally distinct peculiarities). To be direct is, of course, a tenet of feminism. However, it is not part of middle-class English culture. Centuries of colonialism, 'race' and class exploitation require denial. To say directly what you think is considered primitive, not polite. McEwen, reflecting on her upper-class upbringing, explains:

> Being nice meant manners. . . . But it did not, perhaps could not, involve saying what you really thought. That, we were told firmly, was called tactlessness.
>
> It is obvious to me now that both niceness and betterness are maintained on a firm foundation of unasked questions. The pattern of exchange is laid down in childhood, and assiduously reinforced thereafter. People are kept separate from each other, even when they meet and talk and smile. There is small risk, small danger of intimacy. This is bad enough among the upper classes themselves. Across classes, its function becomes altogether more sinister. . . .
>
> [N]iceness is a very useful tool. It gives the upper classes some sort of camouflage to operate behind, at the same time as it aims to distract everyone else from what is actually going on. 'Lord and Lady Bountiful are so generous, so polite . . .'. If you continue to think along these lines, social privilege soon appears entirely natural. (McEwen, 1994, pp. 270–1)

Niceness is used as an armour to keep people at bay. To me it has always appeared as rude and impolite. The message that comes across signifies a lack of interest. Nevertheless, middle-class social graces can also be used to make other people feel at ease. But even this is viewed with suspicion by working-class women:

> If, through your social skills and politeness, you have the ability to make any of us feel comfortable, realize that we know you also have the skills and tools to make us feel *uncomfortable* and that we've seen you use them in this way even if you don't think you ever have. (Elliott, 1994, p. 282)

The English middle class has perfected the skill of saying something without saying it. This often leaves working-class women and women from other cultures bewildered. To feel somewhat uneasy in a 'foreign' culture is exacerbated by a lack of clarity and directness. Outsiders to this culture are not familiar with the taken-for-granted cues. This is known to some middle-class women: see for example a manual on interviewing skills that alerts to possible discrimination when asking a non-English candidate an indirect question that is most likely to prompt a direct, short and insufficient answer (Hedge and Darling, 1992).

I was given the verdict 'sophisticated' when attending interview for undergraduate study, and learned two things while at university. A lecturer informed us that even if we did not learn anything at all in our three years at college we would certainly learn how to become middle-class. This proved correct. The second issue I acquired knowledge of was the mechanism of capitalist exploitation of the male working class. This proved a useful bit of information to which I still refer today, and I certainly miss this understanding in many of my present postgraduate students who, due to the absence of class analysis, are very susceptible to liberal analysis not only of class, but also of sexuality, disability, race and gender.

Having learned how to be middle-class my contacts with my family, who continue to be firmly steeped in German working-class culture (I am still the only one with a university education), keep me grounded. My relatives perceive me as 'successful' (I don't) which produces admiration and resentment, both of which I find difficult to deal with. Like many first-generation academics my education (and even more so my politics, which is connected to my education, albeit not academic) has set me apart from my family in lifestyle, behaviour, attitude, sexuality and language. Words like 'class', 'race', 'lesbian', 'sexist' are still absent from my family's vocabulary; and the need to switch concepts often leaves me very inarticulate.

I am aware, however, that this switching of cultures (albeit disconcerting) is in many ways a privilege that many others who come from a similar class background cannot afford. I had the fortune to grow up in a female-only household with a mother who encouraged independence and self-reliance to a fault. This contributed to me escaping motherhood, marriage and heterosexuality (unlike other women in my family) and largely determined my choice of education, profession, sexuality and lifestyle. Also I am at present able-bodied which enables me to place myself in different regional/cultural/class locations from which I ultimately benefit. In contrast, for many disabled working-class women choice of education and occupation is severely restricted and constrained by a disabling physical and social environment (see Morris, 1991; Kassandra, 1995).

In addition, whiteness opens doors. The underrepresentation of black women at university level testifies to this. However, anti-German xenophobia does not help. Although not subjected to the ridicule, jeering, whistling, Hitler-salutes and name-calling that I have experienced outside the academic community, the deeply ingrained xenophobia, anti-German attitudes are present in a different form. Students at various times have told me that I do not look German (I do indeed not fit the Hitlerite stereotype), that I do not sound German (I do indeed not sound like an English actor unsuccessfully imitating a German accent in an anti-German war movie), and that I could not possibly be German because I am 'so nice'.

This, however, is a slight improvement on the treatment I got as an undergraduate when a lecturer told me that my father was a rich industrialist who had sent me to study in England. I found this bewildering as I knew enough about the rich to know that they send their daughters to somewhat more distinguished universities than the one I was attending at the time. As I had learned English from middle-class teachers I did not speak with a working-class accent and I was often criticized for speaking 'posh'. Few made the effort to communicate with me in my native language which I speak with a regional/tribal accent (accent in German is rarely a signifier of class). I was also told that I did not 'look working-class', i.e. unattractive, unconfident and unsophisticated; and that my looks were 'bought', that is my appearance was a result of my supposedly rich background. Needless to say the university did not have a policy on harassment (academics do not need such things – they are 'nice').

Not being a member of the dominant culture severely restricts my professional mobility. Being dependent on the international community for my sanity has made me reluctant to get a better job 'out in the sticks' with little access to the non-English community. My preference for an international rather than national community is also the reason for my enthusiasm for international political work and my apathy in relation to more localized work.

I have always been amazed at middle-class identification with work. The question 'what do you do?' still feels irrelevant and stilted to me. Academic work is not something that I identify with, that is essential to my self, it is merely something that pays my bills at the moment. As such it is slightly more rewarding than other types of employment that I previously occupied: factory and office work, childcare, cleaning, selling, modelling, designing, translating. Paradoxically, entering university has reaffirmed my belief in equality. Contrary to the implication of recent debates and policies on school selection, intelligence and academic excellence are not the prerogative of the middle class. I entered university in the hope of meeting intelligent people I could learn from. Little did I know that my illusions would be smashed very quickly. In twenty years of university life I have had the constant experience that people who occupy university space are no more and no less intelligent and able than the rest of the world. What I did learn was that academic achievement is circumstantial and not ability-based.

What I also learned was how the academic environment greatly contributes to the perpetuation of class divisions. Therefore, feminists' concerns about 'class' should not consist of the objectification of, and development of theoretical constructs about the 'working class'; more fruitful would be the taking of responsibility for the involvement in the perpetuation of, and participation in, classism. To conclude in the words of Rommelsbacher:

> Identity is not a hermetic concept, just as nation is not a monolithic formation. Identity as subjective reflection of objective belonging has to show in itself the contradictions, the variety and domination that it encounters in reality. For that reason it would be fatal to rely on a hegemonic concept of identity which reduces the complexity in the interest of positions of power. However, to avoid the debate is not a solution either, but rather expression of helpless defensiveness motivated by a need for denial. (Rommelsbacher, 1995, p. 208, my translation)

References

BUNCH, CHARLOTTE and MYRON, NANCY (Eds) (1974) *Class and Feminism*, Baltimore, Diana Press.

(CHARLES), HELEN (1992) 'Whiteness – The Relevance of Politically Colouring the "Non"', in HINDS, HILARY, PHOENIX, ANN and STACEY, JACKIE (Eds) *Working Out: New Directions for Women's Studies*, London, Falmer Press.

DELPHY, CHRISTINE (1984) *Close to Home*, London, Hutchinson.

ELLIOTT (1994) 'Whenever I Tell You the Language We Use is a Class Issue, You Nod Your Head in Agreement – and Then You Open Your Mouth', in PENELOPE, JULIA (Ed.) *Out of the Class Closet: Lesbians Speak*, California, The Crossing Press.

HANMER, JALNA, LUNN, CATHY, JEFFREYS, SHEILA and McNEILL, SANDRA (1977) 'Sex Class – Why Is It Important to Call Women a Class?', *Scarlet Women*, 5.

HEDGE, ANNIE and DARLING, BARBARA (1992) *Fair Interviewing*, Stoke-on-Trent, Trentham Books.

HICKMAN, MARY J. and WALTER, BRONWEN (1995) 'Deconstructing Whiteness: Irish Women in Britain', *Feminist Review*, 50 (Summer).

KASSANDRA (1995) '... dass Du Dir ein selbstbestimmtes Leben kaum leisten kannst', *Ihrsinn*.

KITZINGER, CELIA and WILKINSON, SUE (1993) *Heterosexuality*, London, Sage.

McEWEN, CHRISTIAN (1994) 'Growing Up Upper Class', in PENELOPE, JULIA (Ed.) *Out of the Class Closet: Lesbians Speak*, California, The Crossing Press.

MORRIS, JENNY (1991) *Pride Against Prejudice*, London, The Women's Press.

PHILLIPS, ANNE (1987) *Divided Loyalties: Dilemmas of Sex and Class*, London, Virago.

ROMMELSBACHER, BIRGIT (1995) *Dominanzkultur: Texte zur Fremdheit und Macht*, Berlin, Orlanda.

THUERMER-ROHR, CHRISTINA (1994) *Verlorene Narrenfreiheit*, Berlin, Orlanda.

WALBY, SYLVIA (1986) *Patriarchy at Work*, Cambridge, Polity.

WARE, VRON (1992) *Beyond the Pale: White Women, Racism and History*, London, Verso.

WOLFE, SUSAN J. (1994) 'Getting Class', in PENELOPE, JULIA (Ed.) *Out of the Class Closet: Lesbians Speak*, California, The Crossing Press.

Chapter 11

A Class of One's Own: Women, Social Class and the Academy

Louise Morley

Introduction

A powerful aspect of class oppression is the negation of the intelligence of working-class people. Cultural misinformation and negative stereotyping can contribute to a distorted reading of academic abilities. This chapter critically analyses the coagulation of internalized psychic narratives, and external discriminatory factors as a result of the interrelation of social class and gender oppression in higher education. It will consider how the reification and closure implied by traditional class categories can lead to feelings of fraudulence and contradiction in educated working-class feminists. Using feminist theory, humanistic psychology and personal experience as impetus and frame, I explore the extent to which materialist definitions of social class are replicated in the class system of the intellect.

Getting It Right

It is always a challenge when writing about social class not to overwhelm self and readers with the pain and anger generated by discrimination, injustice and lost opportunities. Whilst autobiography is rapidly gaining credibility as a legitimate research method (L. Stanley, 1995), there is the danger of producing a piece of unrivalled self-indulgence, or worse, a 'literary striptease' (Lewis, 1992, p. 5). As I write these words, my deeply embedded psychic narratives begin to play loudly and clearly. Does this already sound too emotive, too rhetorical, too cathartic? Should I rapidly inject some references to research studies and critical social theories? How might I interrogate the subject in a disembodied, sanitized way, without activating my class distress? For the latter merely serves to remind the ruling class of my inferiority and unfitness to roam the corridors of academia. Or I could situate myself, and announce with pride how my mother is an immigrant from Malta and how my grandfather drove buses in South London for a living. Yet this inverted snobbery sounds clichéd and ingratiating, as if I am desperate to establish class credentials.

You will notice how my locus of accountability shifts from fear of disapproval, rejection and exclusion from the heteropatriarchal hierarchy of dominant institutions, to the voices I have internalized from working-class Britain.

And so the story of social class unfurls, with polarizations and boundaries continually requiring definition by self and others, and yet constantly existing to make one feel 'other'. In the Lacanian concept of the gaze, the powerful describe and define the powerless, positioning them in oppositional status, to react and rant and rave. This raises challenges as to how we speak social class without always 'othering' ourselves. Furthermore, it exemplifies that social class is a process, in relationship, rather than a fixed entity in itself (Shaw, 1995).

An important part of my class identity has always been one of confusion. In my early years, in prosperous post-war Britain, consumer capitalism flourished. Class mobility, in my family, was associated with material acquisitions, rather than intellectual and cultural development. We moved out of the inner city and into the suburbs and tried to acquire signifiers associated with affluence, such as a garden, a television and a mortgage. We began to believe that we could become middle-class by changing postal address or working in an office.

As a young student, I studied Marx and Engels and read research studies on class and education, such as Bernstein (1973) and Lacey (1970). I became angry about class discrimination in education and social reproduction, but for me at that time the working classes were elsewhere, down mines and in factories and living in the poor areas of East London, Glasgow and Salford. While my political analysis of social class was sharpening, I had no notion of my own position in the class struggle. This disembodied knowledge distanced me from my own experiences. Unable to relate analytically the macropolitical to the micropolitical, I, like many young people, blamed my family for everything, believing that they were deliberately holding me back in life. I was unable to perceive how they were enacting their class oppression in their relationship with me. Nor had I any understanding of how my classed and gendered experiences had shaped my inner world, my self- image and sense of worth. Emotionally, I could never identify as middle-class, as I did not come from a background where people read books and played violins, like the families of my schoolfriends. Yet to describe myself as working-class felt hypocritical as my parents had a mortgage and I had entered higher education.

Class definitions are always problematic.[1] Trevithick (1988, p. 63) addressed this issue in her introduction to a working-class women's workshop at the Women's Therapy Centre, London:

> This workshop is for working class women only, which for us means women who have a working class parent. Since we don't accept that higher education should be the monopoly of the upper or middle classes, nor an excuse to dispossess us of our heritage, this workshop is open to women who have struggled through the classism of our education system to acquire a formal education.

My struggle to access higher education exposed class privilege to me, both in terms of what I lacked in relation to the ruling class and what I possessed, compared to other women from working-class backgrounds. The dilemma of divided loyalties has become a cliché of class theory (Phillips, 1987). Discussion is often framed in terms associated with purity and danger:

> To participate in the academic definition of their own class culture, working class people must become part of the colonizing/mediating group; they must become credentialised via higher education. While this does not mean that they abandon their class identity, the fact remains that, by virtue of the lengthy process of participating in education, they will become 'contaminated'. (Lynch and O'Neill, 1994, p. 318)

In my case, contamination came much earlier as my class background was one of denial of working-class origins. My family tried to 'better themselves' by pursuing what they perceived as signifiers of class mobility. We were sent to grammar schools, and to elocution lessons. Merely attending the 'right' school was thought to be sufficient. Working-class families could relax, in the knowledge that their offspring would be inducted into middle-class values and knowledges. Grammar schools contained a hidden promise of quality assurance. As Evans (1995a, p. 61) indicates,

> Being a grammar school pupil has always had status in English society – any grammar school, however inferior or unsuccessful, has been able to make the proud boast that its pupils have been 'selected'.

My convent education schooled me, but failed to encourage me, with cruel teachers playing Cassandra, telling me that I would end up working in Woolworths if I failed to learn the subjunctive mode of French verbs. I was lively, streetwise and challenging. I had always had Saturday and evening jobs. I knew there was a world outside, and school implied the relentless regulation of my sexuality, appearance, social life. Only the quiet, scholarly and somewhat dull young women were encouraged to stay on and apply for university. Nobody in my family had stayed at school a minute longer than they had to. Hence, I left school at 16, with a string of 'O' levels, but also with a distorted view of my identity and abilities, and realized, much later, that I had been misinformed, and that this misinformation was directly linked to not possessing the cultural capital to interpret middle-class readings of my capabilities, or to understand the consequences of educational and career choices.

Identity Politics

In my early twenties, I began to engage critically with feminism, anti-racism and anti-heterosexism. These structures both illuminated and confused my class analysis, as the mania to establish hierarchies of oppression was a feature of the 1970s political scene. As a student in the north of England, I was perceived as a privileged oppressor from the capital, with a pretentious accent (the result of my class-distressed elocution lessons!). And yet I felt angry and oppressed and still resistant to the closure implied in labelling. I could not speak my oppression, because someone else would tell me how privileged I was compared to them. To talk about my own disappointments and hurt felt like special pleading and part of the process of democratizing oppressions. As Epstein (1993, p. 18) indicated,

> The development of subjective identities is both complex and important, and identities themselves are multi-faceted and contradictory. They are formed through a combination of available discourses, personal experience and material existence.... It is by drawing boundaries and placing others outside those boundaries that we establish our identities.

Hence, our identities both define and differentiate us and are dependent on available discursive frameworks. In the 1970s, there was a modernist notion of a unified left. To draw attention to gender, for example, was seen as fragmentation.

The 'working class' was perceived as a homogeneous group, discursively located in opposition to the owning/ruling class. It was left to women and black people to indicate how this approach was yet another variation of white male dominance. The concept of identity politics, as Bourne (1983) indicated, can mean that class is a sanctuary to abdicate responsibility for race-oppressor identity. Class oppression can become something one wheels out, competitively, to convince others of the lived experience of subordination. This can also account for the enormous pain of working on one's racism, as feelings of lack and guilt can be easily activated (Green, 1987; Morley, 1992). Much of the debate on social class and identity politics was couched in either/or dualistic thinking. To theorize social class, we risked subsuming or overlooking other structures of inequality, but focusing on the other structures was seen as a dilution of the class struggle. And so a lifelong elaborate dance was created, with me trying to challenge inequalities as both oppressed and oppressor.

Even in the 1990s, with access to complex theoretical frameworks with which to analyse power relations, such as postmodernism and poststructuralism, it is not uncommon for groups to assert the seriousness of their oppression by differentiating it from the 'easy ride' enjoyed by other oppressed groups. For example, Lynch and O'Neill (1994, p. 307) theorize social class in relation to education, and emphasize how

> working class people occupy a structurally contradictory role in relation to education: on the one hand, social mobility generally requires that they be well-educated. Yet if they are to succeed in the education system they have to abandon certain features of their class

background. They cease to be working class to some degree. Other oppressed or marginalised groups in education, do not lose their defining minority identity or status by being educated: an educated woman never ceases to be a woman, an educated black person never ceases to be black, and a physically disabled person who is educated never ceases to be disabled.

While I can see that the point being argued relates to the problematics of social mobility and identity, I feel it is always unfortunate to compare one oppressed group with another in this way. This type of explanation overlooks the complex, unstable nature of identity and undermines the struggles black people and disabled people encounter in the academy (Mirza, 1995; Potts and Price, 1995; Rassool, 1995; Gibson, 1996). Furthermore, it risks essentializing identity. As Sinfield (1994) argues, all members of oppressed groups have to work hard at ventriloquizing establishment culture in academia, and this 'mimicry' can produce a self-division and painful lack of convergence between the initial culture of family and neighbourhood, and the acquired culture. Lynch and O'Neill also make repeated references to 'a working class perspective', suggesting an enlightenment universality of experiences undifferentiated by 'race', gender, sexualities, disabilities and age.

The challenge remains as to how to keep social class on the political and social agenda without degenerating into rivalrous claims, resorting to universalities, or pursuing the postmodernist preoccupation with dispersed power. Rose (1994, p. 59) draws attention to how the intersection of feminism with postmodernism and poststructuralism has eliminated discussion of social class:

> numbers of theoretically oriented feminists have shifted toward broadly poststructuralist positions, paying attention to subtleties of difference yet somehow not naming class as a major source of difference even at a time when class groups have sharpened.

The discussion of social class has been confounded by the reconceptualizing of identities and subjectivities. The idea that subjectivity is multiple poses some critical questions for standpoint, identity and materialist politics. Walby (1994) indicates that in contrast to the totalizing framework of traditional Marxism, which attempted to tuck all other forms of social inequality under that of class, the focus on complexity and fragmentation expounded in postmodern social theory denies the coherence of classic analytical concepts such as 'woman', 'class' and 'race'. In their dispersal of identity and power, Walby argues that postmodernists neglect the social context of power relations. She believes that, in spite of the reconceptualization of power, 'patriarchy and racism remain potent social forces, and capitalism has not withered away' (1994, p. 226).

With the emphasis on text in some postmodernist thought, 'men' and 'women', 'black' and 'white' are perceived as discursive constructs, rather than materially existing social groups founded upon unequal and exploitative relationships. Lown (1995) expresses concern that the postmodern preoccupation with dispersed power contradicts the possibility of activism. The rejection of the concept of monolithic power embodied in the state, militia or monarchy means the absence of a tangible target. However, as I write, France, the home of postmodernism, has been brought to a standstill as a result of public sector industrial action, suggesting that 'working class' might be more than a discursive category.

Feelings of Fraudulence: Theorizing Internalized Oppression

Classifications of social class inevitably involve closure and reification which leave us uncertain if we have accurately located ourselves in any one category. Shifting identities and social locations mean that there are advantages and disadvantages to being perceived as working-class by some and middle-class by others. Simplistic market-research-type taxonomies utilize income and occupation as indicators. Materialist definitions can be misguiding. For example, it is not uncommon for educational research to utilize indicators of poverty, such as free school dinners, to act as evidence of social class. But there are, as Sennett and Cobb (1977) reminded us, 'hidden injuries of class'. In academia, there is a class system of the intellect, with entry into elite institutions an opportunity to access some of our most painful and powerful feelings of inadequacy and failure (J. Stanley, 1995). This residue of self-doubt and self-blame is often referred to as internalized oppression, a term which Trevithick (1988, p. 72) defines as follows:

> we come to *believe* in our own inferiority, worthlessness and power-lessness, both as individuals and as a group. Whenever we act out negative messages against ourselves and each other, internalised oppression is at work.

For working-class women becoming 'educated' is a complex combination of achievement, struggle and betrayal. It means that wherever we are, there are vast reservoirs of experience and insights we must not speak. It involves learning to reject and to be rejected. Trevithick (1988, p. 63) points out that:

> 'privileges' (e.g. education, high income, etc.) have been used to divide, isolate and confuse our sense of identity with our culture, family, friends and other individuals who share a commitment to end class injustices.

Trevithick makes the assumption that our families and friends want to end classism. Power relations in the class system also construct our desires and wishes. One of the more destructive consequences of internalized oppression is that it keeps the class system alive, by ensuring that social distinctions and a hierarchy of differing values and aspirations embed themselves in our consciousness. The consequences can be an elaborate ritual of separation and connection, with working-class women measuring self-worth in relation to others.

McIntosh (1985, p. 3) uses a different terminology and describes the concept as 'feeling like a fraud'. She argues that hierarchical structures and class stratifications inevitably breed feelings of fraudulence and a sense of being an imposter among 'women and lower class men'. The academy, with its claims to authority and knowledge production, provides perfect preconditions for feelings of fraudulence. The hierarchical nature of its organization reinforces social class hierarchies to provide potent feelings of self-doubt. Miner (1993, p. 81) describes her internalized narratives:

> Like many other college teachers from working class homes, I am amazed when I look around and see myself teaching...I feel a fraud, fearful that someone will discover that I don't belong in front of the classroom.

McIntosh agrees that these feelings are partly the consequences of internalized oppression, but also a deeply wise refusal to collude in the pretence that is required to uphold hierarchies and social divisions.

Elsewhere, the Groucho syndrome, which suggests that everything we acquire becomes devalued once it belongs to us, has some material substance to it. For example, the 1992 Further and Higher Education Act removed the binary divide between polytechnics and universities in the UK. Ainley (1994) argues that this has resulted in the widening of social and academic divisions in higher education. Evans (1995b, p. 74) believes that the transition from elitist institutions to large-scale teaching machines means that 'the *mere* acquisition of a first degree no longer carries the immediate cachet and promise of occupational privilege as it did thirty years ago' (Evans, 1995b, p. 74, emphasis original). Speaking from a different ideological position, Amis said in 1961 that 'if more lower-class people (sic) are let into higher education, standards will decline. More means worse' (quoted in Sinfield, 1993, p. 4). Bourdieu (1979) predicted this development when he argued how culturally arbitrary qualifications can change their worth as badges of distinction acquired by different social groups, and how new signs of exclusion can be evolved by traditional elites to preserve privileged access to the powerful positions they previously inherited but which are now ostensibly open to meritocratic competition. It would appear that increased access seems to be leading to educational inflation and negative equity, with the value of qualifications tumbling as more representatives from marginalized groups acquire them. Rather than associating widening access with enhanced quality and diversity, it is perceived as dilution, or pollution – a situation which challenges the very notion of equity in higher education.

For me, external signifiers of success and badges of distinction acquired in later life, such as degrees and publications, do not seem to have shifted potent internalized narratives installed, at an early age, by the class system. My father, an intelligent man from a poor working-class south London background, was afflicted with such a profound class wound that I unconsciously learned when I was very young that any ability and potential I possessed would always be ignored, negated and resented. Every educational success my father achieved was thwarted by class poverty. His entry to grammar school was delayed while his grandfather worked nights to buy the uniform. Later, he matriculated and won a place to study law at the University of London, but his parents needed his income, and sent him to work as a clerk in an insurance office. Their class background meant that they were unable to differentiate between a lawyer and a clerk, as the central criterion for success was a 'white-collar' job. The war came, he joined the army, and struggled up through the ranks to become a major, only to be told by his colonel that in peacetime men of his class would never have achieved that rank. My father frequently described himself to me as a 'failure', and he gave up struggling, feeling so overpowered by a class system that he could not theorize. Lacking a 'sociological imagination', he blamed himself. In many ways, I have replicated these patterns, constantly berating myself for making wrong decisions, finding out too late the path I should have taken, allowing myself to be held back by the resentments and limitations of others.

Insiders/Outsiders

There is a popular myth that the academy represents an ivory tower, protected from the abusive power relations which exist elsewhere. This dichotomous thinking suggests that working-class people are all on the outside, and mere entry into the academy automatically transforms class experiences and allegiances. Tensions between conflicting cultures were represented in titles of earlier studies on class and the academy such as *Strangers in Paradise* (Ryan and Sackrey, 1984). The relationship of the intellectual to social change has been theorized by Marxists (Gramsci, 1971), and feminists (Morley, 1995a), with Gramsci arguing the need for the working-class to create its own organic intelligentsia to foster a new social organization of knowledge. Critical social inquiry has become a discursive site for the rehearsal of many of these insider/ outsider dilemmas. The interconnection between domination and knowledge production is a subject of a rich debate (Stanley and Wise, 1993; Gitlin, 1994; Maynard and Purvis, 1994), with fears that social research is yet another form of class exploitation.

> The problem is compounded by the fact that most of those who are leaders in sociological analysis do their analysis of class from the comfort and distance of their university chairs. . . . The oppressed are an object of investigation, to be understood, analysed, and, if neces-

sary, structurally located: they are not the people with whom they live, or whose struggles they share. (Lynch and O'Neill, 1994, p. 310)

Stanley (1990, p. 68), herself a working-class sociologist, observes that working-class people are not within academia as participants in the making of socialist knowledge, or subjects, but as 'others' to be studied and observed. My belief is that working-class people are in academia, albeit in disgracefully low numbers, but would consider it fraudulent to name themselves as such (Morley, 1994).

The notion of class relations existing only outside the gates of academia disguises the class structure of the institution (Tokarczyk and Fay, 1993). There are hegemonies and hierarchies both in terms of employment and services. For example, the elitist preference for pure as opposed to applied knowledge means that professional education has relatively low status. It is no coincidence that many working-class women access the academy initially through teacher, community, youth and social work education (Walkerdine, 1990; Morley, 1993; Weiner, 1994). From my experience of working in professional education, I have noticed a strong assumption that a course's academic status is lowered if it attracts black and white working-class students.

Being in the Right Place at the Right Time

A missing discourse in class analysis is that of age. The class system subtly regulates by specifying age-appropriate behaviour and endeavours. The significance of the temporal dimension, in terms both of academic career development and student participation, is particularly relevant in the academy. As the higher education system is so traditionally elitist and hostile to women, it can take working-class women a long time to feel safe enough both to understand it and access it. Lack of guidance and support in youth can mean that socially expected durations can be transgressed by working-class women. So delayed educational timetables reinforce the negative image of working-class women being less scholarly than their middle-class counterparts.

Toren (1993, p. 447) describes how 'Off-time events . . . are frequently problematic and stressful'. This observation is exemplified in Edwards' (1993) study of mature women students. She highlights how working-class older women are being encouraged to enter higher education, while the academy remains unresponsive to their differing needs and lifestyles. This then creates considerable stress as the women have to contain and absorb pressures and expectations, and compartmentalize their student and familial roles. In Britain, the figures show that between 1979 and 1988 there was a 37 per cent increase in full-time mature students, with the proportion of women rising steadily from 41 per cent in 1979 to 48 per cent in 1988 (DES, 1991). However, the normative construction of 'a student' is still the 18-to-21-year-old 'bachelor boy', and mature women students are still termed 'non-traditional' with all the implied connotations of deviancy.

Epstein (1995, p. 61) describes how her former institution was successful in attracting mature black and white working-class students, but how staff were unable to support them and ensure their successful progress through degree courses. This was not, she states, because of lack of goodwill or commitment to equal opportunities, but 'because of the very pressure of numbers resulting from market success of attracting and accepting these students'. In other words, mass expansion led to potential short-changing of the new consumer, as the organization was not geared up to differing educational needs. Epstein also mentions concern expressed by the external examiner in relation to the large proportion of black, working-class women among those who failed the degree or had to resit part of it. This exemplifies the extent to which the market functions as a class strategy and the penalties incurred by recruiting 'value-added' students. As Lorde (1984, p. 115) notes, 'institutional rejection of difference is an absolute necessity in a profit economy which needs outsiders as surplus people'.

Studying full-time in one's youth is perceived as the appropriate path into the professions. Yet this requires access to financial, emotional and intellectual support which many working-class women do not have. I was lucky, in one sense, as I was a student in the 1970s, when it was still possible for young people to find work. I worked in offices for two years before doing my first degree, studying for 'A' levels at evening classes. I was able to finance my higher education, without involving my family at all. On graduating, I taught for two years in a comprehensive school and saved up to do a full-time MA. On completing my MA, at the age of 25, I considered staying on for a PhD but could not conceive how to fund myself. Tutors were only interested in male students, and one of them told me how irregular it was for them to accept students who had gaps in their education (i.e. my periods of work). I had a circle of middle-class friends who automatically turned to their parents for financial aid for housing, education, holidays, transport. I made the mistake of trying to emulate them and was left very hurt and crushed by my parents' resistance and refusal. Gardner (1993, p. 54) describes how working-class academics 'learn very early in their careers that their life-style, general interests, and work are largely incomprehensible to their families'. It is this lack of comprehension, at crucial stages in one's education, that can mean a reevaluation of aspirations and ambitions, as working-class women learn to settle for second best. With no support, I gave up, and like most women from my class background, went out to work and have been working full-time ever since.

Without wishing to sound like a character out of a Dickens novel, it took me a long time to realize the extent to which my internalized oppression made me overwork. In the relentless effort to prove myself in the academy, I prioritized servicing the development of others and frequently overlooked my own interests. This appears to be a familiar pattern.

Working class women academics are more likely to accept heavy teaching loads and committee work because of the psychological toll of crossing gender and class barriers. . . . Many feel a need to pay back. (Gardner, 1993, p. 16)

Two years ago, I finally paid attention to my career development needs and registered for a PhD. Now in my early forties, I am asked by middle-class colleagues why, at my career stage, do I not already have a doctorate. In spite of my strenuous efforts to 'catch up', I am made to feel in deficit. I do not attempt to explain how hard it has been, because that will merely legitimate further oppression.

Healing Ourselves

It would be erroneous to suggest that there is one formula to undo centuries of social and psychological injury to working-class women. For educated working-class women staying silent about class can be a strategy to avoid a commitment to unhelpful bipolarities. Defining our identities risks rejection and disbelief. While I do not wish to seal working-class women into victim identity, there is an issue of isolation in the academy, both for students and teachers. This raises questions about constituency and community.

As Trevithick (1988, p. 71) explains,

Through repeatedly having our hurtful experiences ignored, we are effectively denied an acknowledgment of our own oppression, which leaves us doubting our own versions of events or even our sanity.

Trevithick emphasizes the need for class analysis in order to gain some critical distance from the injustices.

Without this understanding of our oppression, we're left to heal old wounds while we gather new ones, or we're left divided or diverted off course into complaining about or blaming the wrong people (e.g. our parents) for injustices that are initiated at a much higher level in the actions of governments and other institutions. (*ibid.*)

Power relations in dominant organizations, such as the academy, can activate decades of class distress, while simultaneously offering us possibilities to theorize our gendered, classed experiences. Writing this chapter, knowing that the editors are both women from working-class backgrounds, has made a difference to my relation to textual production. I have noticed that my usual internalized narrative of terror and self-doubt when writing is playing at a lower volume (Morley, 1995b). I have also been surprised at how quickly and compulsively I wrote, trying to balance the emotional need to 'client' with the desire to locate my experiences within an analytical framework. Both are important parts of the healing process, as the theory legitimates and explains our feelings and vice versa. This book itself is a counter-hegemonic intervention, creating a community of writers and readers who want to make sense of complex feelings and relationships. Ryan and Sackrey (1984) argued that a working-class background ill prepares a budding intellectual for success in academia and haunts forever those who finally do emerge as university professionals. I would challenge this, suggesting that our anger and theorized experiences can be recycled into creativity and energy for change.

Note

1 Recession and high unemployment challenge the definition of 'working class', with new far right descriptors, such as 'underclass', entering the arena (Murray, 1990).

References

AINLEY, P. (1994) *Degrees of Difference*, London, Lawrence & Wishart.

BERNSTEIN, B. (1973) *Class, Codes and Control*, London, Routledge.

BOURDIEU, P. (1979) *Distinction: A Social Critique of the Judgement of Taste* (trans. Richard Nice), London, Routledge & Kegan Paul.

BOURNE, J. (1983) 'Towards an Anti-Racist Feminism', *Race and Class*, xxv, 1, pp. 1–22.

DEPARTMENT OF EDUCATION AND SCIENCE (DES) (1991) *Mature Students in Higher Education 1975–1988*, London, HMSO.

EDWARDS, R. (1993) *Mature Women Students*, London, Taylor & Francis.

EPSTEIN, D. (1993) *Changing Classoom Cultures: Anti-Racism, Politics and Schools*, Stoke on Trent, Trentham Books.

EPSTEIN, D. (1995) 'In Our (New) Right Minds: The Hidden Curriculum and the Academy', in MORLEY, L. and WALSH, V. (Eds) *Feminist Academics: Creative Agents for Change*, London, Taylor & Francis, pp. 56–72.

EVANS, M. (1995a) 'Culture and Class', in BLAIR, M., HOLLAND, J. and SHELDON, S. (Eds) *Identity and Diversity: Gender and the Experience of Education*, Clevedon, Multilingual Matters, pp. 61–73.

EVANS, M. (1995b) 'Ivory Towers: Life in the Mind', in MORLEY, L. and WALSH, V. (Eds) *Feminist Academics: Creative Agents for Change*, London, Taylor & Francis, pp. 73–85.

GARDNER, S. (1993) 'What's a Nice Girl Like You Doing in a Place Like This?', in TOKARCZYCK, M. and FAY, E. (Eds) *Working Class Women in the Academy*, Amherst, University of Massachusetts Press.

GIBSON, R. (1996) 'Deaf Women in Higher Education', in MORLEY, L. and WALSH, V. (Eds) *Breaking Boundaries: Women in Higher Education*, London, Taylor & Francis.

GITLIN, A. (Ed.) (1994) *Power and Method: Political Activism and Educational Research*, London, Routledge.

GRAMSCI, A. (1971) (Ed. Q. Hoare and G. Nowell-Smith), *Selections from the Prison Notebooks*. London, Lawrence & Wishart.

GREEN, M. (1987) 'Women in the Oppressor Role', in ERNST, S. and MAGUIRE, M. (Eds) *Living with the Sphinx*, London, The Women's Press, pp. 179–213.

LACEY, C. (1970) *Hightown Grammar: The School as a Social System*, Manchester, Manchester University Press.

LEWIS, R. (1992) 'Autobiography and Biography as Legitimate Educational Tasks or Pedagogic Terrorism', working paper presented at the Teachers Stories of Life and Work Conference, Chester, April.

LORDE, A. (1984) *Sister Outsider*, New York, The Crossing Press.

LOWN, J. (1995) 'Feminist Perspectives', in BLAIR, M., HOLLAND, J. and Sheldon, S. (Eds) *Identity and Diversity: Gender and the Experience of Education*, Clevedon, Multilingual Matters, pp. 107–22.

LYNCH, K. and O'NEILL, C. (1994) 'The Colonisation of Social Class in Education', *British Journal of Sociology of Education*, 15 (3), pp. 307–24.

MAYNARD, M. and PURVIS, J. (Eds) (1994) *Researching Women's Lives from a Feminist Perspective*, London, Taylor & Francis.

McINTOSH, P. (1985) *Feeling Like a Fraud*, Work in Progress No. 18, The Stone Centre, Wellesley, MA, Wellesley College.

MINER, V. (1993) 'Writing and Teaching with Class', in TOKARCZYCK, M. and FAY, E. (Eds) *Working Class Women in the Academy*, Amherst, University of Massachusetts Press, pp. 73–87.

MIRZA, H. S. (1995) 'Black Women in Higher Education: Defining a Space/ Finding a Place', in MORLEY, L. and WALSH, V. (Eds) *Feminist Academics: Creative Agents for Change*, London, Taylor & Francis, pp. 116–30.

MORLEY, L. (1992) 'Women's Studies, Difference and Internalised Oppression', *Women's Studies International Forum*, 15, pp. 517–25.

MORLEY, L. (1993) 'Women's Studies as Empowerment of "Non-Traditional" Learners in Community and Youth Work Training', in KENNEDY, M. LUBELSKA, C. and WALSH, V. (Eds) *Making Connections*, London, Falmer Press, pp. 118–29.

MORLEY, L. (1994) 'Glass Ceiling or Iron Cage: Women in UK Academia', *Journal of Gender, Work and Organization*, 1 (4), pp. 194–204.

MORLEY, L. (1995a) 'The Micropolitics of Women's Studies', in MAYNARD, M., and PURVIS. J. (Eds) *(Hetero)sexual Politics*, London, Taylor & Francis, pp. 171–85.

MORLEY, L. (1995b) 'Measuring the Muse: Creativity, Writing and Career Development', in MORLEY, L. and WALSH, V. (Eds) *Feminist Academics: Creative Agents for Change*, London, Taylor & Francis, pp. 116–30.

MURRAY, C. (1990) *The Emerging British Underclass*, London, Institute of Economic Affairs.

PHILLIPS, A. (1987) *Divided Loyalties: Dilemmas of Sex and Class*, London, Virago.

POTTS, T. and PRICE, J. (1995) 'Out of the Blood and Spirit of Our Lives: The Place of the Body in Academic Feminism', in MORLEY, L. and WALSH, V. (Eds) *Feminist Academics: Creative Agents for Change*, London, Taylor & Francis, pp. 102–15.

RASSOOL, N. (1995) 'Black Women as the "Other" in the Academy', in MORLEY, L. and WALSH, V. (Eds) *Feminist Academics: Creative Agents for Change*, London, Taylor & Francis, pp. 22–41.

ROSE, H. (1994) *Love, Power and Knowledge: Towards a Feminist Transformation of the Sciences*, Cambridge, Polity.

RYAN, J. and SACKREY, C. (1984) *Strangers in Paradise: Academics from the Working Class*, Boston, Mass., South End Press.

SENNETT, R. and COBB, J. (1977) *Hidden Injuries of Class*, Cambridge, Cambridge University Press.

SHAW, J. (1995) *Education, Gender and Anxiety*, London, Taylor & Francis.

SINFIELD, A. (1993) *Cultural Politics*, Professorial Lecture given at the University of Sussex on 9 March 1993.

SINFIELD, A. (1994) *Cultural Politics – Queer Reading*, London, Routledge.

STANLEY, J. (1995) 'Pain(t) for Healing: The Academic Conference and the Classed/Embodied Self', in MORLEY, L. and WALSH, V. (Eds) *Feminist Academics: Creative Agents for Change*, London, Taylor & Francis, pp. 169–82.

STANLEY, L. (Ed.) (1990) *Feminist Praxis*, London, Routledge.

STANLEY, L. (1995) 'My Mother's Voice? On Being a Native in Academia', in MORLEY, L. and WALSH, V. (Eds) *Feminist Academics: Creative Agents for Change*, London, Taylor & Francis, pp. 183–93.

STANLEY, L. and WISE, S. (1993) *Breaking Out Again*, London, Routledge.

TOKARCZYK, M. and FAY, E. (Eds) (1993) *Working Class Women in the Academy*, Amherst, University of Massachusetts Press.

TOREN, N. (1993) 'The Temporal Dimension of Gender Inequality in Education', *Higher Education*, 25, pp. 439–55.

TREVITHICK, P. (1988) 'Unconsciousness Raising with Working-Class Women', in KRZOWSKI, S. and LAND, P. (Eds) *In Our Experience*, London, The Women's Press, pp. 63–83.

WALBY, S. (1994) 'Towards a Theory of Patriarchy', in *The Polity Reader in Gender Studies*, Cambridge, Polity in association with Blackwell, pp. 22–8.

WALKERDINE, V. (1990) *Schoolgirl Fictions*, London, Verso.

WEINER, G. (1994) *Feminisms in Education*, Buckingham, Open University Press.

Chapter 12

Classifying Practices: Representations, Capitals and Recognitions

Beverley Skeggs

Charles Taylor (1994) and Nancy Fraser (1995) document the move in the 1990s away from a class politics based on concepts of exploitation to a politics based on the 'right to recognition' by different identity groups who present cultural domination as *the* fundamental injustice.[1] This claim for recognition has been generated by groups who feel proud to be recognized as 'something' (insert as appropriate categories of sexuality, race, nationality). This enables the dispersal of claims for redistribution based on structural inequalities into a movement for identity politics. As many feminist critiques have shown (see Parmar, 1989; Probyn, 1993a) identity politics often restricts political struggle to one singular difference which is promoted as an 'authentic subjective experience' to the detriment of connections to other differences and the making invisible of inequality. This shift from redistributive to recognition politics has significant problems for the articulation of class and has been part of the reason why class has disappeared from the feminist agenda.[2] The ability to claim and promote an 'identity' is often based on access to sites of representation such as higher education and the media; the working class (women and men, black and white)[3] have always had restricted access to where these claims are most frequently made.

Another central problem alongside access is that class is now rarely claimed (other than by academics) by women as a positive label of identity. I argue this point on the basis of the longitudinal ethnographic research I did with a group of white working-class women, many of whom went to enormous effort to dis-identify from being identified as working-class: see *Formation of Class and Gender: Becoming Respectable* (Skeggs, 1997).[4] This made me re-assess the problems of using the term class if it is resisted by those to whom it is meant to apply and it made me ask what is the purpose of classification if it fails to offer any value to those whose lives are meant to improve as a result of acknowledgment of classification (that, of course, is the traditional position taken by Marxists who believe that class consciousness leads to class action and hence change). On a more abstract level it made me question whether identification with categories was central to subjectivity. Dis-identification seemed to be the motor driving this group of working-class women's subjectivity. But to dis-identify we need to know from what the dis-identifications are being made. Recognitions have to be made, resisted, challenged for (dis-) identification to occur. This led me to search for the social and cultural positions that were available for working-class women to occupy, the categorizations through which they could recognize and thereby *know* themselves. Knowing themselves was based on identifying what they *were not* rather than what they were.

So, this chapter firstly explores the representations available for working-class women to recognize themselves through. Secondly, it examines the conceptualization of class through Pierre Bourdieu's models of capital movements, suggesting that his economic metaphors have the greatest explanatory value as a theoretical framework for understanding the lives of working-class women. It then explores issues of access and how they (and I) occupy the class positions available. I do not make the comparison out of self-indulgence but in an attempt to show the implications for identity and class based on different movements in social space. I argue that the politics of class are experienced through 'structures of feeling' (cf. Williams, 1977) in which working-class women can rarely experience security and lack of doubt. The sub-text of this chapter is how we come to know and recognize ourselves via classifying practices.

Representations and Classifications

Although class has a long history as an identity of heroism, rebellion and authenticity for working-class men, an identity which is celebrated across different sites of representation (Tolson, 1977; Willis, 1977), for working-class women recognition is based upon pathologized and sexualized representations. A survey of these representations finds a lot of historical continuity, with very little that is positive and a lot that is pathological (Walkerdine and Lucey, 1986; Nead, 1988; Walkerdine, 1990; Finch, 1993; McClintock, 1995). This is because of the history of the conceptualization which was produced through gendered definitions. The term 'class' came into existence through the attempts by the middle class to consolidate their identities and social position by identifying 'others' from whom they could draw distance. They were able to do this with the use of Enlightenment technologies of social surveys, photography, ethnography and observation. The 'sciences' of anthropology, medicine and biology were used to legitimate these differences which were not only classed but also raced – so that the 'degenerate' other was a conflation of observable and measurable class and race characteristics which were mapped into charts of evolution and civilization with the middle class, of course, positioning themselves as the most advanced and civilized. To position themselves as superior they had to continually position others as inferior.

One of the most effective ways of doing this was through the deployment of sexuality as a 'measurable' means of displaying distance from and to civilized and respectable behaviour. Finch (1993) shows how observation *and* interpretation of the sexual behaviour of black and white working-class women on the basis of their sexuality, and also their care, protection and education of their children, generated the categories of respectable and non-respectable classes. Tautologically, after producing the categories from biased interpretation (and often fantastical projections) which identified what the working class 'was', the behaviour of working-class women was then read back into them. Representations of degenerate women were a central mechanism for legitimating the distance from and hence superiority of the middle classes (Nead, 1988). The representation of working-class women (both black and white) as sexually licentious and depraved (Davis, 1981; Gilman, 1992), unable to care adequately for their children, is continually reproduced through representations and rhetoric which always position the middle class as superior (Wallace, 1979; Finch, 1993).

Just think about the contemporary British Conservative government campaigns (at the 1995 party conference) which demonized single parents thereby (re)presenting working-class women as degenerate, irresponsible and a threat to the national family (yet again). Or refer to popular culture: a recent magazine fashion spread in *Marie Claire* entitled 'Council Estate Slags'[5] which suggests that working-class women are still represented through their 'deviant' sexuality; a quick glance at the programme *Eurotrash* (Channel 4) shows how regional working-class accents are used to signify sexuality, stupidity and degeneracy. To identify as a working-class woman is to have to constantly negotiate the pathological sexualized positions that are available for us to occupy and for us and others to interpret and recognize ourselves through. The women I researched with were constantly aware of how they were being positioned by 'others'. This was especially prevalent when they moved into social space traditionally seen as middle-class as a result of being claimed by the middle class as a site of their legitimacy, for example education, social services, and wealthy shops.

The women of my ethnographic research operated with a dialogic form of recognition: they recognize the recognitions of others. Recognitions do not occur without value judgments and the women are constantly aware of the judgments of real and imaginary others. Recognition of how one is positioned is central to the processes of subjective construction. They produced themselves through the experience of being classified by others and their knowledge of these classifications. In their recognitions, which are felt and experienced, the women learn to navigate themselves through classificatory systems and measure and *evaluate* themselves accordingly.

I began my research as a PhD to show, somehow (I did not know how at the time), that white working-class women were neither stupid, desperate, hyper-sexual, enduring drudges, naive or passive – all prevalent academic and popular representations. Inspired by studies of working-class boys (e.g. *Learning to Labour* (Willis, 1977)), I wanted to show that working-class women too had intelligence and dignity.

The first formulations and representations of 'class' as a concept were not based on any describable reality but were the product of the imaginary, of the political desire to differentiate as a means to consolidate power. Yet they represented a reality for those who did not know any better, i.e., those who did not have any alternative knowledge. Thus, historically these representations were used to construct a 'reality' and generate discourses of difference. As a result of few challenges or alternatives they are still available as a framework for understanding and positioning. This is why to proudly identify as working-class is often lived as a defensive mode, an angry reaction, fuelled by resentment at continually having to begin social interactions with a fear that one is being positioned by the discourses of degeneracy and vulgarity. I am not merely speculating about this – substantial research (especially Kathleen Rowe's (1995) work on *Roseanne*, Ann Gray's (1992) research on women's responses to VCR use, *Video Playtime*, Chris Griffin's (1985) *Typical Girls*, Carolyn Steedman's (1986) account of her mother's life, *Landscape for a Good Woman*, Valerie Walkerdine and Helen Lucey's (1986) account of child development policies for the assessment of working-class women, *Democracy in the Kitchen*, and my own (1996) *Becoming Respectable*) shows how working-class women are usually very conscious of their positioning as the 'other' of little taste and knowledge and as potentially degenerate and sexual. They are aware that these positionings invoke moral evaluations and hence try to generate distance. The social divisions enhanced by the Conservative government in Britain in the 1980s and the rhetoric of Thatcherism enabled more acute divisions to be seen between the working classes (Hall, 1983). The following comments taken from the women with whom I researched show their attempts to dis-identify when asked in 1992 about the working class:

> To me if you are working-class it basically means that you are poor. That you have nothing. You know, nothing. (Sam)

> The real working class are the ones you see hanging round the dole. They're dead scruffy and poor and they haven't a job but I guess they may be working if they are working-class, they may be working. If they're working-class they should be working so they work, I guess, in all the bad jobs. (Sheenah)

> They're rough. You can always tell. Rough, you know, the women are common as muck you know, always have a fag in their mouths, the men are dead rough. You know. (Andrea)

> The ones who batter their kids. (Pam)

These women are able to make these identifications of others and thereby distance themselves on the basis of the knowledge and representations which are available and how they experience these.

I argue, following de Lauretis (1984) and Scott (1992) that we are produced as subjects through our experiences, that these experiences always involve interpretation and that the ability to interpret depends on the discursive frameworks to which we have access. We can only know ourselves through these frameworks of value and processes of interpretation. If, as theorists, we uncritically adopt the term 'class', we reproduce the very categories we are trying to challenge, for, as Scott (1992) notes, the statement 'I am a working-class woman' simply reflects on the facts of historical location. It is to assume that ontology is the ground of epistemology, that what I am determines what and how I know. But how do I know who I am? We thus operate with a constant defining descriptor and all that changes are the descriptions which are sometimes squeezed to fit. We need to know how differences are re/produced and how they are lived. Descriptions of class are not enough: they just operate in the same way as the original classifications, i.e., to fill categories with descriptors which can then be read as the 'truth', when in fact they are constantly being produced and (sometimes) challenged via representations.

This is why I chose to use Bourdieu's formulation of movements in capital to understand how class is lived, formed, reproduced and challenged and to show why certain positions are available and others not, and why investments are made in some forms of identification and not others. His framework enables an understanding of how we interpret, move, recognize, refuse and take up positions.[6]

Class Forms: Forms of Capital

Bourdieu (1979, 1986, 1987, 1989) suggests a model of class which is based on 'capital' movements through social space. The structure of this space is given by the distribution of the various forms of 'capital', by the distribution of their properties, properties which are capable of conferring strength, power and consequently profit on their holder. From this model we can see how class formation operates between abstract structures and concrete specifics of everyday life, noting that because of constant change, class formation is necessarily partial (Sayer and Walker, 1992). Class, for Bourdieu, is neither an essence nor an indeterminate set of fluctuating signifiers, but an arbitrarily imposed definition with real social effects (Moi, 1991). He identifies four different types of capital: economic, cultural, social, and symbolic.

1 Economic capital includes income, wealth, financial inheritances, monetary assets.[7] We are born into certain amounts of economic capital and the more we have the easier it is to generate more (this, after all, is the basis of capitalism).

2 Cultural capital can exist in three forms: in an embodied state, i.e. in the form of long-lasting dispositions of the mind and the body;[8] in the objectified state, in the form of cultural goods and in the institutionalized state, result-

ing in such things as educational qualifications. The discourses of femininity and masculinity become embodied and can be used as cultural resources. This is not to say that gendered relations are purely cultural. They are not. Cultural capital only exists in relation to the network of other forms of capital and hence is always related to the economic. Gender carries different amounts of symbolic capital in different contexts (Moi, 1991).[9]

3 Social capital consists of resources based on connections and group membership. This is capital generated through relationships[10] and again has different value depending on access. Some working-class groups generate social networks as a means to gain employment. The difference is the type of employment to which these social networks provide access.

4 Symbolic capital is the form the different types of capital take once they are perceived and recognized as legitimate. Legitimation is the key mechanism in the conversion to power. Cultural capital has to be legitimated before it can have symbolic power. Capital has to be regarded as legitimate before it can be capitalized upon. All capitals are context-specific. There is very little access to symbolic capital amongst the working class. The attempts by feminist academics to put working-class women on the academic agenda could be seen as an attempt to generate symbolic capital. The representations of working-class women as pathological can be seen as an attempt to delegitimate, devalue and block trading potential.

Thus people are distributed in the overall social space according to the global *volume* of capital they posses, the *composition* of their capital, the relative weight in their overall capital of the various forms of capital and evolution in time of the volume and composition according to their *trajectory* in social space.

The social space we occupy has been historically generated. When we are born, we enter an inherited social space from which comes access to and acquisition of differential amounts of capital assets. This is a space which has been produced from struggle. From being born into the social relations of gender, class and 'race' we also occupy the associated social positions such as 'woman', 'black' 'working-class' (Moi, 1991). We also inherit ways of understanding; we inherit the meanings associated with social positions and positions in discourse and knowledge. Each kind of capital can only exist in the interrelationships of social positions; they bring with them access to or limitation on which capitals are available to certain positions. They become classed, raced, sexed and gendered through being lived: they are simultaneously processed. Gender, class and 'race' are not capitals as such, rather they provide the relations in which capitals come to be organized and valued.

If born into a white working-class family with only small amounts of historically designated legitimate cultural capital the ability to trade with this asset will be circumscribed by the division of labour and the values already ascribed to particular assets generated through historical and symbolic struggle. The women with whom I researched had, by the age of 16, only limited capital to trade: they had very few educational qualifications, so could not increase their access to other social spaces such as higher education or the labour market through the potential 'trade-up' of their qualifications. They only had femininity, sexuality and caring which were tradeable. They used their feminine cultural capital to gain a place on a caring course in a further education college. Yet their caring qualifications gained from the college had only limited value on a diminishing labour market and in a welfare structure which had been drastically curtailed. They could use their caring capital as unpaid labour in voluntary caring or in the family. When the women traded their femininity and appearance on the marriage market they were able to negotiate more power but only in interpersonal terms rather than gaining access to wider institutional power. The trading of femininity, however, also implicated them as the object of the exchange. The women had only limited resources to trade; their ability to increase their capital assets, to convert them to gain material reward, was severely limited.

The inability to trade one's cultural capital because it has only limited value or is not recognized in the places where value can be accrued is a substantial disadvantage to and sign of being born working-class. Entry to the educational system, regulated either via geographical location or via whether one has the money necessary for entry to private education, immediately affects what is achievable. I, for instance, went to a school where only the top 5 per cent were entered for 'O' levels (the predecessors of GCSEs). This meant the other 95 per cent were at the age of 15 disqualified from entering many areas of the labour market and from furthering their education. They ended up at this school on the basis of where they lived and, as Bernstein (1971) and Bourdieu and Passeron (1977) amongst many others note, the cultural capital of the working class is rarely legitimated in formal education. Rather, it is the cultural capital of the middle class which is given value and they are the group who are able early in their lives to begin the capital conversion process. The working class enter not only unequal economic relations but also social, cultural and symbolic relations.

Bourdieu's economistic metaphors are useful for understanding how access, resources and legitimation contribute to class formation and continued class reproduction. For instance, we can understand why those with a small volume of cultural capital will have difficulties increasing its composition and will subsequently have a circumscribed trajectory. To avoid relativizing the different forms of capital we need to understand the mechanisms by which the different forms of capital are enabled or curtailed. We need to know how the structures historically generated from previous movements of capital such as the labour market and the education system institutionalize, that is, provide spaces for the capitalization of the different forms of capital. Class positions are not just relative forms in social space, they are institutionalized positions: the cultural capital of the middle class can offer substantial rewards in the labour market. But we need to remember that the different forms of capital Bourdieu identifies are essentially metaphors,[11] they are not descriptors of empirical positions. They are useful, Moi (1991) argues, because they enable us to identify the interests and benefits of particular groups. The women with whom I researched had only limited trading potential due to their lack of cultural, economic, social and symbolic capital. Moreover, they were positioned by cultural signs and symbolic delegitimation as working-class – a categorization, as was earlier noted, which brings with it delegitimated values of degeneracy.

By a combination of luck, cultural capital (my father was highly interested in politics and had generated in me an interest and knowledge which was convertible in Sociology and Politics), access (I went to a local further education college to do nursery nursing and was moved to Sociology because of my continual critical antagonism to the staff), and social capital (by doing 'A' levels I met public school failures who assumed, even though they were not particularly sharp, that they would go to university – I did not see why I shouldn't), I was able to enter higher education. I can now proudly say I am working-class because I have other aspects of my life which counteract any devaluation and degeneracy. I am an academic. I have accrued economic security and the type of cultural capital which is highly valued. I can deflect any attempts to negatively position me by counteracting them with the middle-class forms of capital that I have acquired through my social movement. Yet. . . .

Wrong Capitals and 'Structures of Feelings'

My first real recognition that I could be categorized by others as working-class happened when I went to university (an upper/middle-class university that often felt more like a finishing school) and I was identified in a seminar group as 'oh, you must be one of those working-class people we hear so much about'.[12] I was absolutely mortified. I knew what this meant – I had been recognized as common, authentic and without much cultural value. For the first time in my life I started to feel insecure. All the prior cultural knowledge (capital) in which I had taken pride lost its value and I entered a world where I knew little and felt I could communicate even less. I was delegitimated. The noisy, bolshy, outspoken me was silenced. I became afraid to speak in case I gave 'myself' (that is my classed self) away. I did not want to be judged and found wanting. Being the object of the judgments of others, whose values are legitimated, is a very uncomfortable position to occupy.

This, however, was a very contradictory experience for I did not really value the people who were making the judgments. They were full of pretensions, a form of behaviour I had learnt to ridicule.[13] So there I was intimidated by people who I didn't rate. But this felt even worse because they still made me feel insecure. Annette Kuhn (1995) argues that one of the central politics of class is the feeling of 'not getting it right'. You are never absolutely sure what 'getting it right' would be but you know that you have not achieved it most of the time. You also are aware that it is other people, unlike yourself, who will be making the judgments. This generates a very contradictory reaction: you want to 'get it right' to overcome the insecurity and doubt, but you would rather not enter arenas where you will be judged lacking. You become aware that you do not have access to the 'right' knowledge to know what 'getting it right' would be. You know that your forms of capital are lacking and have no value (although you probably do not articulate it that way – you just feel permanently awkward). It was this cultural devaluation that was the most obvious and devastating assignment of class for me.

I knew I could never be part of or belong to my new cultural group. But neither could I go back. This can be severely problematic for an academic who has to deal with this on a daily basis. You often choose to block your own access to economic and cultural resources because you would rather not deal with the people who may give you access to them. You have to force yourself to enter spaces in which you never feel as if you belong or will 'fit'. The upside of this is that you are always positioned at a distance and can always see from a distance, you never occupy the normalized class space (although you may simultaneously be occupying normalized spaces of heterosexuality and race).[14] It is the unease which is completely disturbing and the feeling that negative judgments are constantly being made. It is a 'structure of feeling' (cf. Williams, 1977) which can generate a feeling of paranoia if not framed within a class politics.

However, via university I now had access to Marxism. It enabled me to (metaphorically) turn the class system on its head and pointed to the privilege, normalization and lack of 'real' experience of those who tried to patronize me.[15] I learned to avoid being with the really rich and really stupid. I also recognized class difference because I had access to seeing and experiencing privileged groups. For a time I felt more comfortable with Marxism than with feminism. At first middle-class women just appeared to me as privileged. I just could not get/hear/understand their comments on oppression. The only voices I heard were those that were capable of putting me down simply through their existence. I just could not recognize how they could position themselves in any way as oppressed.

Here I was tough, glamorous, sharp, yet made to feel completely inadequate. My appearance was based on years of my mother's and my own labour, skills and knowledge – it was a cultural competence. Yet, I learned to stop wearing make-up, I cut all my hair off, I even managed to put on weight (by drinking pints, of course), I even bought a pair of dungarees, I was so desperate to fit in. I'd always known about inequality, about male violence, about abuse. Prior to university I'd been involved in the local women's refuge and I'd always fought for women's spaces. Yet I didn't seem to do it like they said it should be done. Everything I did seemed wrong. For the first time in my life I felt totally powerless.

My positioning in relation to feminism has never been that of straightforward embrace. I was introduced to academic feminism during a particularly puritanical phase (see Elizabeth Wilson with Angela Weir, 1986). I felt (and it may have been my projected anxieties in the face of such certainties) that I was the wrong class, the wrong sexuality and that most of my cultural knowledge (fashion, football, fighting, femininity and clubbing) was also wrong. The embrace of feminism would require the acknowledgment of how little value I had. It was a difficult move to make – I constantly felt (as had the women of my ethnographic research) that I was judged by appearances which placed me back into the tradition as the object of the 'othered' pathology of the judgmental and voyeuristic middle class: I became the lived sign of working-class women's degeneracy and stupidity, a degeneracy which was being (re)produced through feminism. The emphasis that feminism put(s) on appearance as representative of the 'inner' person just prolongs the long tradition of class judgment,[16] mirroring the ways in which women were classified into worthy and unworthy on the basis of femininity: the unworthy were those who displayed sexuality, the worthy masked displays of sexuality and refigured themselves through femininity (Nead, 1988).

What remains constant is that it is middle-class standards and members of the middle class who instigate judgments. It is also to assume that appearance *is* disposition. It is not. Working-class women have long made ironic and distanced 'feminine' performances before this was recognized as a radical strategy by middle-class feminists: they could never *be* feminine because the sign of femininity was produced for middle-class women to occupy in opposition to the assumed sexuality of working-class women. The constant reading/viewing of working-class women from the position of the knowledge of the middle-classes has produced inadequate theories and conceptualizations. During my research I found that the majority of feminist theory had very little explanatory value in relation to white working-class women. This should not be surprising for it has been produced from the situated knowledge of the middle class, who had little knowledge of 'others' which would inform and/or enable them to challenge their constructions.[17] This lack of knowledge is a structural feature of spatial organization: where do the working class and the middle class come into contact?

Had I not gone to university I would not have known much about the middle class (other than via representations). My social networks just did not include them (due to geographical, educational and cultural factors). At university I learned about the power of middle-class social networks. Many of the people I met did not have to apply for jobs; whatever they did their futures were assured. Most had access to lucrative jobs in the primary labour market from which I would still be excluded. I learned what it meant for people not to have to worry about money. I met those whose confidence in themselves seemed absolute and those who had no doubt that their culture and politics were right. I met those whose 'structures of feelings' were not based on the emotional politics of anxiety and doubt, but on that of security and confidence. It was this intimate positioning of myself with 'others' that enabled me to see differences and feel inequality. Middle-class people are able to operate with a sense of entitlement to social space and economic rewards that would be beyond comprehension to those of the working class for whom limitation and constraint frame their social movement. My access to the middle class enabled me to construct an entirely different framework for understanding my position in social space: the possibilities opened out and I tried to start constructing entitlements. It was from this moment that I started having problems with my family and my working-class friends who saw my adoption of the dispositions of the middle class as a sign of 'getting above myself', of having pretensions.

Conclusions

So, I now may occupy positions of power (I'm co-director of the largest Centre for Women's Studies in Britain) but I rarely feel comfortable. My experience is very similar to that documented by Valerie Walkerdine (1990), I feel a fraud, I feel that one day somebody will find out that I should not really be here. I also feel caught in the contradiction of trying to make a *class* difference by making sure class occupies a space within Women's Studies, but this also enables the matter to be ghettoized by it being associated with me, enabling others to abdicate responsibility. I am marked by class (both by politics and by being recognized) in the same way as Gayatri Spivak (1990) documents being always marked as representative of Black. I am fixed and identified. I just wish sometimes that others would raise the issue, ask the questions, see things. I'm also so terrified of being identified as unworthy that I work myself constantly into physical illness. It is an obsession. I cannot stop. If I stop someone may notice that I'm really not cut out for this job. I want the titles, Doctor, Co-ordinator, Senior, as a sign that I cannot be recognized as unworthy. I do try to re-establish my 'old' cultural capital to engender a space for comfort, but hedonism and the time demands of academia are impossible to hold together. So every hedonist impulse is suffused with guilt. And I'll never have the 'right' knowledge. When people were growing up reading books I was out with my mates. I have missed years of formal education. This is often displayed in my inability to understand references. I did not even know how to write, what grammar was or how to use it. I have had to learn a whole new set of cultural competencies.

And what happens when we become academics? We try to fit others into a system from which we feel alienated. We can give them the skills, the language and the technical competence, but can we give them the feelings of security and entitlement? We can try but we may just engender bitterness and rage. I see the class battles being fought out daily in the feminist classroom often around the division between theory and experience. This can be partly mapped onto distance and immediacy. Distant, unengaged theoretical specu-lation, Bourdieu (1986) argues, has rarely been the prerogative of the working classes: they did not have the time. Humiliation and indignation can generate a retreat into the experiential as a claim for superior knowledge. After all it cannot be taken away. It is something. We turn to black theorists who have been able to use theory in a way that speaks back to them. I read black male autobiographies because they speak more easily to the violence and struggle for respect that I lived, and it makes me wonder why do I do feminist theory? How can I make it speak to me? When it does it upsets me: it's too immediate: Valerie Walkerdine, Carolyn Steedman and Annette Kuhn have reduced me to tears with their powerful, evocative analysis. My own research has generated times of complete despair and powerlessness at my inability to radically change the conditions in which some of the women were forced to live. This powerlessness and realization of my positioning as represrepresenter made me unable to write (for years) about the women of the research for fear of objectifying, of voyeuristically travelling through their experiences, of misrepresenting them.[18] Distance was a privilege to which I had no access.

And whilst I now know why I and the women of the research have all these problems and insecurities it does not help much: there is nowhere else to go or to *be*. My mother still thinks I'm a disappointment (I have no children, I moved away from my home town and I don't drop in to see her every week). Her friends reinforce her feeling of alienation from me. My crime is that I didn't know to stay 'in my place'. The women of the research have mainly 'stayed in their place' but they would rather have left. They and I know that we are recognized, symbolically delegitimated, that our capitals are not the right sort and that we will always be judged and may feel inadequate. We are positioned by pathology rather than normalization. This is the emotional politics of class: a politics of dis-identification, a result of classifying practices enacted on a daily basis by many of those who do not think class is an issue. Yet it is always an issue for those who cannot avoid it. It is a ubiquitous part of their existence, one that cannot be ignored. It is an issue of symbolic and structural violence.

Notes

1 Charles Taylor (1994) shows how claims for recognition have fuelled the multi-culturalism debate in the States.

2 Class has never disappeared from the sociological agenda (see Charles, 1990; Crompton, 1993; and the journal *Sociology*), although an interesting recent trend is the focus on the middle classes (see Savage *et al.*, 1992; Lury, 1996).

3 I purposely choose to use the singular – 'working class' or 'middle class' rather than 'classes' – to make a political point. The use of the singular is to emphasize that class is about conflict, power and opposition rather than just sites of differences. I am aware that there are many different ways of being of either class but what is fundamental is not lifestyles or the numer-

ous proliferations of distinctions (cf. Bourdieu, 1986) but the issue of access to material and cultural resources. I use a model later in the chapter to map this out. In the development of the concept 'class' singularity was necessary to the measurement of observable differences. It is to this history (although with a different politics) that I want to point, i.e., they are historically produced constructs developed to consolidate the power of one group at the expense of the other.

4 Many of the arguments apply to both black and white working-class women. When they are specific to white women I indicate this. The research took place over a period of eleven years, with three years of intensive participant observation and a series of follow-up interviews. The women were aged between 16 and 18 when the research began. They all lived in a northern provincial town and were taking 'caring courses' at a local further education college.

5 Council estates are the UK equivalent to US project housing.

6 The theories of Bourdieu have been used by other feminists for different types of analysis (see Moi, 1991; Lamont, 1992; McCall, 1992; and later footnotes).

7 This should not be confused with the theories of Wright (1985, 1989) and Savage *et al.* (1992) who define assets as either property, skill or organizational. Savage (1992) argues that the cultural and gendered aspects of class formation should also be included in any account: organizational assets are intrinsically vehicles of male power.

8 Cultural capital also brings with it certain dispositions which enable cultural capital to be turned into symbolic capital and hence gain legitimacy. Dispositions such as the 'right' to use social space enable greater capitalization: the arrogance over the control and use of social space by public schoolboys is almost legendary in the UK, although readily contested by other forms of masculinity (Connell, 1989). The constraints over women's use of space puts limits on where and how they can use their cultural capital.

9 Moi (1991) argues that insofar as gender never appears in a 'pure' field of its own, there is no such thing as pure 'gender capital'. The capital at stake is always the symbolic capital relevant for the specific field under examination. We can, however, see how gender is deployed in attempts to gain or not lose capital. The focus on the field of caring enables us to see how femininity is traded.

10 Moi (1991) provides an excellent example where she shows how the relationship of Simone de Beauvoir with Jean Paul Sartre enhanced their total capitals.

11 The use of metaphor involves both substitution and displacement. It is never just a description. The value of the metaphor of cultural capital is that it is a concept that can give back something to those who have always been represented as having nothing. It forces a focus on difference *with* inequality rather than just either difference or inequality.

12 I have always felt uncomfortable with the autobiographical voice. To position myself as an object of academic inquiry is difficult, firstly, because working-class women have rarely found themselves of interest (see Oakley, 1981). Secondly, and more generally, it is difficult because the autobiographical mode was a technology of Western Enlightenment thinking. It was one of the means by which the category 'individual' was constructed. Privileged individuals came to know and construct their 'selves' by defining others as unworthy of knowing, as 'mass'. As Williams (1977) notes, only middle-class men were considered worthy of the categorization 'individual'. It is difficult to use the mode of autobiography without reproducing this bourgeois individualism, although some feminists have achieved this (see Probyn, 1993b).

13 Bourdieu (1986) defines the practices perceived as pretensions as a result of the manifest discrepancy between ambition and possibility.

14 Some sociologists have argued that this liminal space is of great advantage to researchers who are always positioned at a distance (Mannheim, 1936/ 1960).

15 This experiential challenge is institutionalized through feminist standpoint epistemologies which have been used by marginal groups to claim their potential for superior knowledge about the power relations they live (see Harstock, 1983; Collins, 1990; Bar On, 1993; Skeggs, 1995).

16 See Finkelstein (1991) for a discussion of how modernity uses the technique of 'reading' personalities through appearances.

17 This criticism is particularly appropriate to those theories which assume easy movement through social space (for instance, that women have choice over the subject positions which they occupy) and have no sense of constraint or limitation in their analysis.

18 This does not mean that I believe that a perfect representation is possible. I do not. Rather, I believe that some representations do *less* symbolic violence to the group being represented than others.

References

Bar On, B.-A. (1993) 'Marginality and Epistemic Privilege', in Alcoff, L. and Potter, E. (Eds) *Feminist Epistemologies*, London, Routledge, pp. 83–100.

Bernstein, B. (1971) *Class, Codes and Control, Vol. 1*, London, Routledge & Kegan Paul.

Bourdieu, P. (1979) 'Symbolic Power', *Critique of Anthropology*, 4, pp. 77–85.

Bourdieu, P. (1986) *Distinction: A Social Critique of the Judgement of Taste*, London, Routledge.

Bourdieu, P. (1987) 'What Makes a Social Class? On the Theoretical and Practical Existence of Groups', *Berkeley Journal of Sociology*, pp. 1–17.

BOURDIEU, P. (1989) 'Social Space and Symbolic Power', *Sociological Theory*, 7, pp. 14–25.

BOURDIEU, P. and PASSERON, J. C. (1977) *Reproduction in Education, Society and Culture*, London, Sage.

CHARLES, N. (1990) 'Women and Class – A Problematic Relationship, *Sociological Review*, 38, pp. 43–89.

COLLINS, P. H. (1990) *Black Feminist Thought: Knowledge, Consciousness and the Politics of Empowerment*, London, Routledge.

COMPTON, R. (1993) *Class and Stratification: An Introduction to Current Debates*, Cambridge, Polity.

CONNELL, R. W. (1989) 'Cool Guys, Swots and Wimps: The Interplay of Masculinity and Education', *Oxford Review of Education*, 15, 3, pp. 291–303.

DAVIS, A. Y. (1981) *Women, Race and Class*, London, The Women's Press.

DE LAURETIS, T. (1984) *Alice Doesn't: Feminism, Semiotics, Cinema*, London, Routledge.

FINCH, L. (1993) *The Classing Gaze: Sexuality, Class and Surveillance*, St Leonards, NSW, Australia, Allen & Unwin.

FINKELSTEIN J. (1991) *The Fashioned Self*, Cambridge, Polity.

FRASER, N. (1995) 'From Redistribution to Recognition? Dilemmas of Justice in a "Post-Socialist" Age'. *New Left Review*, 212, pp. 68–94.

GILMAN, S. L. (1992) 'Black Bodies, White Bodies: Towards an Iconography of Female Sexuality in Late Ninteenth Century Art, Medicine and Literature', in DONALD, J. and RATTANSI, A. (Eds) *'Race', Culture and Difference*, London, Sage, pp. 171–98.

GILROY, P. (1990) 'One Nation under a Groove: The Cultural Politics of "Race" and Racism in Britain', in GOLDERG, D. T. (Ed.) *Anatomy of Racism*, Minneapolis, University of Minnesota Press, pp. 263–83.

GRAY, A. (1992) *Video Playtime: The Gendering of a Leisure Technology*, London, Routledge.

GRIFFIN, C. (1985) *Typical Girls: Young Women from School to the Job Market*, London, Routledge.

HALL, S. (1983) 'The Great Moving Right Show', in HALL, S. and JACQUES, M. (Eds) *The Politics of Thatcherism*, London, Lawrence & Wishart, pp. 19–40.

HARTSOCK, N. (1983) 'The Feminist Standpoint: Developing the Ground for a Specifically Feminist Historical Materialism', in HARDING, S. and HINTIKKA, M. B. (Eds) *Discovering Reality: Feminist Perspectives on Epistemology, Metaphysics, Methodology and Philosophy of Science*, Dordrecht, Reidel.

KUHN, A. (1995) *Family Secrets: Acts of Memory and Imagination*, London, Verso.

LAMONT, M. (1992) *Money, Morals and Manners: The Culture of the French and the American Upper Middle-Class*, Chicago, University of Chicago Press.

LURY, C. (1996) *Consumer Culture*, Cambridge, Polity.

MANNHEIM, K. (1936/1960) *Ideology and Utopia*, London, Routledge & Kegan Paul.

McCLINTOCK, A. (1995) *Imperial Leather: Race, Gender and Sexuality in the Colonial Context*, London, Routledge.

McCALL, L. (1992) 'Does Gender Fit? Bourdieu, Feminism and Conceptions of Social Order', *Theory and Society*, 21, pp. 837–67.

MOI, T. (1991) 'Appropriating Bourdieu: Feminist Theory and Pierre Bourdieu's Sociology of Culture', *New Literary History*, 22, pp. 1017–49.

NEAD, L. (1988) *Myths of Sexuality: Representations of Women in Victorian Britain*, Oxford, Blackwell.

OAKLEY, A. (1981) 'Interviewing Women: A Contradiction in Terms', in ROBERTS, H. (Ed.) *Doing Feminist Research*, London, Routledge & Kegan Paul, pp. 30–62.

PARMAR, P. (1989) 'Other Kinds of Dreams', *Feminist Review*, 31, pp. 55–66.

PROBYN, E. (1993a) *Sexing the Self: Gendered Positions in Cultural Studies*, London, Routledge.

PROBYN, E. (1993b) 'True Voices and Real People: The "Problem" of the Autobiographical in Cultural Studies', in BLUNDELL, V., SHEPHERD, J. and TAYLOR, I. (Eds) *Relocating Cultural Studies: Developments in Theory and Research*, London, Routledge, pp. 105–23.

ROWE, K. (1995) *The Unruly Woman: Gender and the Genres of Laughter*, Austin, Texas, University of Texas Press.

SAVAGE, M. (1992) 'Women's Expertise, Men's Authority: Gendered Organisations and the Contemporary Middle Classes', in SAVAGE, M. and WITZ, A. (Eds) *Gender and Bureaucracy*, Oxford, Blackwell, pp. 124–51 (reprinted from *The Sociological Review*).

SAVAGE, M., BATOW, J., DICKENS, P. and FIELDING, T. (1992) *Property, Bureaucracy and Culture: Middle-Class Formation in Contemporary Britain*, London, Routledge.

SAYER, A. and WALKER, R. (1992) *The New Social Economy: Reworking the Division of Labour*, Oxford, Blackwell.

SCOTT, J. (1992) 'Experience', in BUTLER, J. and SCOTT, J. (Eds) *Feminists Theorise the Political*, London, Routledge, pp. 22–41.

SKEGGS, B. (1995) 'Introduction: Processes in Feminist Cultural Theory', in SKEGGS, B. (Ed.) *Feminist Cultural Theory: Production and Process*, Manchester, Manchester University Press, pp. 1–33.

SKEGGS, B. (1997) *Formations of Class and Gender: Becoming Respectable*, London, Sage.

SPIVAK, G. C. (1990) (ed. Sarah Harassym) *The Post-Colonial Critic: Interviews, Strategies, Dialogues*, London, Routledge.

STEEDMAN, C. (1986) *Landscape for a Good Woman: A Story of Two Lives*, London, Virago.

TAYLOR, C. (1994) 'The Politics of Recognition', in GOLDBERG, D. T. (Ed.) *Multiculturalism: A Critical Reader*, Oxford, Blackwell, pp. 75–106.

TOLSON, A. (1977) *The Limits of Masculinity*, London, Tavistock.

WALKERDINE, V. (1990) *Schoolgirl Fictions*, London, Verso.

WALKERDINE, V. and LUCEY, H. (1986) *Democracy in the Kitchen: Regulating Mothers and Socialising Daughters*, London, Virago.

WALLACE, M. (1979) *Black Macho and the Myth of the Superwoman*, London, John Calder.

WILLIAMS, R. (1977) *Marxism and Literature*, Oxford, Oxford University Press.

WILLIS, P. (1977) *Learning to Labour: How Working Class Kids Get Working Class Jobs*, Farnborough, Saxon House.

WILSON, E. with WEIR, A. (1986) *Hidden Agendas: Theory, Politics and Experience in the Women's Movement*, London, Tavistock.

WRIGHT, E. (1985) *Classes*, London, Verso.

WRIGHT, E. (1989) 'Women in the Class Structure', *Politics and Society*, 17, pp. 35–66.

Chapter 13

Northern Accent and Southern Comfort: Subjectivity and Social Class

Valerie Hey

'How would you define your working classness?'
Hilary: 'It's a little like being asked to define your femaleness.
You just *feel* working class.' (*Spare Rib*, undated)

Class is not just about the way you talk, or dress, or furnish your
home; it is not just about the job you do or how much money you
make doing it; nor is it merely about whether or not you have 'A'
levels or went to university, nor which university you went to. *Class
is something beneath your clothes, under your skin, in your reflexes, in
your psyche, at the very core of your being.* (Kuhn, 1995, p. 98;
emphasis added)

Introduction: Sound Bites (1)

There is a funny and self-knowing series of advertisements for Boddington's
Beer.[1] Their theme extends the slogan which markets the beer as the 'cream of
Manchester'. The three advertisements are unified by one joke –
WYSI(N)WYG – what you see is *not* what you get or, more accurately,
what you *see* is contradicted by what you eventually *hear*. The ads all turn
on the dislocation between 'the look' and 'the sound'.[2] I frame my discussion
of subjectivity and class through an interpretation of one of these advertisements.

In *Sun Cream* the focus of our gaze is the woman as aspirational
hi-fashion icon – as sex-goddess – the reference is to the *femme fatale* of the
Ambre Solaire ads. Then Vera emerges demanding a 'rub down with some
chip fat' – at this cue, cameras pan to show the setting as Blackpool rather than
the supposed exotic playground of the jet set. The glamour is simultaneously
parodied and domesticated.[3] The broad Manchester accent is key, since now it
codes an altogether different femininity – working-class northern glamour
rather than aspirational southern chic.[4]

The ad wouldn't work without the voice – and it wouldn't work unless
accents carried these sedimented and constantly reactivated meanings linking

the demography of class to the geography of accents and their place in a hierarchy of social positioning (see Honey, 1989).[5] Compelled to resolve the contradictions between text and talk we draw upon social knowedges that are saturated with binary (class) meanings. As soon as Vera opens her mouth we 'know' we are no longer in the world proposed by the visual codes. We have moved from middle class to working class; from South to North; from the elite to the vulgar; from the 'toffs' to the 'oiks'.

The ad is personally emblematic, providing a powerful reminder of times when, like Vera, I too have (less triumphantly) disrupted the dominant code, finding myself in the wrong class (code) at the wrong time. Valerie Walkerdine's discussion of mispronunciation (1995) and Annette Kuhn's discussion of 'passing' (1995) resonates here.

In sum, it is common sense to presume a link between place, voice and a class location. We are invited to share preferred meanings which code success as middle-class and southern and no-nonsense banality and ordinariness as working-class and northern. The Vera figure connects because the text dramatizes the dilemma as well as the cultural pleasures to be had moving across, as well as desiring to stay identified with/in, the borders of (working-) class identity. The rest of the chapter explores how these cultural dialectics currently play across my own working life. In order to do this I need to explore two sets of ideas: firstly, those related to class as an identity and secondly, some current issues about working in an elite sector of education. My most immediate experience of class allegiances and gender politics are played out within the restructuring of academic life through marketization (Arnot, 1982).

Social Class and the Dialectics of Dialect: Sound Bites (2)

I spent the first seventeen years of my life in the north in an almost totally working-class council estate world. The nearest I got to the middle classes was when along with a few of my peers I moved into the A stream in the primary school in my last year. The only real flesh-and-blood (as opposed to fictional) middle-class children in the whole world appeared to me to be in this class. These girls had completely different names to my friends. They drank rose-petal tea and ate exotic food. One girl invited me home for her birthday tea which included olives (I thought these were grapes and was appalled by the new taste!). Such girls weren't allowed to watch television and read *Bunty*. The middle class was a different country. The girls lived in the only owner-occupied houses in the vicinity. These girls undeniably did things differently there. They also spoke differently – a fact which seemed the most compelling reason why they should all have passed the 11+ whilst the promoted ginger group of working-class children failed the selection test.

I cannot stop myself compulsively (and reductively) fitting people into class boxes merely on the evidence of their accent.[6] It took me a long time to believe that there were working-class people anywhere other than the north![7] Giving up this deeply embedded habit has proved illusive. My subjective sense of working-classness is pervasive despite my objective re-moval from these roots and my intellectual and political antipathy to identity politics. It is precisely this contradiction which intrigues me. Why do I continu-ally adhere to this girl I once was before the longing and the wanting? Why is my affective home still 200 miles north of the southern comforts I have acquired? Part of the answer lies in my experience of a context where I have long experienced myself being read through the grid of elitist values – a powerful complex of ideologies and cultural practices which splits cleverness not only from femininity (Walkerdine, 1987) but also from working-classness/ northernness.

My negotiation of these class relations is literally carried, condensed and expressed most acutely in my voice – more particularly in the dis/location between my accent and my vocabulary – precisely between the flat vowels, the unaspirated *h*'s and the analytical elaborated code I now speak. Not only is this split read by others as evidence of my outsider status, it allows for the performance of cultural language games not unlike those enacted in the Boddington's ads. The following section explores this cultural arbitration in more detail.

'Voice Over'

Resolving the contradictions to make my voice has meant more than learning a new vocabulary, it has also demanded self-reflexivity. I have long felt frus-trated by the constraints of written academic discourse. Spoken discourse is more spontaneous and open to more instantaneous forms of disruption and self-commentary. Voices are particularly sensitive to contradictions because of their versatility. As an instrument a voice can be tuned and attuned and can reference as well as respond to different cultural histories.

I play games through my accent. Whilst I have generally modulated my accent in response to how I experience other people reading me as a 'thicko' (cf. Stanley, 1995), I continue to constitute my accent as something of a tribal trophy. I frequently and deliberately exaggerate its broadness as a reminder that I am *not* an endemic member of the class that is invisible to itself. Moreover I have to admit to a childish frisson as I undercut the stifling discretions of academic formalities with my Northern vernacular. After all I have been mimicked – flat vowels and unaspirated *h*'s are the favourite targets.

We all know the phenomenon of the 'telephone voice': the switch into standard English seems almost compulsory when we talk with strangers who cannot see us. I take up a more elaborate version when I routinely move between two heritages in the course of my work – to speak from both codes, mixing speech genres, forms of language, intonations and cultural references so as to move across different cultural knowledges in writing and speech (cf. hooks, 1993). Such schizophrenia is exhausting and undoubtedly over-determines how I occupy a dominant expert voice and its opposite. I try, in other words, to make the making of language evident through, firstly, de-naturalizing language and, secondly, self-parody.

The first is accomplished by deliberately switching from the register of academic specialization into northern vernacular, to indicate that each dis-course is a social accomplishment – more particularly that academic jargon is *another* language acquired by practice. I can often move through the trajectory of my own auto/biography in the space of a sentence (cf. Walkerdine's (1985, p. 74) discussion of 'lasting and pasting'). Taking up and putting down postmodernism (for example) expresses the critical distance between my/self and this particular intellectual fashion. A certain sardonic stance reflects my delight in, as well as resistance to, some of academia's more seductive mind games (cf. Kenway, 1996).

These switches might be read in multiple ways. Those who have not had to translate their own language to fit into academia might consider them inappropriate but I suggest (though I have never checked this out) that my uses of classed in-jokes are available to other women for whom my cultural references to certain working-class forms (football, soap operas, watching non-serious television)[8] resonates with their secret (low-class) passions (Hey, 1995).[9] It is of course equally feasible that some students consider these appro-priations either shocking or patronizing – worse than being addressed through dominant middle-class speech forms.

Finding my voice(s) in higher education has meant and continues to mean a constant negotiation with a cultural code that is not natural. Indeed the production of an educated self has necessarily had to be made out of what Bhabba calls, in another context, 'translations' (1990, pp. 209–10). He points to how cultural meanings work as 'symbol-forming and subject-constituting interpellative practices'. By this I take him to mean that despite what he cites as the 'incommensurability' of cultures, there is redemption in the possibility of counter-identifications since the desire for representation is common to all cultures. It is this which makes it possible to translate ours and others' mean-ing. He indicates the need of translations through political negotiation so that alliances are formed in a new or 'hybrid' space which stands apart from 'the sovereignty of the self'. It is only in 'letting go' that we can 'gain the freedom of a politics that is open to the non-assimiliationist claims of cultural differ-ence' (Bhabba, 1990, p. 213).

But living in 'difference' is no mere matter of representation – differences are lived, as Kuhn argues, 'at the very core of your being' (Kuhn, 1995, p. 98). In my case and ironically, no amount of fascination with poststructuralist accounts of 'decentred' subjectivity can erase the 'under the skin' sense of an intractable (working-class) class identity. On the contrary whilst class splits and translations condition the production of this territory of self in education they do not efface this feeling. Like other subjects who are not white, male, anglo and middle-class, my relationship to the preferred position is one of ambivalence, subordination and struggle. Sometimes splits prevail; then the predominant feeling is that it is *not me* who is writing this paper or that book (see Walkerdine, 1987) – there is an uncertainty – a failure of nerve and a sense that my masquerade (cf. Kuhn's (1995) discussion of 'passing') will be denounced. However, successful translations result in a sense of euphoria – the outcome of feeling whole, as multiple selves are held in play in language that recovers all forms of one's cultural capital in classrooms or text.

I certainly agree with Bhabba's insistence that we have to make political alliances across difference. Equally we need to recognize that making a culture on the basis of a 'non-sovereign notion of the self' (Bhabba, 1990, p. 212) is a lot more difficult or ambivalent for those who have seldom experienced their selves as sovereign in the first instance. As numerous feminists have insisted, the getting of a gender identity is always a condition of instability, frequently lived as a painful cultural contradiction (Walkerdine, 1987). Significantly, as Jane Kenway (1995) and others (Donald, 1985) have shown, we have hardly begun the task of recognizing how our selves are invested by the relations of power and desire.

Identities are constructed out of history and culture. Making ourselves means, as Debbie Epstein claims, making ourselves in conditions of material and social inequity. Furthermore, 'we have investments in the differences and inequalities by which we are produced and which we ourselves produce' (Epstein, 1993, p. 19). It is the role of our affective and psychic stakes in difference which indicates that letting go of these affinities is neither definitive nor unproblematic. Indeed my own struggle emerges as one of ambivalence and frustration – that no matter how much *I* might want to let go of crude allegiances established in my working-class past (on the grounds of an abhorrence of identity politics) I am saturated both by its legacy and its appeals. Furthermore the situation of tension between intensification and residualization expressed in my middle-class profession (contract research) incessantly reinscribes my tribal allegiances in the face of the reproduction and reformulation of dominant hierarchies.

My own experience of making *and sustaining* a 'radical educated self' periodically and repeatedly falters on the grounds of an older unreconstructed and heavily invested self – that part of my self that seems essential and integral both to my identity *and* resistance (see Epstein, 1993). The following indicative narrative suggests we need to pay a great deal more personal and analytical attention to these ghosts in our own machine.

Class and Gender Locations: Contract Cultures

It is no longer fashionable to talk about class as difference and this is as true in the discourse of the New Right world of entitlement cultures and consumer choice as it is in the white heat of postmodernist high theory. Now we have the conditions for the formulation of 'plastic sexualities' and identities (Giddens, 1992) in what Lash and Urry (1987) call the economics of 'disorganized capitalism'. There is certainly overwhelming evidence of global shifts which have made for more permeable class structures. However, the imposition of new technologies and the construction of more diffuse patterns of consumption (Kenway, 1995) have meant that class relations are being re-articulated around patterns of consumption rather than around the means of production.

If theoreticians are moving helter-skelter towards deconstructionism my own subjectivity has not quite caught up. Urgent formulations that 'all that is solid melts into air' (Berman, 1983, citing Marx) makes it difficult to retain a singular, or indeed *any*, analytic focus on class. I want to retain a focus on class and gender since these relations are currently being re-articulated and amplified rather than deconstructed in the marketized academy.

To make a banal and obvious initial point – working as a researcher in higher education in an elite institution is a lot more privileged than working on the tills at Tesco's supermarket. There is still some scope for controlling the terms and tempo of work – for exercising some choices despite the intensification of higher education (see Holland *et al.*, 1993). I have worked behind bars, in cotton mills, in a welding factory; in Littlewoods, and in cafés, and I do not underestimate the difference between my material past and my material present! However, if there are differences there are also some stunning resemblances between the endemic insecurity of working-class unskilled labour and the conditions of employment in contract research.

As I now locate my/self through both my past as well as my present, I am increasingly aware of the brittleness of my claims on elite work. Ironically in one sense I have come home! The intensification of academic life in general and the residualization of research contract culture in particular complicates the already precarious position of being a working-class educated women. Now the identity at stake is not so much declassed intellectual as re/class(ifi)ed peripheral flexible specialist (Kenway, 1995).

I want to take up and hopefully extend Ann Oakley's analysis that 're-search work is the housework' of the academy (Oakley, 1995). Oakley argues that the relations of contract research units to the core business of teaching and academic work undertaken by tenured staff in higher education resemble the relations which exist between the invisible unpaid work of housework and the publicly acknowledged status of male labour. Certainly the analogy is at one level highly persuasive because most contract researchers are women and most professors and senior staff in universities are men. Whilst Ann Oakley makes many accurate not to mention funny points about the semi-detached status of research units, she does not address how these relations might also be classed. I want to track aspects of the intensification in higher education as a reassertion of class and gender. For me these shifts articulate another relation between my working-class past and my middle-class present. I consider next the unacknowledged cultural capital of being an educated working-class women.

If my voice is the link to this past, it is also part of my stock of current social capital because as a social researcher it is a particularly rich basis for negotiating social exchanges. The social relations of gender have been part of a cogent critique of classic interviewing texts (see Oakley, 1981) but there has been little reference to how class constructs the social processes of research. This silence suggests that class is largely naturalized in interviews and it also indicates who is interviewing whom (see Hey, in press). I will not forget the sense of shock I experienced when reading some transcripts of interviews between middle-class feminist researchers and their male working-class respondents, in which highly educated social researchers asked what seemed to me to be almost unaskable questions because they were framed by a 'lifestyle' discourse completely disconnected from the material realities of working-class men's lives. Having a 'lifestyle' implies notions of choice whilst it was very clear to me that the compulsions of poverty and need drove the biographies of the men interviewed.

It is not that the 'working classes' should not be spoken to, more that the specificities and limitations of middle-classness should be acknowledged. This points to the need for more self-reflexivity on the part of interviewers. Conversely my working-class background means that I am more conscious of difference. I am only too aware of what I sound like and what I am 'read' as.

Predictably such readings are context-sensitive. My mother calls my voice 'posh'; colleagues describe it as a 'northern' voice, though they usually locate me on the wrong side of the Pennines.[10] I like what I sound like which is just as well since I spend a lot of time transcribing interviews. It has interesting qualities usually described by others as 'warmth' and 'animation' – it has qualities which make people feel reassured and non-threatened in my interviews – it elicits and offers sympathy – it can seduce confessions at twenty paces so I am also aware that it is quite a dangerous instrument. It is in many ways an ideal value-added medium for driving a whole range of sensitive interview exchanges – it seems to work across age barriers (I have some wonderful data from young children and extremely old people), it can do the trick across gender – I have memories of adolescent males waxing lyrical in unsolicited personal talk (here no doubt I was positioned as sympathetic mum) – and it has got me into and out of interviews and seminars with powerful men. In other words, the cultural resources I use from both sides of my/self are central to my strength as a social researcher. These cultural skills are continuously exercised in the course of my academic work. Skills which draw (often unconsciously) upon speech forms, ways of being, habits, observances and understandings help me manage those difficult invisible moments in research usually condensed in the term rapport. It is paradoxically precisely those attributes which have sometimes been stigmatized that work to my advantage in interview situations. And it is precisely my skill in translation between forms of differently evaluated cultural capital which contributes to corporate intellectual capital.

Locations and Dis/Locations: The New Politics of Subjectivity

Calls for a new politics of identity within the debate about radical pedagogies (see Ellsworth, 1989; Giroux and McLaren, 1994) reflect demands for new political subjectivities (see Hall, 1990; Bhabba, 1990; Mercer, 1990; Rutherford, 1990). My concern has been to raise some of the practical, emotional and social difficulties of this project, since my excursion into making an/other subjectivity suggests that it is a lot more difficult than the exhortations of the male radical intelligentsia would have us believe.[11]

(Classed) subjective identities and identifications are powerful markers. I have argued that they can be wittingly and unwittingly provoked back into existence alongside newer and more diffuse plastic selves (see above). If we simply erase class and its tenacious hold through calls for a third position, we erase any way to think about people who are not so much plastic as only too intractable (Hey, in press). The glamour of the postmodern conceptualization of hybridity promises more pliable terms for the construction of alliances and notions of community which move the debate away from the bloody battles of difference, but we should be aware that the seductions of theory are one thing, the task of constructing political visions which embrace the systematic lived oppressions of people, another.

This is not some mindless privileging of either empiricism or 'ordinary' people – it is just the insistence that we need to think through the tenacities which invest us in some desired as well as un/desired places (Donald, 1985). It seems to me now as a reluctant hybrid (a casualized professional in an elite institution) that we are in danger of being pushed into forms of high abstraction incapable of holding onto the social realities the majority of people live in conditions of commodification. The differential experience of marketization in academic employment should alert us to the abiding tyrannies which can all too easily persist in the masquerade of entitlement cultures when it seems that some of us are more 'entitled' than others.

In short, the imprecise concept of 'hybridity' needs empirical elaboration if it is not to remain on an academic wish-list. Crucially we need to factor into 'the (educational) politics of subjectivity' (Walkerdine, 1987, p. 277) the persistence of past social experience – to recognize, in other words, the power of previous as well as current (class(ed)) allegiances and their associated forms of subjectivity. Shifting identifications with/against my working-class past have been orchestrated through repeated encounters with an equally recalcitrant identity, namely that represented by the dominant face of higher education – middle-class, masculine rationality – which is generally oblivious to its own partialities but all too vigilant about an/others. For example, a director of a research project subsequently wrote about my gendered participation as showing 'complicity'[12] between myself and girls. Needless to say his own complicity with the boys he interviewed remained unremarked.

I have discussed why I currently come to feel myself *more, not less* 'working-class' through the prevailing conditions in academic life (Aziz, 1991; Morley and Walsh, 1995). This position is held at the same time that I know I cannot (neither do I want to) return to that past. This does not make such feelings irrelevant – to be dissolved by the application of rational argument – on the contrary it is precisely these cleavages within my current identity which feed both upon and back into the material uncertainties of my current position.

My experience of shifting (and being shifted) in academic culture indicates the inadequacies as well as the seductions of identity politics. I have argued that identities are productions and co-productions (see Davis, 1994) which are spun out of the powerful allegiances of the past as well as the power relations of the present. Valerie Walkerdine spoke of 'femininity as performance' (1987, p. 267); I speak of class as endlessly elicited through performance. The case is overwhelming that we need more theorizing about, as well as recognition of, the power and determinacy of our emotions. We need, in other words, emotional as well as political literacy; or, more accurately, we need to attend to the making of a political language which is emotionally literate.

Notes

1 The trio are called *Face-Cream, Ice-Cream* and *Sun Cream* respectively (New TV Campaign 1994). I am grateful to the Whitbread Beer Company for their assistance in supplying me with a copy of the *Sun Cream* advertisement.

2 The promotional video for the campaign sets the tone, 'red hot and coming to your TV screen this summer, a litany of . . . bronzed bodies . . . sun-kissed beaches . . . scandalous cover-up . . . the perfect antidote . . . and the last resort . . . all in the shadow of Blackpool Tower'.

3 There is an associated genre of advertisements which re-position, quote or reflect upon yuppiedom (see the recent Audi advertisement).

4 It is related to the feminine images proposed by television soap operas – principally *Coronation Street*. I am thinking of Elsie Tanner, Bet Lynch and Rita Fairclough. There is another northern stereotype – the battle-axe: Ena Sharples/Nora Battie – but that is another story.

5 These cultural associations are currently being played out in Britpop around the southern band Blur and the northern (Mancunian) band Oasis. Martin Wainwright talking on Radio 4 mapped literary classed locales in

the following way: stories about a 'life of perpetual hardship' are set in the North; lives of passion are told about the West Country; and the South specializes in genteel middle-class dramas.

6 I certainly located myself politically in residual forms associated with working-class solidarity far earlier than I became aware of sexual politics – it wasn't men who were my 'other' but the owners of the means of production. My family would boo the 'one nation' Tories on television and heckle and mimic their voices and ways of speech. I learned my place against 'them' as the bosses and 'us' as 'the workers'!

7 Rather like the characters in the Monty Python 'shoe box' sketch I too shared the compelling set of identifications of multiple deprivation with a sense of place – with home.

8 I have always been amused by the ways in which a lot of my middle-class friends 'hide' their televisions in their bedrooms – presumably on the analogy that, like participating in sex, watching TV is something undertaken between two consenting adults. In the course of researching into 'television literacy' I was constantly struck by the ways teachers agonized over the viewing practices of their pupils – the stigmatizing discourse linking watching TV to forms of moral turpitude, feckless parenting and commercial capture and the consequent corruption of the young is so dissonant from my own childhood. I can remember the TV being kept on even when visitors arrived. Equally the middle-class obsession with quality time bears no relation to the social mores in my childhood when as a child I was not allowed to speak at the table.

9 I have another concern here which it is only possible to note, namely that the allegiances of class inflect forms of femininity and thus the language of middle-class feminist critique frequently degrades those forms which are taken up by working-class girls and women (see Kenway and Blackmore, 1995).

10 I always find the use of the word 'regional' amusing, a bit like the response of someone to the idea of having a conference in Stirling ('That's a long way,' said a Londoner – 'It all depends where you start from' came the exasperated reply) – in other words London is a region to those of us unfortunate enough to be born outside of the sound of the M25. Incidentally I am always intrigued by the sign on the M1 which signals 'The North'; as far as I am aware there is no equivalent one on the other carriageway for 'the South'!

11 Whilst the literature about political renewal is surely right in theoretic principle it is noticeably reticent on specific strategies about how to get to this desired position.

12 Given that gender as well as social class constitutes my social and cultural capital and given that interviewing demands the ability to build a bridge between one's self and the interviewee by identifying and drawing upon shared social capital it is impossible to construct an interview situation that is not complicitous! Someone else's complicity is my rapport.

References

ARNOT, M. (1982) 'Male Hegemony, Social Class and Women's Education', *Journal of Education*, 164(1), pp. 64–89.

AZIZ, A. (1991) 'Women in UK Universities: The Road to Casualisation', in STIVER LIE, S. and O'LEARY, V. E. (Eds) *Storming the Tower: Women in the Academic World*, London, Kogan Page.

BERMAN, M. (1983) *All That Is Solid Melts Into Air: The Experience of Modernity*, London, Verso.

BHABBA, H. (1990) 'The Third Space: Interview with Homi Bhabba', in RUTHERFORD, J. (Ed.) *Identity: Community, Culture, Difference*, London, Lawrence & Wishart.

DAVIS, K. (1994) 'What's in a Voice? Methods and Metaphors', *Feminism and Psychology*, 4(3), pp. 353–61.

DONALD, J. (1985) 'Beacons of the Future: Subjection and Subjectification', in BEECHEY, V. and DONALD, J. (Eds) *Subjectivity and Social Relations*, Milton Keynes, Open University Press.

ELLSWORTH, E. (1989) 'Why Doesn't This Feel Empowering?: Working through the Repressive Myths of Critical Pedagogy', *Harvard Educational Review*, 59(3), pp. 297–324.

EPSTEIN, D. (1993) *Changing Classroom Cultures: Anti-Racism, Politics and Schools*, Stoke on Trent, Trentham Books.

GIDDENS, A. (1992) *The Transformation of Intimacy: Sexuality, Love and Eroticism in Modern Societies*, Cambridge, Polity.

GIROUX, H. A. and McLAREN, P. (1994) *Between Borders: Pedagogy and The Politics of Cultural Studies*, London, Routledge.

HALL, S. (1990) 'Cultural Identity and Diaspora', in RUTHERFORD, J. (Ed.) *Identity: Community, Culture, Difference*, London, Lawrence & Wishart.

HEY, V. (1995) '"A Game of Two Halves": Complicities and Simplicities in the Debate between Right and Left about Education Markets: Notes towards a Feminist Agenda', paper presented at one-day seminar organized by CREG, 'Shopping for Ideas': Feminist Analyses of Education, Marketization Institute of Education, University of London, 20 September.

HEY, V. (in press) *'The Company She Keeps': An Ethnography of Girls' Friendships*, Buckingham, Open University Press.

HOLLAND, J., HEY, V. and MAUTHNER, M. (1993) 'Behind Closed Doors: Researching the Family', BSA Conference Paper, University of Essex, 5–8 April.

HONEY, J. (1989) *Does Accent Matter?: The Pygmalion Factor*, London, Faber & Faber.

HOOKS, B. (1993) 'Keeping Close to Home: Class and Education', in TOKARCZYK, M. and FAY, E. (Eds) *Working-Class Women in the Academy:*

Laborers in the Knowledge Factory, Amherst, University of Massachusetts Press.

KENWAY, J. (1995) 'The Marketisation of Education: Mapping the Contours of a Feminist Perspective', paper presented at ECER Conference, University of Bath, 14–17 September.

KENWAY, J. (1996) 'Having a Postmodernist Turn or Postmodernist Angst: A Disorder Experienced by an Author Who is Not Yet Dead or Even Close to It', in SMITH, R. and WEXLER, P. (Eds) *After Post-Modernism: Education, Politics and Identity*, London, Falmer Press.

KENWAY, J. and BLACKMORE, B. (1995) 'Measure and Rain: Beyond Feminist Authoritarianism and Therapy in the Curriculum', paper presented at the Unesco Colbzuium, 'Is there a Pedagogy for Girls', Institute of Education, University of London, 10–12 January.

KUHN, A. (1995) *Family Secrets: Acts of Memory and Imagination*, London, Verso.

LASH, S. and URRY, J. (1987) *The End of Organized Capitalism*, Cambridge, Polity.

MERCER, K. (1990) 'Welcome to the Jungle: Identity and Diversity in Postmodern Politics', in RUTHERFORD, J. (Ed.) *Identity: Community, Culture, Difference*, London, Lawrence & Wishart.

MORLEY, L. and WALSH, V. (1995) *Feminist Academics: Creative Agents for Change*, London, Taylor & Francis.

OAKLEY, A. (1981) 'Interviewing Women: A Contradiction in Terms', in ROBERTS, H. (Ed.) *Doing Feminist Research*, London, Routledge & Kegan Paul.

OAKLEY, A. (1995) 'Public Visions; Private Matters', Professorial Inaugural Lecture, The Institute of Education, 26 September.

RUTHERFORD, J. (1990) 'A Place Called Home: Identity and the Cultural Politics of Difference', in RUTHERFORD, J. (Ed.) *Identity: Community, Culture, Difference*, London, Lawrence & Wishart.

STANLEY, J. (1995) 'Pain(t) for Healing', in MORLEY, L. and WALSH, V. (Eds) *Feminist Academics: Creative Agents for Change*, London, Taylor & Francis.

WALKERDINE, V. (1985) 'Dreams from an Ordinary Childhood', in HERON, L. (Ed.) *Truth, Dare, or Promise: Girls Growing Up in the Fifties*, London, Virago.

WALKERDINE, V. (1987) 'Femininity as Performance', *Oxford Review of Education*, 15(3), pp. 267–79.

WALKERDINE, V. (1995) 'Reading History', in BARRS, M. and PIDGEON, S. (Eds) *Reading the Difference: Gender and Reading in the Primary School*, London, CLPE, London Borough of Southwark.

Chapter 14

Interpreting Class: Auto/Biographical Imaginations and Social Change

Val Walsh

Introduction

The life history process[1] makes class and gender visible as enmeshed and contingent, social and performative processes, and therefore implicated in, even a function of, women's personal and social creativities. Class and gender may be viewed as performative, to the extent that they are 'acted out' and 'improvised' on the basis of culturally acquired codes, norms and taboos, within personal and social arenas not entirely or hardly of our own making. (Does this make them fact or fiction?) Class and gender may also be understood as instrumental and coercive: as social forces influencing and guiding those individual performances and versions. However problematic, contested and ambiguous, class is a body of experience/consciousness which is ours, individually and collectively. For women from working-class backgrounds, class is not simply a deficit position, but can and must be an important aspect of our power, our Wild Woman:

> Wild Woman is the health of all women. (Pinkola Estés, 1994, p. 10)
> The Wild Woman carries the bundles for healing; she carries everything a woman needs to be and know. . . . She carries stories and dreams and words and songs and signs and symbols. She is both vehicle and destination. (*ibid.*, p. 12)
> She is the one who thunders after injustice. . . . She is the one we leave home to look for. She is the one we come home to. She is the mucky root of all women. (*ibid.*, p. 13)

In this chapter, I start by considering the importance of feeling and internalized narratives of oppression in the lives and works of women from working-class backgrounds, and the consequences for feminist work and relations between women. I sketch in my own hybrid class background, and some of the ways in which this contributes to my identity and understanding of class and gender now. I also consider the impact of education and feminism in my life, as both partial and essential. I conclude by advocating narrative resources which emphasize interpretation, creativity and healing, as both means and end.

Linking knowledge production and the making of meanings with healing and reconstruction challenges the demarcations between everyday and specialized knowledge, between 'experts' and Others. Research is the province of the academic, storying the lifeline of peoples and cultures. As 'strangers' within, women from working-class backgrounds have both a special place and a crucial role to play in changing academic practices and purposes, and their relation to social change.

Throughout, I allow and represent my own class hybridity, uncertainty and ambivalence, by sometimes saying 'I', sometimes 'we', sometimes 'you', sometimes 'they' in my references to women from working-class backgrounds. I also mix formal referencing to the work of other writers with first-name references to writers themselves, in an attempt to embody them within my text, both as a gesture of appreciation and affection, and as a way of avoiding objectification, making them abstract and textual, as opposed to personal and social. I feel the need to produce a text (one day?) which reflects, as well as speaks about, the ambiguities and ambivalences which mark my own life history (see Shilling and Mellor, 1994; Sparkes, 1996a). This means taking liberties with academic formalities, perhaps being 'over-familiar', and mixing the academically respectable with the taboo. . . .

Class Feeling / Class Healing

I am aware of my own *taboo thresholds*, of how I have constantly censored myself for not wanting to be perceived as 'too powerful' or 'too middle class' – depending on who I am speaking to and how 'safe' it feels to reveal myself. Every day, in a variety of situations, I carefully choose my modes of address, whether or not to signal my 'authority' or 'knowledge' or 'superiority'. On the other hand, when in an amenable or *'therapeutic space'*, I am less guarded, more vulnerable and in consequence I am able to speak in a more fractured, tentative, incoherent way. (Spence, 1995, p. 159, emphasis added)

Healing takes place within us as we speak the truth of our lives. . . . There is no healing in silence. (hooks, 1993, pp. 19, 25, emphasis added)

Lives and works are by no means neatly distinct; the life that is lived makes continual use of a rich variety of *representational means*, while such representations are predicated on lives that are actually lived. (Liz Stanley, 1994, p. i, emphasis added)

> Once a story is told, it ceases to be a story: it becomes a piece of history, *an interpretive device.* (Steedman, 1993, p. 143, emphasis added)

In the statements above, four feminists, women of different working-class origins, draw attention to the relation between silence and oppression, life and art, experience and theory, history and women's herstories, representation and healing. They imply that the relation between cultural production, self-recovery and empowerment is significant. The implicit questions concern the conditions for women's creativity, that is the means to continue, maybe to flourish. The terrain they mark out is charged with personal/political resonance, as they locate themselves in terms of their own feeling-laden performances, for example as artists, writers, academics; or as friends, neighbours, partners. Their words testify both to the complexities and pressures of negotiating social and institutional structures of discrimination and exploitation, and to the power and persistence of internalized narratives of oppression. They simultaneously occupy and map a borderland where experience and identities meld and reform in the light of both what is 'out there' and what is 'in here'. In this place, lives and works entwine, neither superseding the other in importance: a symbiotic dance of significations. This formulation overturns the polarization in Western epistemologies between the everyday and the specialized, experience and theory, identity and representation, life and art: *fact and fiction.*

The gendered class performances of these women, as embodied in their lives and works, appear variously provisional, tentative, exploratory, experimental, incoherent and articulate, on the one hand; self-censoring and guarded on the other. At the very least they lack certainty and singularity, as they construe, construct, coordinate and rework the materials available to them. I see this as a richness, rather than a failure. As these women and other marginals demonstrate, interpretation/performance/improvisation/representation are simultaneously forms of resistance/recovery/creativity.

In Mary Evans' exposé of a girls' grammar school education in 1950s Britain (Evans, 1991), she describes how, as a middle-class girl and young woman she endured the coercive pressures of an education designed to elicit conformity to a contradictory muddle of bourgeois values and expectations. For example, the school strove to suppress and exclude feeling and desire. Both public and private grief were denied a place, ostensibly in the effort to construct a suitably 'rigorous' intellectual and academic environment. Desire is glimpsed, as a 'natural' fact of life, which the school tried hard to disregard, while affording it implicit recognition in school policies directed at its containment and management. These took the form of dress/uniform rules and restrictions, and homophobic and heterosexist assumptions about 'normal' sexuality and domesticity. The achievement of emotional and sexual *decorum* was clearly imperative: a classed and gendered performance comprised of repeated acts of self-control.

Women's accounts of class differ of course in many ways. In contrast to Mary Evans' account, bell hooks (1989, 1991, 1993, 1994), Carolyn Steedman (1993) and Jo Spence (1986, 1992, 1995) exhibit and explore *damage, pain and distress*, as central to their experience and understanding of class. Shame, inferiority and anger act as lens and frame for these writers. Social class is represented as something pervasive, even suffocating: absorbed and felt, before it is thought. In a class-based society, in which guilt and shame are inscribed in a unitary working-class identity, for women of working-class origin disclosure is unavoidably also *exposure and confession*, with attendant social, academic and professional risks. It is likely to be received and resisted as 'personal stuff' (I quote), rather than political, by other women, including feminists who are not yet unready to confront their own internalized oppression and pain, and/or collusion with class oppression. If, in a class-based society, working-class means *lack*: of decorum and beauty, education and influence, knowledge and power; if it means *wrong*, as in uncultured, unskilled, unintelligent; if it signifies poverty and dependence: how can it be admitted, let alone celebrated? How can a language be created which does not reproduce these social stereotypes and stigmas? How can working-class women present/ represent themselves, without either functioning as the exotic and exceptional Other for middle-class and ruling-class women and men, or, in acts of self-presentation and representation, self-destruct by camouflaging our class roots as we head further and further away from those familial (and political) ties? bell hooks, speaking as a black woman, assures us that 'assimilation, imitation, or assuming the role of rebellious exotic other are not the only available options and never have been' (hooks, 1991, p. 20). Thank goodness.

There can be no denying that an education such as Mary Evans describes inflicted itself upon girls, and differentially according to class background, with consequences for identities, subjectivities and social confidence, for example. But despite its feminist register, Mary's perceptive and stringent account can be accommodated as social and political critique, however scathing. While rooted in anger, hers is not an angry text, and her middle-class identity provides some social and academic continuity and cover. The voices of bell hooks, Carolyn Steedman and Jo Spence resist such recuperation, for they are also *grieving voices*, as much as they are critical and political. There is emotional turmoil in their accounts, as much as political analysis, and this register, perhaps more than the events and moments in the accounting, pushes them beyond the academic and sociological, towards art (literature) and/or therapy (confession). Their marks of origin – *they know* – are less a badge of honour, more stigmata, and integral to the life histories of women of working-class origin. *Risk is therefore attached to their creativity*, as a consequence of their identities both as women and as of working-class origin. Acquiring the accoutrements of 'success' (that is, middle-class, professional identity or lifestyle), may be accompanied by guilt, about denial, pretence or masquerade, and the risk of being found out (McIntosh, 1985). While approving Audre Lorde's invocation that 'pretense has never brought about lasting change or progress'

(Lorde, 1985, p. 57), I would also suggest the need for a nuanced and political understanding of 'pretence' in the lives of all marginals, and specifically women (see Lerner, 1993) in a society where white, non-disabled, middle-class and heterosexual identities function as social 'ideal(s)'. This work could usefully extend to the much underexplored area of the aesthetics of class (see Spence, 1986, 1995; Martin and Spence, 1986; Martin, 1991). The need for interdisciplinary and multimedia work is immediately apparent. Rather than accepting victim-blaming discourses, which leave middle-class and ruling-class identities as the unmarked categories, perhaps we should at least, for example, consider the possibility of masquerade as, on occasion, a knowing, artistic and honourable performance, in/as life as much as in/as art.[2]

Drawing on and articulating internalized oppression, rather than focusing exclusively on structures of discrimination and exploitation, is likely to disturb and hurt readers, as much as it might move, strengthen and motivate them. It is this shamanistic sharing of wounds (Spence, 1995, p. 163; see also J. Stanley, 1995a) which may variously empower, heal, embarrass, offend, even repel other women, whatever their own class backgrounds. It is this, too, which renders such work available and meaningful to those (women and men) whose hybrid identities, liminal sensibilities, and liberatory politics have been forged on the moving margins of social demarcations and power. *As art*, the work functions as reminder, exemplar, inspiration and vision: models of women's efforts towards integration and healing, as much as indictment. The indeterminacy and multiplicity of working-class experience, both fugitive and persistent, requires interpretive devices and representational means which can work with and through complexity and ambiguity, without schematizing or reducing that experience to disembodied bits and abstract notions, no longer recognizable to subjects themselves. For example, black American women first spoke their lives in song, poetry and story, before entering the academic arena of theory. They have now produced a body of academic work which maintains and promotes continuity between their lives and work: *between poetry and discourse, art and politics, feeling and theory, body and soul.* The works of Patricia Hill Collins, bell hooks, June Jordan, Audre Lorde and others continue to provoke in me a sense of identification which is sustaining. This surely reaches beyond my identity as female, British and white, to connect with both my class roots and my art background, and the importance of feeling and integration within both. Carolyn Steedman also refutes the separation and hierarchy of emotion and thought, the everyday and the specialized:

> Once a real child in a real situation is seen making these efforts (reading books, thinking, furnishing an imagination) then it becomes impossible to separate intellectual life from emotional life. (Steedman, 1993, p. 106)

Carolyn declines the invitation to deny (body, sex and class), and defies this resilient and persistent binary, around which the academy is organized.

Asserting the importance of interpretation over analysis, of feeling as integral to health, identity, subjectivity and knowledge, is to advocate purposes and methods for the academy which emphasize diversity and multiplicity, relational process and holistic practice (Walsh, 1996). It is also to agree with Carolyn that 'to enter the arena of subjectivity does not mean abandoning the political' (Steedman, 1986, p. 114). This is a contentious issue amongst feminists, the tug of war between what is seen by some as private, personal and (worse) therapeutic – marks of inadequacy/femininity – and the 'real' business of feminism, that is politics, social policy and upward mobility in a man's world . . . Class, disability and race issues bristle in this weary binary opposition.

So, there are real risks and problems for women from working-class backgrounds who speak as/of ourselves, particularly in academic contexts, and even in feminist ones. In acts of presentation/representation, we perform incoherently/imaginatively/bewilderingly: for how can we be both working-class and educated/working-class and academic or artist? How can you speak out of an identity which is supposed to be shameful and inferior? Women, of course, have, as it were, Other relevant experience in this matter, having, in increasing numbers and for some time now, taken up the challenge of re-inventing ourselves despite a culture which would have us conform to a narrow range of sexual stereotypes.[3]

Hybridity and Ambiguity: Class and Gender Tensions

My own gendered class experience and biography produced a growing tension and ambivalence regarding working-class culture, and uncertainty and hesitancy in relation to what I later glimpsed of the early Women's Liberation Movement in my twenties. I think the former was a function of my developing independence as a young woman getting educated (and my incipient feminism), and the problems this increasingly presented for my father and brother in particular: so that to me as daughter and sister, white working-class culture looked more and more sexist and male-dominated (Walsh, forthcoming). I suspect my early ambivalence about the Women's Liberation Movement was a class-based hesitancy. Disentangling class from other structurations is not easy. It is always implicated: you can recognize its presence and influence, but not separate and isolate it. The continuity in my own class identity has been political rather than social, and centres around my early commitment to and identification with working-class movements and causes – socialism, the labour movement, trade unionism. My class identity is thus tangled with my class politics, and an early political identity which meshed, for example, peace politics, socialism, CND, Vietnam War and Free Angela Davis activism. These activities link me to my father, and his biography and identity. In fact he took me to the first CND rally in Trafalgar Square, London, when I was 14.

My experience and understanding of social class provide me now with an emotional and political base which feels enduring, if somewhat ambiguous. I am a woman rooted, albeit problematically, in white working-class history and politics, which is the line of descent from and connection with my father. But the life history process has made me aware of my *hybrid* origins and their significance. I had one parent who was an educated, white, (lower?)-middle-class, commercial artist, singer and ballroom dancer from south London, turned housewife and mother. My other parent was a white working-class socialist, who grew up in poverty in the midst of an extended family in the East End of London; left school at 14 to work as a pageboy in a restaurant; left this to seek an apprenticeship, and, at the age of 16, organized the whole shopfloor of a print works to join the union, as a result of which they were all sacked. Thirty years later he was elected Assistant Secretary of the same union, and later elected Branch Secretary (Rule, 1954).

Sociologically and conventionally, a child takes her class from her social father (where he is known), and I always thought of myself as straightfor-wardly, if not typically, working class. I say not typically, because questions and comments from neighbours and relatives, from when I was about 15 till I was 22, about still being at school or college, were regular reminders of my atypicality as a girl on the estate. The life history process has disturbed this unitary identity and illuminated the relation between my biography and what is an ambiguous and ambivalent class identity. I feel as if a fog is beginning to clear. In particular, I have become aware of how an account of my background and identity as 'working-class' marginalizes *my mother's* presence, identity and class background, and her contributions to and significance for me as girl/woman/feminist. I should have realized this sooner. For my *cultural* roots connect me with my mother. This is partly because my interests (apart from current affairs, politics and modern languages) lay mainly in the direction of the arts (visual arts, theatre, cinema, music, literature, poetry); aesthetics (nature, clothes, domestic interiors, architecture); and interpersonal relation-ships. And it is partly because I followed her route into formal and selected education, and into art school, like her via a scholarship. Although in my teens and twenties I identified myself as 'ordinary', one of the majority class in society, I never felt fully and comfortably a part of the working class with whom I identified politically. I did not properly belong.

Class as a social and political issue has been fairly determinedly 'disap-peared' by politicians, academics (including women and feminists) and media alike (see Dunne, 1996). According to Roy Greenslade, in a follow-up study of his year group, ten years after leaving his (and my) old school, the working class have colluded in this process (Greenslade, 1976a, 1976b). However, dispensing with the working class as a unitary sociological category highlights the difficulty of *anybody* speaking about class. If it has become so difficult to demarcate and pin down, how can it be part of discourse and theory? Morwenna Griffiths has noted that girls living in a society within which the term 'slag' is operational cannot simply behave as if the label does not exist (Griffiths, 1995, p. 119). The same is true for 'working class'. Máiréad Dunne provides a recent reminder that, while social class is irrefutably and persistently linked to educational achievement and life chances, it has also been the most neglected (avoided?) factor in equal opportunities research, policy and practice (Dunne, 1996).

The Life Histories,[4] including my own, demonstrate the personal/ political significance of hybridity, multiplicity and liminality, for our subjectivities, theory, creativities and politics. But, as I suggested at the beginning, this is in the face of social censure, for as anthropologist Mary Douglas noted: 'Cultural intolerance of ambiguity is expressed in avoidance, by discrimination, and by pressure to conform' (Douglas, 1984, p. 53); 'Not only marginal social states, but all margins, the edges of all boundaries which are used in ordering the social experience, are treated as dangerous and polluting' (*ibid.*, p. 56).

Over the last thirty years, feminists have produced a body of work which has articulated and deconstructed women's dangerous and polluting status. In addition, liberatory and feminist activists have qualified Mary Douglas' insight, as we have spoken out of and about our experiences of marginality, as 'a site of resistance, as location of radical openness and possibility' (hooks, 1993, p. 22): as productive, even pleasurable. This is the kind of work which tackles and explores the problems of authenticity and empowerment which are central to both liberatory politics and personal well-being (see Griffiths, 1995; hooks, 1989; West, 1990). But equivalent work on class from a feminist perspective and feminism from a class perspective has been lacking. It would appear that women and men from working-class backgrounds have felt less empowered to speak out of *their* 'dangerous and polluting' social identities. Is this because it is too painful (and dangerous), or is it because the working classes are no longer dangerous and polluting, because they have been incorporated and silenced, or turned into an underclass and silenced?[5]

Education: Glimpsing Class and Gender

In my teens and early twenties, class meant politics rather than identity, and it was a strong and purposeful place to be and from which to speak. I was lucky enough to grow up during the early years of the Welfare State in Britain, and I saw myself both as ordinary and as evidence of an emergent society, a new and better world. There were no visible precedents to follow, no ready place being kept warm for me, no signs saying 'this way'. Education has been many things for me: impetus, stage, means, reward, and, intermittently during my career as teacher and academic, a real danger zone. In Mary Evans' girls' grammar school

What was important was class-based social order. . . . On the whole, given the nature of our social backgrounds, there was a close corre-

> spondence between the school's expectations and our behaviour. Our departure from the values of the school was only ever minimal and our rebellion limited. (Evans, 1991, p. 111)

There are visibly places being kept warm for rightful occupation. But while the new grammar schools were busy preparing middle-class girls for middle-class life and prospects, they also took in 'strangers' (Walsh, 1995b). The new tripartite system, based on selection and categorization, was being used to alter the social fabric, by providing different kinds of education for supposedly different kinds of children, as well as one kind, the grammar school, which was to include children of unequal birth but equal ability. There were 'rebellious' girls in the new grammar schools. I was one (Walsh, 1995b, forthcoming). How much was this class? Politics or astrology?[6] How much my inchoate feminism? Probably all these and more. At the time, I think it was seen as more a question of 'personality'. . . . In the post-war period, at primary school and grammar school, I was part of an educational obscuring and neutralizing of gender and class as constraint and disadvantage. At the grammar school I did not feel I was being (successfully) educated as 'girl' as opposed to 'boy', nor did I particularly identify my difference as class-based. This may be because, according to Greenslade (1976a) the school's intake was overwhelmingly white working-class children, with only a tiny number of white middle-class children in any one year. My sense of difference was, rather, always connected to my 'seriousness' as a student: from a very early age I enjoyed studying and learning, and worked very hard. Between the ages of 3 and 18, I encountered personal warmth and robust nurturing in the institutional setting of my schools, mainly, but not exclusively, at the hands of female teachers. This was influential in helping me feel real and alive, in sustaining me in the process of self-actualization, to which education can contribute so vitally.

My experience at grammar school differed from Mary's, not just because my home background was different. Perhaps it was because my grammar school took in boys as well as girls, and was located in the middle of the largest council estate in the world (at the time), rather than in the home counties. Perhaps it was as a result of individual, committed teachers and their particular combination. Individuals make choices within the context of social structurations, which are not simply determined by these pressures. For example, teachers are not just members of a particular class and professional group, and their pedagogic performances can act to dislodge and subvert the influence of dominant structures of discrimination inside and outside school (Walsh, 1996). In marked contrast to Roy Greenslade's account of his year group (four years behind mine) (Greenslade, 1976a), I believe I was extraordinarily fortunate in the teachers I encountered. For example, at the end of the fifth year, before we left or went on into sixth form, the ritual was to rush around getting teachers' autographs. One of my English teachers, Peter Day, wrote:

Let your mind be quiet, realising the beauty of the world, and the immense treasures that it holds in store.

All that it holds in store for you, all that your heart desires, all that your Nature so specially fits you for – that or the counterpart of it awaits embedded in the great whole, for you. It will surely come to you. (Edward Carpenter)

At the time, I did not know who Edward Carpenter was, only much later taking pleasure in the knowledge that he was a socialist and active in sexuality campaigns. Another of my English teachers, Kay Day, had not long married Peter. She was one of my important early role models, and over the page from Peter she wrote:

May your studies provide for you the romance of 'magic casements, opening on the foam of perilous seas in faery lands forlorn'. (John Keats)

These poetics, so carefully chosen, moved me then, as they do now. Years after, reading these two passages again (and again), I marvel: how did they know? And I think, yes, that's just how it's been, and still is, and partly thanks to them.

My experiences as a child at primary and grammar school provided a sense of personal possibility and intellectual excitement, which Mary says her school failed to communicate (Evans, 1991, p. 3). At her 'good school', above all the girls were expected 'to appreciate order, emotional continence and self-discipline' (*ibid.*, p. 101); and continence is a word which recurs in her account. The corollary to this was that passion, involvement, commitment were suspect, for both relationships and study (*ibid.*, p. 81). Even enthusiasm seems to have counted as a lack of continence (see *ibid.*, pp. 77–101). By contrast, whatever emotional turmoil I experienced during my grammar school years, there is no doubt that I succumbed to the seductions and pleasures of learning and performing (in class, in debate and on stage). Later, deciding to teach was a class-based, political decision, which arose out of this conjunction of class and educational experience. I wanted to try to do for others, especially ordinary, working-class children, what I felt had been done for me. I knew in my heart, and from experience, what was possible: I knew the difference one person can make to the life of another. I took with me the energetic, good-humoured, idiosyncratic and generous pedagogic models I had encountered. But the first thing I did on leaving grammar school was to disappoint most of my teachers, by deciding to go to art school instead of to university to study English or Modern Languages. My art teacher, Pat Cope, was a striking personality and an intellectual woman from the West Riding of Yorkshire. She really stood out amongst the other teachers, but though I feel she was liked and respected by her colleagues, there was clearly something in the school's disappointment at my decision, which echoes what Mary remembers of how, at her grammar school,

> Art, music, the visual and creative arts in general were part of a peripheral world. From the point of view of serious, grown-up people, only slightly mad, eccentric people engaged in lifetime commitments to art, music or literature. (Evans, 1991, p. 119)

Unwittingly, I was compounding my liminal status. This was to be the pattern throughout my life.

Although I was seen as independent, even 'rebellious', as a girl and young woman, my upbringing and education left me without a coherent sexual politics. My feminism was implied rather than articulated in my life, perhaps more visible to others than myself. The gender-neutral schooling I remember suddenly left me vulnerable as I embarked on the art school experience immediately after sixth form, and I was ill-prepared for its contradictory sexual messages for me as a young, educated woman entering the anti-intellectual wing of higher education (Walsh, 1990). Perhaps my upbringing, politics and education had provided me with a certain confidence, even audacity: from an early age, I presumed a place in the public sphere and within its debates (for example at public meetings and on street corners). I assumed that as members of society we all had a right to speak and be heard, and social and political discussions with my father over the years helped foster this idea.

My subsequent movement across and in between societal layering and demarcations as a result of grammar school, art school and university, followed by a full-time career mainly in higher education, combined to produce, rather than reproduce, an identity and subjectivity which conformed to neither working-class nor middle-class models, and perhaps, therefore, remains indecipherable to those whose social class has been confirmed by upbringing, education and employment experience – whether working-class, middle-class or ruling-class. My current class identity (whatever it is) affords a specific and useful vantage point, because it incorporates ambiguity and multiplicity; the experience of crossing-over, moving between; resisting incorporation and assimilation; and the frustration of stereotyping and repeated *mistaken identity*. My consciousness of these mingling processes and connections is of course a crucial ingredient.

The question is, once educated, *where's home*? It's difficult to speak unproblematically of 'back home', because while the cliché is that home is where the heart is, for educated white working-class women, it is more likely to be where the heartache is – but maybe that's true for everyone? So home (and community) has to be prospected for, found and created as much out of the materials of our imaginations, as from memory or previous experience. It is a fiction of which we are not yet a part – until we realize it in here/out there. I remember an early sense of trying to live out ideas and possibilities prefigured in my political imagination, to 'show it can be done', rather than copying alien class models. I felt enormous energy and optimism. It was a hopeful time.

Feminism: For Better, For Worse, For Good

From an early age, I had a sense that the modern world had arrived, and I was part of it. Only now, after what seems like an eternity of accelerating New Right politics, I no longer feel so celebratory. This is not what I struggled for. But then there are the women. . . .

> While it is true that certain kinds of political activity are and have to be possible between persons who are not friends, both politics and friendship are restored to a deeper meaning when they are brought together – that is, when political activity proceeds from a shared affection, vision, and spirit and when friendship has a more expansive political effect. (Raymond, 1986, p. 8)

Here, Janice Raymond speaks of and out of the knowledge, politics and relationships which have become familiar to so many women during the last thirty years of feminist activism and struggle.

Feminism was implicit in my life long before it gathered momentum when, just before my thirtieth birthday, I started teaching in higher education. Eighteen months later I moved north. In Britain, the class divide is a north/south divide too. Even after over twenty years, I still worry about being stereotyped as 'posh', not just because of my academic identity, but because I can still be identified from my voice as both (formally) educated and from the south. Even my daughter and son went through a phase when they were preoccupied with this equation: south equals posh/Other. At some point I started to masquerade, by altering my vowels, to alleviate my sense of otherness. I told myself this was a political move in Thatcherite Britain: I was identifying with the north she so despised and ignored, and attempting to dissociate myself from the class politics which underpinned this binarism (this was true, but . . .).

As a young woman, my relatively inchoate feminism and lack of feminist contexts left me without the means for engaging with my class roots *as a woman*. Feminism has to develop to aspire to adequacy in relation to class differences, just as it has to work to embody disabilities, ethnicities and sexualities into its body politic, rather than constructing them as Other to a normative and élitist feminism. As I moved through my twenties, my socialism was in turn inadequate to the task of addressing my position and experience as female in a male-supremacist society. It is the conjunction of class and gender that the life history process has spotlighted for me as a major tension in my own biography and identity. However, moving in feminist, women-only and

Women's Studies environments over the last ten years or so has had other consequences.

Encountering white middle-class women and would-be middle-class women, in greater concentration and closer than ever before, I nonetheless did not immediately recognize that these were middle-class environments, only run by women – probably because I had expectations about 'sisterhood'.... Along with other women, I began to acknowledge my dis-ease, even disapproval. For despite being educated and a 'professional educa-tor' all my life, I cannot identify *as* middle-class – or do I mean *with* the middle class? It feels like a mix of resistance and incapacity. Looking back now, the 'problem' – that is, *the creative problem* – remains: you 'get out' of one class (sort of and without trying), but you don't want to get into another. So white, middle-class feminism has intensified my awareness of class differences *be-tween women*, in particular in the academy. I suspect this is something to do with our differential positioning with regard to feeling and what Patricia Hynes has called 'passionate thinking' (Hynes, 1989, p. 4). Understanding this means I don't hurt (well, not much!), but I am disappointed (sometimes angry).

These contacts with other women and feminists have been instrumental in a growing awareness that my own feeling-laden performances are rooted in a very specific conjunction: my gendered class identity, and a continuing politi-cal commitment to values which derive from this; and my initial training and identity as an artist, which still underpins and informs my life and my work as an academic. At the same time, I have become increasingly aware of class as a factor within female friendship. Finding myself more and more close to women whose backgrounds turn out to be similar to my own has alleviated my sense of disappointment within feminist environments and networks. I have experienced this as a healing process, which suggests a deep-seated wound, injury or absence, of which I have been hardly or only intermittently aware. These relationships, and the feminist environments within which they have flourished (even against the grain) have refocused my attention on and inten-sified my concern with the significance of class for feminists and for women's creativity.

As a full-time academic for twenty years, I could choose to foreground or mask my class identity, in a way that ethnicity and disability cannot be man-aged. I am now moved to consider, critically, the extent to which, as an academic, I lived not only as if there were no limits – both because anything was possible (I had imagination, ideas, apparently limitless energy and a sturdy body), and because consuming singularity of purpose was and is promoted as professionalism – but also, and consequentially, as if I had no background (Spence, 1995, p. 208) and no body to speak of. To what extent did I live as if there was only one order of experience, that of the fictive text (the work and the lifestyle), while denying the order of the body, until it reasserted itself in protest (see Sparkes, 1996a, 1996b), reminding me that 'not all experience is fictive, subject to the limitless power of imagination to transfigure and invent'

(Kirmayer, 1992, p. 323, cited in Sparkes, 1996b)? During those years, I saw and experienced the pain and damage women suffer, both as women in society and in academia, and not least in our relations with each other. All these factors, together with the life history process itself, have refuelled my sense of liminality, as both vulnerability and politics.

> We must now continue to identify each other so that we can form alliances and create cultural groupings which are more complex than simply being 'black' or being 'women'. Now when I lecture, teach or lead workshops, instead of my previous confusions over my identity. . . . I see that I am no longer an ugly duckling trying to be a swan but that I belong to a very specific and previously unlabelled group. (Spence, 1995, p. 163)

Feminism reworked and expanded my life materials, not in one go, but in waves which built up over the years. The basic framework was thus altered in a fundamental way, which in turn has helped me see the extent to which my class identity is not 'pure' or simple, but marked simultaneously by a sense of continuity as well as disruption and displacement; by ambiguity, ambivalence, tension, as well as a sense of excitement and adventure. It is other feminists and my own feminism which now provide the context, confidence, means, and justification for a process of re-construction which is political: towards a politics of my own becoming which connects me to and draws strength from the political struggles of other women. I can do this now, knowing that my story will join with other women's stories to help make sense of our struggles and differences, our resistances and ambivalences. By fostering inner strength, rather than independence, feminist process and co/creativity work to counter past fragmentation, providing materials for recovery and healing. These materials reside in and re-order the relation between the order of the body and the order of the text, the polarization of life and art, lives and works. While still recognizable in themselves, these orders of experience are perhaps better seen as continually emergent and changing, and as more or less entwined over time and on occasion. Feeling is not therefore peripheral, or mere 'grit in the machine of living', but both reason and reward.

Morwenna Griffiths suggests that the most significant relationships are ones of love, resistance, acceptance and rejection, and that these are 'connections of belonging, deciding whether to belong and of being given or refused permission to belong' (Griffiths, 1995, pp. 85, 86). These issues are implicit, and often explicit, in life histories, and central to any feminism. As Joanna Bornat has highlighted in relation to oral history work, it is also a question of 'having to come to terms with the limits of sharing while we reflect on the divisions of class, race, age, culture and impairment (sic)' (Bornat, 1994, p. 21). The openness, interrogation and political instrumentality she commends as virtues of oral history (*ibid.*, pp. 22–6) are also central principles for any feminist work on social class, as is the value Joanna places on the origins of oral history as dialogue. bell hooks, among others, has reiterated the urgency that women, as marginals, tell our own stories before someone else tells them, 'claiming to know us better than we know ourselves' (hooks, 1991, p. 22). Similarly, during her recovery from breast cancer, Jo Spence demonstrated and testified to the importance of inhabiting our own history (Spence, 1992). In considering the narrative resources available and useful to women from working-class backgrounds, I have implied that stories and storying loom larger than sociological or cultural theory, particularly if the latter are perpetrated by middle-class scholars or working-class researchers in denial.

> Stories set the inner life into motion, and this is particularly impor-
> tant where the inner life is frightened, wedged, or cornered. Story
> greases the hoists and pulleys, it causes adrenalin to surge, shows us
> the way out, down, or up, and for our trouble, cuts for us fine wide
> doors in previously blank walls. . . . (Pinkola Estés, 1994, p. 20)

To repeat Carolyn Steedman (1993, p. 143), 'Once a story is told, it ceases to be a story: it becomes a piece of history, an interpretive device' (see also Jo Stanley, 1995b). The significance of stories connects powerfully to issues of shame and guilt, scars and secrets, as well as to the achievement of community. No stories, no community. As feminist, Jungian analyst and as *cantadora* (storyteller), Clarissa Pinkola Estés knows that:

> The keeping of secrets cuts a woman off from those who would give
> her love, succour, and protection. It causes her to carry the burden of
> grief and fear all by herself, and sometimes for an entire group,
> whether family or culture. (Pinkola Estés, 1994, p. 377)

Bundles for Healing

The task of transforming gendered class experience and identities into a resource, not just for ourselves, but hopefully for other women, including those from different backgrounds and in different circumstances, is feminist work which produces new knowledge. New knowledge is a change agent; in part a product of feminist networking, collaboration, co/creativity, which in themselves can transform gendered class experience and identities. This network of feeling and meaning has been one aspect of what has become, over the years, an increasingly pivotal theoretical/political/professional/personal imperative and joy: the friendship, affection and love of women for each other, in active association and alliance – always precarious, also surprising. In 1993, three women of different white working-class backgrounds were amongst those who read the life history work-in-progress I had started that year. As a way of returning to the central problematic I set out at the beginning of the chapter, I will share extracts from their responses, as examples both of co/

creativity and of the dilemma faced by women from working-class back-grounds when we try to uncover 'a wound that will not heal until the matter is given words and witness' (Pinkola Estés, 1994, p. 377).

Comments on the manuscript from feminist historian and cultural worker, Jo Stanley, included stylistic improvements, questions, suggestions for development, encouragements like 'Yes!' or 'Lovely!', to pointing out where something was particularly useful or significant for her in relation to her own life history. She also drew attention to places where I was switching into the impersonal, and suggested I look at whether or how the meaning changed when I replaced this with 'I'. Aaah. In addition, there was a string of comments which I will summarize in her words:

> It might be instructive to look at all the points where you omit yourself and go off into theory. What do these absences hide, that can assist your project?

She said she hoped she was not being too 'intrusive', and described these as 'a therapist's responses to areas that seem significantly buried'. (Jo is also a trained Gestalt therapist.) Artist Rosy Martin, experienced co-counsellor and well-known for her groundbreaking work (with Jo Spence) in developing phototherapy, wrote something very similar. The parts she enjoyed most, she said, were the most autobiographical. Sociologist Jean Hardy, who is also trained in psychosynthesis (see Hardy, 1996), sent detailed reactions and observations, including:

> My main reaction to your material is that it is beautifully written – and that you've left yourself out of it!
> I think that this is one thing that we learnt very well – not to take ourselves seriously, and not to think and feel, experience, how we were becoming persons. Most working-class people learn this, I reckon. . . .

Considering the sense of *exposure* I had felt on the way to my first life history presentation at the second annual Women's History Network Conference, these observations took me by surprise, but I realized they were among the most important I received.

Writing about the Crisis Project, unfinished at her death in 1992, Jo Spence describes the wider scope of the work: 'Not only does it celebrate, but it also mourns, accuses and attempts to heal' (Spence, 1995, p. 219). This evokes the holistic multiplicity and complexity we must attempt, in our work, as in our lives. It is, of course, more art than science, if we understand art as 'not so much the investigation of human life as its extension and creation' by means of symbolic form 'whose function is to connect' (Pacey, 1977, p. 58). Patricia Hynes, comparing the writing of a well-known male eco-warrior with that of Rachel Carson, the author of *Silent Spring*, the book which first triggered the environmental movement in the West, sums up the difference in this way:

> Mediated by prose, the difference is more than one of writing style; it is the difference between rational and passionate thinking. In his work we are critical onlookers. She wrote with a 'feeling mind and thinking heart'. In her work we enter the problem. (Hynes, 1989, p. 4)

For marginals in society, there is no value in the stance of critical onlooker. This has considerable implications for our academic practices: research and teaching, as well as writing (Walsh, 1996). For in entering a problem, we offer ourselves to it, locate ourselves in its terms. We relinquish the (relative) safety of our boundaries and risk losing ourselves, as well as finding ourselves and each other in new ways. How do we develop ways of entering the problem (any problem), of feeling sufficiently courageous and responsible? In this case, empowered to imagine and perform against the grain of expectation and coercion.

There is no doubt in my mind that my own personal stamina, social and intellectual creativity, my capacity for connection, humour and irony, my political energy and at times furious determination and independence, *such as they are*, are all rooted in these gendered class positionings, experiences and identities. My vulnerability and fragility, my brokenness and self-doubt, my uncertainty and frustration, my dis-ease, stubbornness and despair; my wounds and my anger: these too are rooted in experiences of class and gender in a class-based patriarchal society. And like everyone else, both my health (I mean of course, *my body*, which I took for granted as sturdy and reliable) and my ill-health are products of and marked by my particular biography. My hybrid identity and liminal sensibility provide a vantage point on the world, which provokes in me political anguish and perseverance; aesthetic and spiritual exhilaration; laughter and hope (still).

I believe creative process and cultural action and production are rooted in these liminal locations and experiences (Swift and Walsh, 1995/1996). Perhaps liminality can be understood as the *consciousness* of these marginal locations and identities, and their possibilities; the achievement of a working level of self-esteem *as a marginal*. Not as neither this nor that, nor even 'both', but something new and valuable, a basis for a politics of both identity and creativity. Theodore Roszak has considered the problem of finding a middle term between continuity and discontinuity in evolution (1993, p. 195), and suggests that ' "Potentiality" is exactly that term. It is the zone of possibility that lies waiting to be crossed between hierarchical levels' (*ibid.*).

Hybridity, multiplicity, and marginality are after all the majority experience and location in society: all those on the margins, all those pushed to the boundaries and limits of one or more social and political categories. These are the materials to hand. Either these locations and experiences result in emotional, social and ecological disruption, or they provide the basis for renewal and recovery. The question is: what are the factors which make the difference between liminality as creative impetus and resource, or as the mark of oppression only?

Education does not solve the problem of class oppression, and as Jo Spence realized, 'You can't get rid of class conflict through therapy' (Spence, 1995, p. 208). As signalled at the start of this chapter, these experiences and issues are not amenable to conventional analysis, which separates and divides, which produces and works in terms of the binary dichotomies of private/public, feeling/thinking, body/mind. Auto/biographical imaginations are at the heart of this revolution, both outside and inside the academy: as a bridge between the two, and in redefining purposes and boundaries. As Liz Stanley has argued, 'Auto/biography intends an epistemological revolution within the social sciences' (1994, p. i). Also at issue is the relation between women academics, and between women who are academics and those who are not. As a woman from a working-class background, and as a feminist, I have always been conscious of this dilemma. We occupy territory which is not yet mapped. We are working creatively and collectively for our lives, recognizing uncertainty, fragility, corporeality, as nature's way, rather than marks of failure in a competitive, consumerist and technicist culture.

Chris Shilling and Philip Mellor have pointed to the dislocation of texts from contexts and bodies as a feature of post-Reformation society. They see 'the liberation of the text from ritual contexts [as] the hallmark of the production and consumption of modern auto/biography' (Shilling and Mellor, 1994, p. 119), where 'meaning is apprehended increasingly in cognitive terms, and the role of feelings and bodily states is devalued in terms of their importance for knowing and understanding' (*ibid.*, p. 122). Academic disembodiment is not a useful model for women (Walsh, 1995a). What we need are 'texts-in-context' (Shilling and Mellor, 1994, p. 122): both texts and contexts as far as possible of our own making and for feminist purposes – but not, of course, a feminism which reproduces the hierarchies and injuries of the host society.

What are the agencies of healing and creative transformation which convert the injuries and distortions of class and gender into lives and works which are more than their sedimentation and exposure? The processes of self-recollection and re-construction, of responsible feminist reflexivity and critical scrutiny, are vital features of any feminist epistemology, and of the recovery process itself, as we try out ways of being with each other and ourselves, which sustain authenticity, intimacy, social diversity and psychic and political empowerment. Tracing the agency and influence of class and gender in my life via life history process is helping me understand the dynamic between class and gender, and between class consciousness and feminist consciousness. It has also brought me closer to other women of working-class origin, who are willing to share their own social and psychic journeys. Thanks are not enough.

Notes

1 In February 1993, at the instigation of feminist historian Jo Stanley, I began life history work, taking as my starting points (at her suggestion) education, art and feminism. Jo had drawn these themes from reading an earlier paper of mine, which, on rereading, I saw was replete with life history material, both my own and other women's (see Walsh, 1990). My first reaction to her suggestion was: 'But I am not an historian'. However, I trusted this woman, so I headed three pages with each of these words, and waited to see what came up. In this chapter I draw on some of this material, parts of which I presented as 'Digging Up Tangled Roots: Feminism and Resistance to Working-Class Culture' at the second Women's History Network annual conference (1993) in London, and at the BSA (British Sociological Association) Study Group on Auto/Biography annual conference (1994) in Manchester. This prompting of one woman by another, and the trusting of one woman by another, is a good example of feminist co/creativity: we make each other possible, we give each other permission to go down roads we had not noticed ourselves. We encourage each other to *dare*.

2 Masquerade is defined in the *Concise Oxford Dictionary* as 'false show, pretence'; 'appear in disguise, assume false appearance'. This of course presumes the Western binary demarcations between fact and fiction, science and myth, life and art, which are themselves at issue here. Once the creativity and performativeness of our daily lives and identities is acknowledged, life moves closer to art. Contemporary women artists (too numerous to list) have been prominent in using performance and masquerade as ways of exploring, deconstructing, re-imagining and embodying the oppressive constraints of the social order, Woman; the processes of resistance and transgression required for survival; and the wealth of possibilities we can access via our auto/biographical imaginations. In this work, art both models and remodels life; demonstrates the reciprocity between the two, and the living dynamic between these overlapping arenas of symbolic action and ritual. See for example, Boffin and Fraser, 1991; Spence and Solomon, 1995; and the work of Addela Khan, Rosy Martin, Brigitte Potter-Mael, Lesley Sanderson, and Jo Spence in a forthcoming international interdisciplinary and multimedia anthology edited by Jacquie Swift and myself. While masquerade is used by artists to reveal, expose and invent, in daily life masquerade may be used in addition quite differently: for example, to protect from exposure and/or injury; to create distance, space and/or privacy; and as playfulness, in varying degrees exploratory and/or celebratory. For fun?

3 The significance – *and potential* – of shame is tackled imaginatively by Judy Purdom (forthcoming) in her discussion of the work of American artist Nancy Spero. Judy's aim is 'to use shame as a force of difference and to produce a body politics (as opposed to an identity politics) which engages with the actual experience of women'. Her method is 'to voice our shame, to

show up, subvert and to exceed patriarchy'; to move, *via auto/biography*, towards 'an aesthetic of shame, not a conception of shame'. See note 5 below; Jan Zita Grover, 1980; Jo Stanley, 1995a.

4 In November 1995, I extended my own life history by setting up a three-year life history and peer group project, Degrees of Change (referred to as the Life Histories here), which documents and explores the experiences, self-understandings and theories of a group of women from white working-class backgrounds who became academics. See Walsh, 1995b.

5 This suggests that while both class and gender may be seen as performative and open to negotiation and reconstruction, the narrative resources available with regard to class are less rich than for gender. This reduces opportunities for change and empowerment. This disparity is in part because for thirty years feminists have been expanding and enriching the narrative resources available with regard to gender and sexual difference, and within this work, class has been relatively, even largely, neglected. So, class has continued to shape feminist work by default, because class continues to shape relations between women, including those in academia (see Jo Stanley, 1995a). In addition, New Right and New Labour would have us believe that class has been displaced as a major structuring agency in British society. This denial/manipulation of reality internalizes social class as unspeakable within conventional politics. Hence the need for marginals and academics to find common cause – and marginals who are academics to find voice – in forging purposes for the academy which establish its responsibility and value in terms of a healing politic, *towards knowledge that will help save lives* (see Walker, 1984, p. 14).

6 This is a specific, if oblique, reference to an astrological reading and interpretation provided by Paul Mayo (2 November 1995). It is also a reminder that multiplicity includes what we cannot know or understand fully or even at all, certainly within the constraints of Western epistemologies. Note, too, how including this word, 'astrological', alongside and co-terminous with conventional sociological terms, risks *spoiling* the academic status of my text, and the credibility of my narrative, depending also on the reader. . . . 'Spoiling' needs reconsidering, when waste and damage are routine, and ruin or renewal are at stake.

References

BOFFIN, TESSA and FRASER, JEAN (Eds) (1991) *Stolen Glances: Lesbians Take Photographs*, London, Pandora.

BORNAT, JOANNA (1994) 'Is Oral History Auto/Biography?' in special double issue of *Auto/Biography*, 3:1 and 3:2, pp. 17–30.

CARSON, RACHEL (1962) *Silent Spring*, Harmondsworth, Penguin.

COLLINS, PATRICIA HILL (1991) *Black Feminist Thought: Knowledge, Consciousness and the Politics of Empowerment*, London, Routledge.

DOUGLAS, MARY (1984) *Implicit Meanings (Essays in Anthropology)*, London, Routledge & Kegan Paul.

DUNNE, MÁIRÉAD (1996) 'The Power of Numbers: Feminism, Equity and Quantitative Research', in MORLEY, LOUISE and WALSH, VAL (Eds) *Breaking Boundaries: Women in Higher Education*, London, Taylor & Francis, pp. 160–79.

EVANS, MARY (1991) *A Good School. (Life at a Girls' Grammar School in the 1950s)*, London, The Women's Press.

GREENSLADE, ROY (1976a) *Goodbye to the Working Class*, London, Marion Boyars.

GREENSLADE, ROY (1976b) 'Never Had It Good', *The Guardian*, 11 June, p. 7.

GRIFFITHS, MORWENNA (1995) *Feminisms and the Self: The Web of Identity*, London, Routledge.

GROVER, JAN ZITA (1980) 'Phototherapy: Shame and the Minefields of Memory', *Afterimage*, 18, 1 (summer).

HARDY, JEAN (1996) *A Psychology with a Soul: Psychosynthesis in Evolutionary Contex*, London, Woodgrange Press.

HOOKS, BELL (1989) *Talking Back: Thinking Feminist – Thinking Black*, London, Sheba Feminist Press.

HOOKS, BELL (1991) *Yearning: Race, Gender and Cultural Politics*, London, Turnaround.

HOOKS, BELL (1993) *Sisters of the Yam: Black Women and Self-Recovery*, London, Turnaround.

HOOKS, BELL (1994) *Teaching to Transgress: Education as the Practice of Freedom*, London, Routledge.

HYNES, PATRICIA H. (1989) *The Recurring Silent Spring*, Oxford, Pergamon, The Athene Series.

JORDAN, JUNE (1989a) *Moving Towards Home: Political Essays*, London, Virago.

JORDAN, JUNE (1989b) *Lyrical Campaigns: Selected Poems*, London: Virago.

KIRMAYER, LAURENCE (1992) 'The Body's Insistence on Meaning: Metaphor as Presentation and Representation in Illness Experience', *Medical Anthropology Quarterly*, 6(4), pp. 323–46.

LERNER, HARRIET GOLDHOR (1993) *The Dance of Deception: Pretending and Truth-Telling in Women's Lives*, London, Pandora.

LORDE, AUDRE (1985) *The Cancer Journals*, London, Sheba Feminist Publishers.

MARTIN, ROSY (1991) ' "Don't Say Cheese Say Lesbian" ', in BOFFIN, TESSA and FRASER, JEAN (Eds) *Stolen Glances: Lesbians Take Photographs*, London, Pandora, pp. 94–105.

MARTIN, ROSY and SPENCE, JO (1986) 'Photo Therapy: New Portraits for Old. 1984 Onwards', in SPENCE, JO. *Putting Myself in the Picture*, London, Camden Press, pp. 172–93.

McINTOSH, PEGGY (1985) 'Feeling Like a Fraud', Work in Progress, The Stone Center, Wellesley College, No. 18, pp. 1–11.

PACEY, PHILIP (1977) *A Sense of What is Real*, London, Brentham Press.

PINKOLA ESTÉS, CLARISSA (1994) *Women who Run with the Wolves: Contacting the Power of the Wild Woman*, London, Rider.

PURDOM, JUDY (forthcoming) 'Shame', in SWIFT, JACQUIE and WALSH, VAL (Eds) *Intimate Roots and Tender Visions: Auto/Biography/Art/Education*.

RAYMOND, JANICE G. (1986) *A Passion for Friends: Toward a Philosophy of Female Affection*, London, The Women's Press.

ROSZAK, THEODORE (1993) *The Voice of the Earth*, London, Bantam Press.

RULE, LEONARD G. (1954) 'Page Boy from Bow BECAME AN AGITATOR at sixteen. Organised Shop: Lost His Job', *The Paperworker*, National Union of Printing Machine Minders (later SOGAT). London, pp. 21–2.

SHILLING, CHRIS and MELLOR, PHILIP (1994) 'Embodiment, Auto/Biography and Carnal Knowing: The Protestant Reformation and Modern Self Identities', in special double issue of *Auto/Biography*, 3:1 and 3:2, pp. 115–28.

SPARKES, ANDREW C. (1996a) 'The Fatal Flaw: A Narrative of the Fragile Body/Self', *Qualitative Inquiry*.

SPARKES, ANDREW C. (1996b, under review) 'Performing Bodies: Illness and the Death of Selves', *Auto/Biography*.

SPENCE, JO (1986) *Putting Myself in the Picture*, London, Camden Press.

SPENCE, JO (1992) 'The Artist and Illness', *Artpaper*, 11, 5, pp. 11–13

SPENCE, JO (1995) *Cultural Sniping: The Art of Transgression*, London, Routledge.

SPENCE, JO and SOLOMON, JOAN (Eds) (1995) *What Can a Woman Do with a Camera?: Photography for Women*, London, Scarlet Press.

STANLEY, JO (1995a) 'Pain(t) for Healing: The Academic Conference and the Classed/Embodied Self', in MORLEY, LOUISE and WALSH, VAL (Eds) *Feminist Academics: Creative Agents for Change*, London, Taylor & Francis, pp. 169–82.

STANLEY, JO (1995b) 'Accounting for our Days', in SPENCE, JO and SOLOMON, JOAN (Eds) *What Can a Woman Do with a Camera?: Photography for Women*, London, Scarlet Press, pp. 17–28.

STANLEY, LIZ (1994) 'Introduction: Lives and Works and Auto/Biographical Occasions', in special double issue of *Auto/Biography*, 3:1 and 3:2, pp. i–ii.

STEEDMAN, CAROLYN (1993) *Landscape for a Good Woman: A Story of Two Lives*, London, Virago.

SWIFT, JACQUIE and WALSH, VAL (1995/96) 'Intimate Roots and Tender Visions: Auto/Biography/Art/Education. A Performance', at Free International University Social Sculpture Colloquium, Goethe Institut, Glasgow, Scotland, 11 November 1995; and at a Theoros Seminar, *Tender Passions: The Female and the Aesthetic*, in the School of Historical and Visual Studies, University of Wales Institute, Cardiff, 23 April 1996. This project is also being prepared as a book proposal.

WALKER, ALICE (1984) *In Search of our Mothers' Gardens: Womanist Prose*, London, The Women's Press.

WALSH, VAL (1990) '"Walking on the ice": Women, Art Education and Art', *JADE (Journal of Art & Design Education)*, 9, 2, pp. 147–61.

WALSH, VAL (1995a) 'Unbounded Women? Feminism, Creativity and Embodiment', in JASSER, GHAISS, VAN DER STEEN, MARGIT and VERLOO, MIEKE (Eds) *Travelling Through European Feminisms: Cultural and Political Practices*, Utrecht, The Netherlands, WISE (Women's International Studies Europe), pp. 149–61.

WALSH, VAL (1995b) 'Women Academics of White Working Class Origin: Strangers in Paradise? Or Just Other? Or the Impossible Dream/er Herself?', presented at the BSA Study Group on Auto/Biography Annual Conference, Auto/Biographical Imaginations, Rome, Italy, 16 December.

WALSH, VAL (1996) 'Terms of Engagement: Pedagogy as a Healing Politic', in MORLEY, LOUISE and WALSH, VAL (Eds) *Breaking Boundaries: Women in Higher Education*, London, Taylor & Francis, pp. 187–207.

WALSH, VAL (forthcoming) 'Digging Up Tangled Roots: Feminism and Resistance to Working Class Culture', in POLKEY, PAULINE (Ed.) *Women's Lives into Print: Theory, Practice, Product*, London, Macmillan.

WEST, DAVID (1990) *Authenticity and Empowerment: A Theory of Liberation*, Hemel Hempstead, Harvester Wheatsheaf.

Chapter 15

To Celeb-rate and Not to Be-moan

Jo Stanley

Once upon a time there was a girl who lived among lions who had no time for the likes of her. Whenever she put her head up they roared. She learned to lie low, low, low, and almost died of silence and starvation.

Then she discovered there were girls there. Indeed, they and she had all grown to womanhood despite their privations. They had somehow become beautiful, albeit sometimes in slightly distorted ways: their trunks were weary with the bending; their hearts were fluctuatingly weak and strong, with the terror and hiding – and so could not always be relied on. Their legs usually seemed quite good for walking with heavy weights, running and even standing firm.

And they found – having company for the first time – that they had voices. These voices could sing. Together they sounded wonderful. And so, quaveringly at first, then loudly and sometimes jaggedly and sometimes with a harmonious and deeply enjoyable raucousness, they sang.

They sang together. They discovered that some of their number were of another species – male. And some of the women said, 'we can sing together'. And some others said, 'no, we can sing better on our own'. And some women were part of both groups, singing sometimes with women, sometimes with women and men. And together, whatever their sex, their voices loud, they found that they could frighten the lions off. That they could build worlds. That they knew about collective upraising of voices and actualizing of dreams in a way that the lions did not.

The end of the story, dear Reader, is not yet known. Did the lions die of the singing that overpowered them? Did the lions and the humans find ways to live harmoniously together? Was it half and half? What common bonds did they find? Or did they just take themselves off to separate worlds recognizing that lions will never stop roaring and tearing but that humans will always be interested in surviving differently – and in singing beautifully and happily?

The ex-girl tried many paths in a life that seemed almost too full of challenges for her survival. She lived not happily ever after but on the edge of the lion pit. And the times when 'happy ever after' felt almost possible were when she and the others reminded themselves to sing, and to construct new worlds with their songs. And they sang both the exploratory just-invented new songs and some of the old ones that seemed to speak about justice and co-creativity.

Dear Reader, what's your ending for this?

Friends, sisters, countrywomen, resisters all, lend me your ears. I come not to bemoan working-class difficulties but – in cautious gladness – to praise the solidarity that we manage to achieve sometimes. I come to revel in what we do well, not to grieve over all the places where we fail. To exhult in some of the fleeting paradisical moments of correspondence between substantial self and situation (Sparkes, 1994, p. 103), when I see I fit my world, and it fits me beautifully – me as working-class oh-so-critical feminist. A moment of being spiritally *and* socially 'at home'. To temporarily focus on the positive while holding in my breast the knowledge of absolutely good reason for existential despair and awareness of the dangers of projecting my personal difficulties into collective distress (Green, 1987, p. 189). To remind myself and maybe you of a non-negative side to being working-class: the pleasure of being 'us' and not solely 'I', of being a part of 'us', that resistant working class, that gang whose bodies metaphorically can sing anywhere in the world that – as the anthem asserts – 'the *Internationale* unites the human race'. And for a minute it does.

And who is this I who speaks, shouts, and seemingly sings? Not just a leftie from a skint and marginalized family (Dad an insurance man, Mum a mother and part-time artist), but a female leftie: a heart-possessing feminist one. Specifically one who enjoys being part of what I call 'us working-class, educated, resistant progressive sisters'. It's my tricky joy – to en-joy this going for our common goals: spiritual and material. The emblem is the profound embodied pleasure of joining in with the US protest-song-singer/writer Joan Baez – together and alone – in any renditions anyone likes of 'We shall overcome some day'.

Yes we will.

And believing it.

Yes we will.

That's what we're going for. That's the key.

Why celebrate? Because for years I've complained – aloud and silently – about the negative truths (the difficulties) of being working-class. Stage one has been these decades of what bell hooks (1991) has called a narrative of struggle in which the subjectivity of an oppressed individual reasserts itself. It's time for a reappraising break; time to absolutely see, in Koestler's terms, 'the importance of not being ernest' (Koestler, 1970, p. 63).

So this is what I am: a resistant, collectively-aspirational woman who challenges the material and spiritual oppressions of a society that devalues people of my class and gender. A woman who is also miserable. I do want to moan. Many of the keywords I associate with my working-classness are negative. My list goes: us, deprivation, unease, pride, shame, unjustness, not fair, fight, other, them, us, us, us, we. I spring (active passive) from it, derive from it, abandon it. I am of it. I hurt. And bits of it were good. Are good. Dispossessed. I see that things (not just me) need changing. I see that the scale of the necessary change is so great that it can't be achieved alone. Nor would it be right to attempt to do so because this is *our* change – and not individual personal consumerist salvation.

Why Politically Active?

My chronology of seeking out other justice-seeking working-class women and men begins with the Youth Campaign for Nuclear Disarmament from 1963; the underground movement from 1968, including anti-psychiatry initiatives;[1] the Women's Liberation Movement from 1969; the labour movement and the Communist Party of Great Britain from 1972: all before I was 23. These separate[2] strands continued to be evidenced through lifestyles (hippy clothes forever, rainbow Filofaxes, anti-consumerist homes, left-wing papers on my daily doorstep) and into subsequent groups: world peace movements and women-focused radical organizations. Sometimes there has been solidarity, which Jonasdottir (1988, p. 55) defines as 'a relatedness which does not necessarily presume personal friendship but, when practised, involves sacrifice and sharing of burdens, [which] should be possible among *many*'. Sometimes temporary and beautiful sisterhood has come my way: that bond which Jonasdottir sees as 'a bond of relatively deep affect, of friendship and sometimes love, [and] only possible between a *few*'.

Since the 1970s, my milieux have included the Educated Working-Class Women's Group from 1989; SWOMP (Socialist Women on Men's Platforms) from 1992; various women's and radical history groups; and the women's committee of my union, the Writers' Guild. Many and heartening are the overlaps in the 1980s and 1990s.

This is not to claim uncomplicated membership of any de-problematized community. In most progressive movements (Hearn, 1987, pp. 175–7) tensions between the individual and collective are ferocious, between the lust to participate and the aching need for private space. My psychic survival during reporting a People's March for Jobs was achieved by escaping from the muddy slog to tearooms and country house novels (but I did so with the backing of my mate from the Trades Council women's committee). I have cringed at pronouncements by my party's leaders, but find some of my greatest moments of unity in recognizing how many others feel the same critical way. Member of two sections of the population, I bring two sets of knowledge: as working-class person I am activist and lover of community. As woman I am affiliator (Miller, 1988) and one who has shared enough feminist talk about the political to have gained wisdom about the tensions within that community, too.

For me these three decades have been full of ideas about revolution if possible, reform in the meanwhile.

Why haven't I – as ambitious working-class 1960s-raised individuals did – gone for personal aggrandizement? Partly it is personal – and maybe my fears are/were shared by other women who were also disabled by class and gender socialization. Fear of my success being taken from me, fear of it not feeling real or OK if I alone got it. Uncertainty about my rights to any private boon (as a girl, as part of a hard-pressed family still enduring no-longer-war-induced deprivation.) In common with many children (Sennett and Cobb, 1972, p. 132), my rebellion against my parents necessarily included rebellion against their disavowal of their working-class roots. In opposition to them, I *invested* in my class. That shift in loyalty and new socialization (Purdey, 1979, p. 151) was enabled by the social and economic attitudes of the times which meant my sense of class shame was less sharp than my parents', because *my* direct experience of poverty was less harsh and *my* radical chic world embraced us proles (though nominally). Also, social desires at that time looked likely to be met. More positively, my generosity and self-sacrifice (the former the product of genuine kindness, the latter occasionally sometimes a way to manipulate others in order to avoid my own fear) (Sennett and Cobb, 1972, p. 40)[3] impelled me, too.

And why a feminist? Partly because it looked exciting; other alternatives such as working-class marriage did not.[4] I like company. I like fun. I love doing things together with other people – our bodies acting together for a common goal (yes, including orgasms). I want to be with other sharp and lively women who, as friends and co-activists, determinedly continue to expect and organize for a future full of justice, equal rights, the finest life for all.

But why do others think a woman (like me) comes to choose such a path? A disturbing number of social psychologists and political geographers see relative deprivation as a key motivating factor for left-wing affiliation.[5] Lack. Lacking what we want and what others seem to have, we turn to violent annexation. ('We' is also male. Women's socialist commitment is little considered among the accounts of generic male Marxist activism – see Hearn, 1987). Few works deal generously at all with the motivations of people who want extreme change: revolutionary action is mixed up as synonymous with terrorist action on London's Senate House library shelves. The writers of the forty or so books on these shelves generally assume that radical action is destructive action. Too many view it as a consequence of socially caused psychological damage: that radicals are acting from chips on shoulders rather than from reasoned and principled views. Anti-racist and anti-disablist campaigners have, of course, been similarly charged in the last decades. Feminist activists, likewise, were written off in the 1970s as driven by bitterness at being ugly and man-less, and portrayed as wild and irrational bra-burners rather than seers or political leaders.

But my experience of our (my working-class women friends') motivations for pursuing change is that it comes not from a reactive poisoning kernel but from a healthy well-spring of knowing what we need to go for to create a saner world. I celebrate our respectful wisdom. Yes, there is some pain at the core, some desire for reparation too.

The ache of exclusion is complex. Do I want to belong to the dominant club? No, but I do want to belong to something, to be in something. And I do want my values – not 'theirs' – to be dominant; I believe in their efficacy and appropriateness. An argument derived from social psychology would propose that oppressed groups (e.g. women) seek to minimize their social ambiguity (at best) and to deal with the pain of exclusion by taking one of three steps: first, by rejecting the rejecting dominant group (by 'being the oppressors', taking the offensive), second, by presenting ourselves as not really so bad – trying to make ourselves likeable by the dominant group – or third, by denying that we are experiencing any rejection. Also we choose at different times different strategies and different actions within that whole scale of choices.

As feminist and socialist in a patriarchal capitalist society, I see that I/we mainly use the first strategy listed above: seeking the value of my own group, my working-class and woman selves. Gay Pride, Black Pride: such reclamation is a standard tactic. I need and gain from my groups and their cultures. These counter-cultures both educate and reinforce our chosen oppositional life.

Pageant and Physicality: The Creative Culture of Progressive Movements

Spectacle matters. Physicality matters in this acting together to create a society that values us more and has peace and justice at its core. Suffragettes knew that: marching shoulder to shoulder in their white and lavender and green costumes, draped in flowers, sashes, carrying lilies, singing suffragette anthems (Tickner, 1987). The labour movement knew it:[6] think of miners' galas; think of New Labour's use of US-style political jamborees. Think of how much better a Nicaragua fundraising fête looks if there is bunting; how much better a march is when there are balloons and clowns, streamers, masks and PA systems.

Of course I am talking about socialization, participation in situations that have apparently common meanings. In this case, a key meaning is that resistance and solidarity means empowerment and pleasure. If the culture of an organization emphasizes joy and fun in membership, then the cohesion and collective self-love grows and the darts of enemies' disparagement hurt a little less.

Something to have fun in. Progressive experiments in children's development (e.g. Axline, 1969, pp. 91–6) show how much more happily and readily learning takes place when play, not 'work', is the method. If the parent/movement encourages 'play' then people made nervous by life can – together and at their own speeds – enjoy actions through no-fail experimentation. A place to practise and explore with relative light-heartedness.

Something to belong to. Something to be proud of ourselves in. The Labour Party in the inter-war decades stressed the importance of (non-exploited) leisure for the working class; Marxists went one further and organized alternative cultural activity: touring agit-prop theatre groups, workers' photography groups, Left Book Clubs. The reason 'was political – to further the class struggle and to disseminate the principles of British Communism ... Communists were implicitly and explicitly challenging dominant bourgeois values and making it possible to develop a proletariat aware of its own creative abilities and potential' (Jones, 1986, p. 154; see more generally *ibid.*, pp. 134–63). Fox example, the Workers' Music Association with its choirs of women and its classes 'set out to encourage the composition and performances of music which expresses the ideals and aims of humanity for a betterment of society where social justice is seen as being the norm. It believes further that genuine art has in the past moved people to work towards these aims and will continue to do so in the future.'[7] Women were part of this culture in tiny numbers and limited roles, but at least we were there.[8]

The peace movement marched to a new music that reflected its values. One of the leading folk singers and CND (Campaign for Nuclear Disarmament) activists of the time, Ian Campbell, points out:

> The jazz revival and the rise of CND were more than coincidental: they were almost two sides of the same coin . . . the great flowering of the peace movement went hand in hand with the folksong revival . . . the CND's first great anthem, *The H-Bomb's Thunder* . . . was uniquely effective in generating a proud sense of unity and identity among the demonstrators; its slightly hymnal tune was easily learnt and . . . its strong rhythm made it an ideal marching song. (Minnion and Bolsover, 1983, p. 115)

Music never wholly unites, of course. The 1960s Communist Party was riven by debates over tuneful music versus the challenges of Shostakovich, between those who backed home-grown skiffle and those who preferred US commercial rock'n roll.[9]

Speech – the opening of the mouth, especially collectively – helps create a counter-culture that works. Ideally it even promotes discussion and thrives on the different metaphorical notes and rhythms of all concerned. And as bell hooks has said (1989), talking back is important for women. It's the thing we're not supposed to do: open our traps, give lip, shoot our mouths off, voice it! Shouting a counter-call is always empowering, if only temporarily. It shows us we have the power to refute, to express our own desire. As the sex taught to be silent, as the class whose accents are mocked, whose very ability to speak is doubted or negated, this refutation matters. And if fight we must, then sound can be used as a weapon to frighten off enemies. North African women ululating can send attackers cowering, for example; Belfast women bashing bin lids freak out the troops. War cries help our own side because we hear our power but they also assist pyschological warfare: they stress the might of us against them.

Music provides rhythms by which to collectively and harmoniously do shared and sometimes otherwise unendurable tasks. It uses the right brain, it involves our creative sides and not just our logical sides, our dutiful super-ego. Song can put pleasure into politics. 'People do not "work" music. They "play" it', music therapists argue (Dewhurst-Maddock, 1993, p. 47). Also, there's a selfish pleasure for me in collective singing: if I sing in a gang it doesn't matter that I do it so technically badly that I was booted out of the school choir. To sing in a gang, whose main interest is not artistic excellence, is to be comfortably subsumed, happily overwhelmed. Being part of that collective identity can sometimes help me feel less bad about my individual identity.

Most importantly, when we celebrate with our bodies we can cross language li(n)es and achieve temporary unity: dancing, marching, singing. At big international socialist and feminist gatherings I've felt that dangerously apolitical feeling: if there are so many of us – rumbling the same rhythms but using different words – despite coming from such different places ergo I/we must be a bit right; we must belong to something important; we must be heading towards approximately the right thing. There must be a bit of hope. Maybe the world isn't such a frightening place, maybe we can all be united.

My Trail of Bunting

I would like to explore some of my own experiences of shared collective working-class feminist joy in detail, in order to celebrate having experienced so many moments of being one of millions of women (and men) going happily and proudly for justice. I see it as bunting: small complex flags on a string of hope.

First Flag: Youth Campaign for Nuclear Disarmament

In 1963, at our YCND group in Crosby, the break-time records on the Dansette[10] taught me far better than speeches that I was connected – somehow through vibrations in my belly – to US Civil Rights struggle in Alabama. We shall overcome. We *shall* overcome. Joan Baez refused to pay her federal income taxes (Jacobs and Landau, 1966, p. 327) and the US-British-Soviet treaty banning nuclear weapon tests in the atmosphere was signed just a few months after I joined. That meant *our* sung, spoken and demonstrated warnings were being recognized; that CND was a temporary community[11] that could change things. It had power. And I, a working-class girl who was part of it, thereby also gained some power and pride in my ability to effect. At last.

I discovered I could go comfortably on outings with gangs of others: not with the unease of a Brownie or the misery of a press-ganged daughter but as a needed member of a group selling *Sanity* on Southport Pier. I acquired blokes, saw new places, gained friends. It was the first place I'd ever heard talk about the immorality of capital punishment, the connecting egalitarian function of Esperanto, the merits of anarchy versus Communism, and the use of unions. I got a thousand informal lessons, given largely by middle-class progressives. And I received them hungrily, as do people lunging for a different way of seeing. I did so out of knowledge of the 'perceived need deficiency'[12] of the contemporary power structure.

Second Flag: Women's Liberation Movement (WLM)

Between YCND in the early 1960s and the new wave of feminism in the late 1960s came the underground movement. In London and Liverpool, in psychedelic clubs and serious arts labs I learned about the counter-culture, tripping and fucking with the privileged men who created it. But my working-class self was absent, and I was chick (ergo hanger-on) not woman. The start of the WLM, however, showed me that I could be a central actor in these changes. Part of the power was again in the physicality of being with a gang of women like me in a public site. We entered – took swaggering possession of – universities and City Halls for our conferences. I'd never been in one before. Is that a portcullis I see before me? Away it goes. Corridors and Council Chambers fell to our booted tread (beneath long flowered skirts). Walking between workshops as sites of new knowledge – that was the life I needed. This was where power was: and we – anyone – could enter it, organize in it, shout in it, laugh at cabaret skits on gender in it.

Putting 'politics' and 'women' together was a bitty process.[13] But at least it had its own culture, that I could take home to my room: records by singer-songwriters such as Holly Near who sang about why nuclear protestor Karen Silkwood died; records distributed by Women's Revolutions Per Minute. Through them I found women's blues albums such as *Wild Women Don't Get the Blues*. Feminist theatre groups showed I was not alone. With Spare Tyre on stage, dieting and contraception and anxiety were all nameable. I was part of one of the earliest feminist media action groups and went barefoot in the rain carrying red tulips to plan campaigns. My bits were coming together.

And at least the Women's Liberation Movement nominally understood the extra oppressions of class and race (even if some members still carried on being clueless about it). *Ourwrite* magazine posited an international politicized women's movement – not exactly of women who would sing the *Internationale*, for it now seemed rather European – but women who naturally accepted that there had to be spiritual as well as economic elements in our struggle. Bread and Roses. Sweat and Spinach. Love and (maybe if we have to) Guns.

Third Flag: Union Women

I joined the labour movement in 1972, slumming it as machinist and shop steward in a Brighton soft toy factory. The labour movement was a hard place to be for a woman who felt lone: it was so male. But going away to collective events – again physically relocating as part of a gang sharing food, rooms, parties and trips – created my joy in collectivity. The unions took on women's issues with the proposed Equal Pay and Sex Discrimination laws and I went to day schools full of women who belonged to both my camps: left and feminist. Again it was not an unproblematic community. I was aware of our very different feminisms and aware of middle-class lawyers' and leaders' inability to do other than patronize working-class women. It was uncomfortable, for at WLM conferences I felt pain at the way radical and socialist feminism seem so divided. I hated attacks being made on trade unions as if they were composed only of bloated male bureaucrats instead of full of effective women: my friends.

Fourth Flag: Within the Communist Party

I hung around Communist circles from 1971 and began working for its paper, the *Morning Star*, in 1979. The point was to be the daily paper that showed what was being done and – some believed – what should be done. There, in that five-storey office built by comrades on their weekends off, I was housed by a revolutionary culture: *my* class were *our raison d'être*. My gender were at least nominally respected – even though an argument was still raging about feminism being a bourgeois diversion. It was a fraught community – divided into right and left. It was so full of codes and traditions, I needed a map to find a way round its culture. This was no place of light-hearted festivity. Some of the journalists were shockingly snobbish. But it was a site of daily respectful celebration of a struggle and a proudly oppositional life. The proof was in the paper and print, the hot metal and fraternal (sic) visits. The movement was on the map. To the side, along with several other women, I wrote a women's column and turned out features for the women's page, reviewed the new feminist women's books (in Virago's first successful years) and in doing so educated myself in Cora Sandel and Kay Boyle, Mary Daly and Alexandra Kollontai. I saw we were something to write home about – and did so.

As the only woman industrial journalist on any national daily newspaper, I covered events such as hospital picket lines: a woman talking to women shop stewards, women strikers. The daily experience of witnessing resistant action and talking to the working-class women who took it showed me implicitly that I could do it too. Being on a picket line after a few weeks can be tedious. Seeing what people do to keep up their spirits, to not moan, but to be proud of the challenge they are mounting, showed me how even the tiniest physical gestures of solidarity can have immense spiritual impact: car horns tooting, a passer-by handing over a sweetie, a postman turning back instead of crossing your line. As part of the movement, rather than capitalist media spy, I was invited to report the coups: the first women's conferences of many unions. Learning and partying, chatting and eating in baronial halls taken over by Co-ops and unions, again demonstrated that working-class women could build the good spaces we need.

Fifth Flag (The Boldest): Revolution Enacted

My most important experience of witnessing and taking part in a change for the benefit of *us* was Grenada in the Caribbean. I went out twice during the revolution (1979–83), once for International Women's Day. It's one thing to talk of wanting to make change but another to be part of establishing it. There I actually witnessed not only a will to succeed, but action to succeed and many actual successes. These ranged from rural women lovingly decorating roadside boulders to make their island more beautiful, to sisters setting up the co-operative sauce factory designed to utilize previously wasted windfall paw-paw, to quiet girls taking part in the People's Revolutionary Militia to defend the island from US invasion. Sitting in a flag-strung field seeing US militant Angela Davis speak or sheltering from a tropical thunderstorm hearing Peter Tosh's reggae distinction about priorities (*I don't want no peace, I want equal rights and justice*) I learned with my whole body, through joy and comradeship. I learned that if people struggling for change do not occasionally (preferably frequently) witness that good change can occur, they get disheartened. They stop fighting. This is why so many British people made trips to socialist countries from the 1920s to the 1970s. It made the progressive movement strong if its members had seen with their own eyes that oppressors can be overturned and that a better future for all can be worked for. For all that so much went wrong in socialist countries and was damaged by occuring within capitalism, it was important to see living examples.

Sixth Flag: Community Publishing

Throughout the last two decades, the community publishing I have been involved in – as student and tutor – ensures that marginalized voices are heard[14] and working-class experience validated. For me the point is to be critically and resistantly working-class and so I struggle with a triumphalist tendency within the Federation of Worker Writers and Community Publishers which sometimes implies that working-class *per se* is necessarily 'good' and ignores politics. Class identity is more fractured than some romantics like to believe (Stanley *et al.*, 1987). There have been some livid rows within the Fed about feminism – often with writer Jimmy McGovern near their core. But oh the pleasure of book launches and Raymond Williams Prizes won, of the annual conferences of the Fed – including coach trips to it, the noisy meals at it, the dancing and readings at its Saturday nights. They offer collectivity and reassurance that being working-class does not mean being a piece of trodden offal. In these cases it means mouthily and creatively uttering statements (often of wit and precision) that illustrate class experience and shatter the silences.

Seventh Flag: The Educated Working-Class Women's Group

Between 1989 and 1993, I became a member of the Educated Working-Class Women's group, along with Helen Lucey, Joan Solomon, Jo Spence, Valerie Walkerdine and for a time Pam Trevithick. With its monthly London meetings it was a space in which to voice the complex experience of being educated out of our original social class, and doing so in a free and theorized way. Sitting on homely floors drinking hyacinth tea to the smell of Chinese herbs brewing, moaning about cars and jetlag, families and jobs, bodies, bodies, bodies (Stanley, 1991, 1995), these meetings were a kind of advanced conciousness-raising group. We collectively wrote an unbroadcast series of skits for TV, turning pain into pedagogy and laughter. Many books, papers, and workshops have emerged from our experience (see references). It was also so frustrating that I nearly left several times. But it was a rare body that was drawing the strands of class and gender together: I needed it and miss it.

Eighth Flag: SWOMP

On-going now: my membership of SWOMP – Socialist Women on Men's Platforms. It's famous for frightening male leaders into non-sexist behaviour. One of the first initiatives was to award a pink plastic handbag to a TUC leader, in reference to all the handbags that officials routinely awarded to retiring leader's wives. It worked. No more handbags. On International Women's Day 1996 we celebrated in the TUC's best suite pleased not least that three key labour movement positions were uniquely held by women this year. There was booze, there were babies; decorous busts of former labour leaders were bedecked with earrings. There was gossip and the best of networking – for these are some of the liveliest women in the labour movement. And we were there as women, women activists who determinedly enjoy life. Every bash we have, from St Valentine's Day Massacre to mega events at the annual Trades Union Congress, has awards for best frocks and competitions for most outrageous earrings. The determination to be upbeat no matter what particular hell we might be enduring acknowledges that enjoyment as activists is often best achieved in groups. Fun is useful. Ritual – and repeated contact – work.

Conclusion / The End of the Bunting

This chapter has been about metaphorical singing, political singing: its ability to uplift, unite, and engage whole bodies. It's my deeply selective narrative of bits of my history as a working-class woman who wants better for all of us. I'm still *en route* to change and I'm so happy to be doing it in company. The metaphor is of gangs singing on coaches on the way to demonstrate that change is needed and that solidarity exists: Bandiera Rossa on charabancs to Spanish Civil War commemorations,[15] to Moscow, to peace camps, to women's events.

My body has celebrated best with song. One final image. I'm singing, along with over a thousand of we justice-lovers who finally standing inside that South African Embassy outside which we had shouted for so long. Together we sing the anthem that means apartheid really is no longer in full control:

Nkosi sikelela lafrica. As usual I'm singing (badly) at the side of a woman, in a mixed gathering of people who do actually care about the future. I'm enjoying the gestures of standing with my fist clenched (Yes, it says, I can fight if I have to) and on my feet (Yes, I will not be cowed) and with lots of people who for those few moments share goals. It offers a temporary, luxurious home: a moment of actual existing community. And that's what gives me heart. That's what makes the ex-girl who fled the lions think that it's worth carrying on, possibly even that it's good to carry on.

I'm wearing my Wild Women Don't Get the Blues lapel button that I picked up from the feminist bookstore in San Francisco. It's alongside an old union badge: Public joy, not private sorrow: stop privatization. It could be any version of any badge, any sash, any banner, any poster that says Stop the Cuts, Stop the Cuts, endlessly Stop the Cuts – to benefits, to opportunities, to rights, even to subsidized music courses for working-class women. Stop the cuts.

Start the collective singing that'll build up hearts and tear down weapons dumps and racist barriers and chemical warfare plants and all the power structures that work against our free singing and living. Wild working-class woman sometimes don't get the blues. But often we do: rightly. There is cause to grieve appropriately but not to be-moan inactively. There is need to celebrate, because it rates us as worth singing about and for and with alongside. Together.

Notes

1 The politics of the anti-psychiatry movement at that time (see Cooper, 1967), were socialist and anti-racist but had not then taken feminism on board. Juliet Mitchell's writings, including *Woman's Estate* (Penguin, 1974) and *Psychoanalysis and Feminism* (Penguin, 1974) were some of the first published manifestations of a change in this course.

2 It is not accident nor solely personal inability to connect that made this separation. As Juliet Mitchell pointed out (in an interview in Rowland, 1984, pp. 74–6), Marxist men in the 1960s simply did not see women as a social group: it's difficult to see ourselves as groups if others do not validate that. I felt like a member of several mutually exclusive groups which were not recognized by the others as equally valid groups.

3 Richard Sennett and Jonathan Cobb (1972) propose the following tendency amongst working-class people, which seems a harsh but approximately correct explanation for my and perhaps others' flight into selfless do-gooding at times: 'Sacrifice is . . . the last demonstration of competence. It is the most fundamental action you can perform that proves your inability to be in control; it is the final demonstration of virtue when all else fails . . . you, oppressed, in your anger turn on others who are also oppressed' rather than on the society that causes the problems.

4 Mirra Komarovsky's (1967) unfeminist but useful work, *Blue Collar Marriage* (New York, Vintage), found that educated wording-class wives were

both more pained and more creative in their marriages than less educated wives.

5 For a range of explanations for 'protest politics' see for example: J. Craig Jenkins and Bert Klandermans (eds) (1995), *The Politics of Social Protest* (London, UCL Press); Alan Marsh (1977) *Politics and Political Conciousness* (Beverley Hills, Sage); Ted Robert Gur (1970) *Why Men Rebel* (New Jersey, Princeton University Press).

6 Gorman (1985) summarizes some of the visual spectacles of labour as badges, posters, banners (sewn by women and paid professionals) etc. See also Philip Foner and Reinhard Schultz, 1985, *The Other America: Art and the Labour Movement in the United States* (London, Journeyman). Eric Hobsbawm discusses the gendered nature of these images in *Worlds of Labour* (1984, London, Weidenfeld & Nicolson).

7 Workers' Music Association publicity leaflet, *c*.1993. The association can be contacted via Anne Schuman (Hon. Sec.), 240 Perry Rise, London SE23 2QT; tel. 0181 699 2250.

8 O'Rourke (1988) records the working-class women's writings omitted from the all-male account in the classic Kraus (1985). Chambers' (1989) history of Unity Theatre reflects women's limited on-stage roles rather than their numerically large participation. Smith (1987, pp. 148–51) usefully discusses Doris Lessing's role in its socialist movement context.

9 Debates within the Communist Party about popular music are discussed in Ian Watson, *Song and Democratic Culture in Britain* (London, Croom Helm, 1983). See also Mike Waite's writings, for example in Geoff Andrews, Nina Fishman and Kevin Morgan (Eds) (1995) *Opening the Books* (London, Pluto), and in his 1992 MPhil Thesis, *Young People and Formal Political Activity: A Case Study: Young People and Communist Politics in Britain, 1920–1991; Aspects of the History of the Young Communist League*, Lancaster University, unpublished.

10 These included songs by Pete Seeger, Woody Guthrie and the Spinners. Titles included *Little Boxes on a Hillside*, *The Family Of Man*, *Dirty Old Town*, *Where Have All the Flowers Gone*?

11 See veteran activist Peggy Duff's memoir, *Left, Left, Left* (Allison & Busby, London, 1971), for her analysis of why CND failed by 1964.

12 See the discussion of V. Le Clair's 1969 notion of 'perceived need deficiency' as one way adults choose to go into further education in Sean Courtney (1992), *Why Adults Learn: Towards a Theory of Participation in Adult Education* (London, Routledge), p. 56.

13 In the 1990s the feminist historian Anna Davin told me that in the 1960s she started looking for, then singing, folksongs about/by women because she noticed the lack of them at her University Folk Club. It was DIY time for some women.

14 For discussions of these initiatives by feminists see Eileen Cadman, Gail Chester and Agnes Pivot (1981), *Rolling Our Own: Women as Printers, Distributors and Publishers* (London, Minority Press Group). For a discus-

sion on class see D. Barton and R. Ivanic (Eds) (1991), *Writing in the Community* (Newbury Park, Sage); Ken Warpole *et al.* (1982), *The Republic of Letters: Working Class Writing and Local Publishing* (London, Comedia).

15 One of the main sources of song lyrics at that time was the *Big Red Songbook* (1977), compiled by Mal Collins, Dave Harker and Geoff White (London, Pluto). See also Roy Palmer (Ed.) (1974), *A Touch of the Times: Songs of Social Change 1770–1914* (Harmondsworth, Penguin Education).

References

AXLINE, V. M. (1969) *Play Therapy*, New York, Ballantine.

CHAMBERS, C. (1989) *The Story of Unity Theatre*, London, Lawrence & Wishart.

COOPER, D. (1967) *Psychiatry and Anti-Psychiatry*, London, Paladin.

DEWHURST-MADDOCK, O. (1993) *The Book of Sound Therapy*, Stroud, Gaia.

GORMAN, J. (1985) *Images of Labour*, London, Scorpion.

GREEN, M. (1987) 'Women in the Oppressor Role: White Racism', in ERNST, S. and MAGUIRE, M. (Eds) *Living with the Sphinx: Papers from the Women's Therapy Centre*, London, The Women's Press, pp. 178–212.

HEARN, J. (1987) *The Gender of Oppression: Men, Masculinity and the Critique of Marxism*, Brighton, Wheatsheaf.

HOOKS, B. (1989) *Talking Back*, Boston, South End Press.

HOOKS, B. (1991) 'Narratives of Struggle', in MARIANI, P. (Ed.) *Critical Fictions: The Politics of Imaginative Writing*, Seattle, Bay Press, pp. 53–61.

JACOBS, P. and LANDAU, S. (1996) *The New Radicals*, Harmondsworth, Pelican.

JONASDOTTIR, A. G. (1988) 'On the Concept of Interest, Women's Interests, and the limitations of Interest Theory', in JONES, K. B. and JONASDOTTIR, A. G. (Eds) *The Political Interests of Gender: Developing Theory and Research with a Feminist Face*, London, Sage.

JONES, S. G. (1986) *Workers at Play: A Social and Economic History of Leisure 1918–89*, London, Routledge & Kegan Paul.

KOESTLER, A. (1970) *The Act of Creation*, London, Pan.

KRAUS, G. (1985) *The Literature of Labour: Two Hundred Years of Working-Class Writing*, New York, St Martin's Press.

MILLER, J. B. (1988) *Toward a New Psychology of Women*, Harmondsworth, Penguin.

MINNION, J. and BOLSOVER, P. (Eds) (1983) *The CND Story: The First 25 Years of CND in the Words of the People Involved*, London, Allison & Busby.

O'ROURKE, R. (1988) 'Were There No Women? British Working Class Writing in the Inter-War Period', *Literature and History*, 14, 1.

PURDEY, M. (1979) 'Socialisation and Language: The Object of Study for Social Linguistics', in WHITE, G. and MUFTI, R. (Eds) (1979) *Understand-*

ing Socialization, Nafferton, Drifield, Yorkshire, Studies in Education, Ltd, pp.

ROWLAND, R. (1984) *Women Who Do and Women Who Don't Join the Women's Movement*, London, Routledge & Kegan Paul.

SENNETT, R. and COBB, J. (1972) *The Hidden Injuries of Class*, New York, Knopf.

SMITH, D. (1987) *Socialist Propaganda in the Twentieth Century British Novel*, London, Macmillan.

SPARKES, A. C. (1994) 'Self, Silence, and Invisibility as a Beginning Teacher: A Life History of Lesbian Experience', *British Journal of the Sociology of Education*, 15, 1.

SPENCE, J. (1986) *Putting Myself in the Picture*, London, Camden Press.

SPENCE, J. (1995) *Cultural Sniping: The Art of Transgression*, London, Routledge.

STANLEY, J. (1991) Unpublished journal of the Educated Working-Class Women's Group.

STANLEY, J. (1995) 'Pain(t) for Healing: The Academic Conference and the Classed/Embodied Self', in WALSH, V. and MORLEY, L. (Eds) *Feminist Academics: Creative Agents for Change*, London, Taylor & Francis.

STANLEY, J., (1987) with HUNTER, B., QUIGLEY, M. and WALLACE, J. 'Class Conflicts', in CHESTER, G. and NIELSEN, S. (Eds) *In Other Words: Writing as a Feminist*, London, Hutchinson.

TICKNER, L. (1987) *The Spectacle of Women: Imagery of the Suffrage Campaigns 1907–14*, London, Chatto & Windus.

TREVITHICK, P. (1988) 'Unconsciousness Raising with Working-Class Women', in KRZOWSKI, S. and LAND, P. (Eds) *In Our Experience*, London, The Women's Press, pp. 63–83.

WALKERDINE, V. (1990) *Schoolgirl Fictions*, London, Verso.

WALKERDINE, V. and LUCEY, H. (1989) *Democracy in the Kitchen: Regulating Mothers and Socialising Daughters*, London, Virago.

WHITE, G. and MUFTI, R. (Eds) (1979) *Understanding Socialisation*, Nafferton, Drifield, Yorkshire, Studies in Education Ltd.

WILSON, E. with WEIR, A. (1986) *Hidden Agendas: Theory, Politics and Experience in the Women's Movement*, London, Tavistock.

WOLPE, A. (1977) 'Education – The Road to Dependency', in *Some Processes in Sexist Education*, London, Women's Research and Resources Centre.

Chapter 16

Finding a Voice:
On Becoming a Working-Class Feminist
Academic

Gerry Holloway

The writing of this chapter has come at a time when other aspects of my work have also caused me to reflect on my life history. Firstly, I have recently completed my thesis and I used a piece of my life history to introduce my thesis and make connections between my research and my life. Secondly, I had been asked to teach the Life Histories course of the MA in Women's Studies at the University of Sussex. Although, during my teaching and research, I have read many biographies, autobiographies, diaries and oral histories and read much theory concerning these sources, I had not thought too seriously about writing about my own life. I have from time to time kept a journal but I've always thrown it away. I am ambivalent about such an exercise. On the one hand, as a historian I know the importance of texts which deal with ordinary lives; on the other hand, it seems arrogant to think that anyone would want to read about my life. However, as the students on the Life History course were expected to reflect on their own lives, it was unreasonable to expect them to reveal themselves to the group if I was not prepared to do the same.

I have spent quite a lot of time over the last few months thinking about myself in ways that I am not accustomed to do. When I first agreed to write this piece I naively thought that writing about being a working-class academic would be relatively straightforward. I have long recognized the relationship between my own life experience and the type of work I have chosen to do. For me, teaching Women's Studies to mature women is a political choice rooted in my own journey through feminism into academic study. However, I have found that there is a chasm between what I know in my heart and mind and what I feel able to articulate on paper. I began working on this piece in the only way I felt comfortable, that is by using my skills as a historian. I plumbed the depth of my memory, retold the story of my childhood as I see it now, reflected on some of the issues I teach my students to consider, such as the fallibility of memory and issues of disclosure, and I read and reread autobiographical writings of other professional women born within a decade of myself (Heron, 1985; Steedman, 1986; Walkerdine, 1990).

As usual my research and reflection raised more questions than it answered. How do we find an entry into our past where it is possible to explain to others our relationship to it? In the construction of the word on the page, rules of grammar, vocabulary, language itself, take away our meanings, re-shaping them so that we think – 'No it wasn't quite like that, but I can't get any nearer'. The problem of articulation is more pertinent when one feels that one is writing from the margins. How do we convey to others who have not necessarily shared our experience the sense of what it was like to be our younger self, the person who is still very much part of who we are today? The problem of articulation is central to the way I feel about my place as a working-class woman working in an elite institution. Finding a voice has always been important to feminists and as a historian I participate in the feminist project to recover lost voices from the past. But how do I, as a working-class woman, find my own voice when I have been taught since childhood to 'put up and shut up' and to be 'seen but not heard'?

So this chapter is an approximation, the story it tells was never quite like that, it was something like it, but the sense of my life seems just beyond my grasp. I cannot adequately convey the essence of what it was to be the younger me, so I shall try to chart the events which, at this moment, when I have been reading so much theory about autobiography, class, feminism, difference etc., seem to offer some account of my relationship to feminist agency and feminist research.

Thinking about Class

In my recent reading of women's autobiography, especially the autobiographies of educated working-class women of around about my age, I have been struck by the differences between their stories and mine. Like Alison Fell, Carolyn Steedman and Valerie Walkerdine, I grew up as one of the first generation of working-class children who would benefit from the new system of secondary education, easier access to higher education, free orange juice and the like (Fell, 1985; Steedman, 1986; Walkerdine, 1990). Yet unlike these women, I never had the burning ambition to escape my background although, like them, I passed my 11+ and went to a girls' grammar school. Steedman claims that her book *Landscape for a Good Woman* is 'about lives lived out on the borderlands, lives for which the central interpretative devices of the culture don't work' (Steedman, 1986). Similarly, as Steedman writes against the conventions of male working-class autobiographies, I write from the borderlands of the story of the working-class girl with the ambition to succeed. What are the factors in my life that made me resist the openings offered by the Welfare State to a different life from that of the rest of my family? I think this question is important. Perhaps my experience will help us understand why clever working-class girls give up on education? This is a particularly important question both for the women's movement and for those of us who teach girls or adult women returners. Perhaps it will offer some insight into why working-class women have so often been represented in middle-class texts as politically apathetic and difficult to organize? Again, this is important for those of us keen to promote women's issues to the widest possible constituency. And finally, on a personal level, perhaps reflection on my life will explain why I am ambivalent about being an academic and reluctant to plunge into that world on a full-time permanent basis?

Many feminist theorists find it difficult to write about class between women and I have found that when I have given papers on the subject, many of my largely middle-class audience are uncomfortable with my analysis and tend to play down class and want to focus on gender as our main oppression whereas working-class participants nod furiously in recognition of the points I am making (Holloway and Stuart, 1995). Phillips argues that this problem of tackling class stems from the early days of women's liberation when socialist men attacked feminists as middle-class (Phillips, 1987). Feminist historians have often bypassed the issue by arguing that a woman's relationship to class is associative and is linked to the class of her father/husband/brother (Levine, 1990). This position is problematic because it concentrates on the economic characteristics of class and ignores the cultural influences. Firstly, this argument denies that any women have power derived from their class position, as with all those middle-class social reformers at the beginning of the century who sought to represent working-class women in debates around legislation which affected women's working conditions without asking the women what they wanted. Secondly, it undermines the role of women in the family as transmitters of cultural values as it places undue emphasis on the role of the wage-earner as the focus for class categorization.

Unlike some feminists who regard class as of secondary importance to gender, I have always found class oppression pervasive, unavoidable, difficult to challenge, less straightforward than gender oppression but often more pernicious in its effect. The main problem seems to be its seeming invisibility, yet under the surface of social relations it is there for those who experience it to acknowledge but those who practise it to deny, either explicitly or implicitly. This causes problems for those of us who are seeking to work together because, as Audre Lorde (1984) has so eloquently argued,

> It is not the differences among women that separate us, but rather our refusal to recognise those differences and to examine the distortions which result of our misnaming them and their effects on human behaviour and expectation.

I shall now examine some of the early influences of my life to explore some ways in which both class *and* gender have formed and informed this particular working-class feminist academic.

Growing Up Working-Class

During the first seven years of my life, my parents lived with my paternal grandparents in a small terraced house in a poor part of Islington. Our large extended family all lived within a two-mile radius. My grandfather was a self-employed, semi-retired coal merchant and my father worked with him delivering coal from a horse and cart. My grandfather also looked after me, taking me out and about tending to the horses or visiting his business cronies in various pubs in the City and Docklands. (My grandmother would have been outraged if she had known that I spent my time hovering around the entrances of these bastions of male immorality; the smell of alcohol and tobacco have always suggested wickedness and complicity to me.) So for most of my early years, I was influenced not only by my parents, who grew up during the 1930s and the war years, but also by my Victorian, conservative, working-class grandparents. My grandparents' philosophy was based on working-class notions of respectability which included hard manual work, knowing your place and, for my agoraphobic grandmother, keeping oneself to oneself.

As children, we learn our place in the social order from our immediate environment. These roles are internalized and become part of our perception of ourselves (Holloway and Stuart, 1995). Two phrases from this period of my life still ring in my brain – 'you should have been a boy', uttered whenever I did anything that transgressed my family's notion of femininity, and 'that's not for the likes of us', for any suggestion that might have involved us not keeping to our place in the world. I have long since come to the conclusion that these two phrases have been crucial to the way I perceive myself as an adult.

I have never really had any problem contesting the perceptions that underpin the first phrase, 'you should have been a boy'. For me the normative role for girls, playing with dolls, wearing pretty dresses and so on, was always an anathema. I liked being a tomboy. I liked boys' games. I played in the streets with boys – football, climbing lampposts and carting – and I wore trousers whenever I could. Throughout my early school life I was known as aggressive because I fought with the boys. Not that I was really aggressive, but of course any girl who stood her ground rather than dissolving into tears was labelled aggressive. I think that my attitudes towards gender roles emanate from the role women play in my extended family. All the women were, and are, strong-minded and possessed a degree of economic independence. My mother, grandmothers and aunts all did paid work, made the decisions, managed the household accounts, and kept their homes, children and husbands in order. It is a standing joke in my mother's family that all the sisters kept their youthful looks while their husbands aged rapidly and this was attributed to their energetic ways which sapped their husbands' strength!

The second phrase, 'that's not for the likes of us', has been far more problematic for me. Gender difference I could challenge. Class was another matter. In *Schoolgirl Fictions*, Valerie Walkerdine writes of struggles to escape the 'ordinariness of working-class life'. Walkerdine chose academic work as the way to attain a bourgeois lifestyle (Walkerdine, 1990). As a child and young woman I had no desire to escape my working-class life. I knew my place and, moreover, I had been taught to be proud of it. I enjoyed the rebellion I felt was implicit in being both a tomboy and working-class. Both my parents and grandparents were contemptuous of 'toffs'. Like the Victorian servant Hannah Cullwick, my family felt pity for people who had to rely on other people's labour for their livelihood (Cullwick, ed. Stanley, 1984). However, their contempt was shot through with fear of the people they despised, people like the bank manager, boss or landlord, who had the power to take away their means of independence, their work and their home. These people spoke and acted with an assured articulacy which comes from a good education, secure career and general sense of being well placed in the world. In our home the vicar and the doctor were treated with due reverence. The only person who could silence my loquacious mother was the doctor: my first experience of the silencing involved in class relationships.

When I was 7 my grandfather died. The business was bankrupt so my parents took a tied cottage in the classy, ultra-respectable seaside town, East-bourne. My father became a coal porter for a large coal merchant. It was a precarious life relying on the same person for one's home and livelihood and the ghost of my father's employer hung over the family and in my mind personified omnipotence. It was around this time I stopped believing in God. For the first time I met middle-class children at school and I was bullied because of my 'cockney' accent which I soon learned to moderate: my second experience of silencing in class relationships. I also discovered that my father's work was regarded as shameful because it involved getting dirty so I learned to conceal his occupation and make sure that my friends were not around when he came home: my third experience of silencing in class relationships. However, these experiences of silencing did not make me want to escape my class; they just made me resentful and resistant to relationships with middle-class children.

Unlike Walkerdine, I passed my 11+ examination without realizing its significance. This was partly because the event took place at a time when we were being evicted from our home. My father had lost his job through ill-health and we eventually moved into a council house. However, as far as I can recollect, we had never talked about what the 11+ examination meant in my family until I passed it. Then I was told I could go to the Girls' High School if I wanted to. Raised on Enid Blyton's *Malory Towers* books I thought a girls' school meant sports and producing Christmas pantomimes, both of which appealed to me. Somehow the classed nature of Blyton's books passed over my head. Thoughts of university or a career never entered my reveries. At the High School my dreams were quickly shattered. I found myself in a world where fathers were doctors, bank managers and all the other professions we had always held in awe. My peers often lived in large detached houses, both their parents had cars and they went abroad for holidays. We had none of these things except a mini. Unlike Walkerdine and Fell, who worked hard to be good girls and do well so that they could join this middle-class world, my experiences as a tomboy and my resentment towards what I regarded as middle-class snobbery meant that the last thing I wanted to be was academic. I became a rebel. A popular rebel, I was voted form captain one year, but I was never really comfortable with my middle-class friends. I regarded our largely middle-aged and unmarried nicely spoken teachers with contempt and resolved to leave school as soon as possible and get a job, any job. Therefore, although I was in the top stream, I did well by default. In my youth I had a photographic memory and this served me well in the old-fashioned 'O' levels of unseen exams. I infuriated my teachers by doing well without working and I think they were pleased to see the last of me when I left at 16 with seven 'O' levels. Girls' High Schools were no place for female rebels with a cause. So how did this rebel become an academic?

Unlike many of the women whose lives I have read about, I came to education through feminism rather than the other way round. When I left school, I joined what Alison Hennegan (1985) describes as 'the dreary and disheartening procession of girls who left school . . . to submerge themselves in marriages to men they'd outgrown half a decade later'. For me, marriage at 17 had seemed an escape, the only possible escape, from family constraints rather than class constraints. My husband and I had a flat, a car, an adequate income and a hectic social life, and for a while this suited me. But although I had not worked hard at school, I had enjoyed learning in my own anarchic way and missed intellectual stimulus. My husband was dyslexic (although we did not call it that) and had not done well at school. He hated to see me reading as it was something he could not and did not want to participate in. So I never read when he was around. Like most of the men in my family he was a manual worker, first a mechanic then a lorry driver. Looking back, it is no wonder that the marriage was a disaster. I was the strong one, the one who took decisions, controlled the money. My husband was irresponsible and unfaithful, and relied on me to sort out his problems. When I suggested that I leave my job in an insurance company, where all promotion went to seemingly inadequate men, to go to teacher training college – the only possible option, I thought then – he responded by panicking and arguing that we could not afford it and it was just an excuse to leave him. Instead, he found a new job, in a new town with a new house. We brushed our differences under the carpet and started a new adventure. It was doomed to failure and, removed from the family's gaze, the marriage soon disintegrated. I moved on, he found a new strong woman to look after him.

At 25, I found myself in a new job, in a new town where I knew no one. It was the first time in my life that I had lived alone and in some ways I was like an 18-year-old undergraduate away from home for the first time. This was in the late 1970s when the media was full of the activities of 'women's libbers', so I joined the local women's liberation group – partly for social reasons and partly because I thought that I might at last be able to do something about the injustices I felt had been meted out to me because of my sex both at work and in marriage. The problem seemed straightforward. Men oppressed women and if women united and worked together we could change this.

At this point in my life I was not political in the normal sense of the word. I came from an apolitical family and had lived in a small town. I worked to earn a living and despite recognizing that I was 'very bright' I did not see education and an academic career as an appropriate avenue for me. Working-class, from a grammar school background, yet from a family that placed little value on a girl's academic education, I wanted to change my life but I could not see how to do it. My involvement with feminism helped me to some extent but class was still an obstacle. I had begun to connect my life with the experiences of other women and I began to read books, especially women's history. Like many other women at the time, the first women's history I read was Sheila Rowbotham's *Hidden from History*. The chapter that particularly struck me was the last one, 'Feminism and Socialism after World War 1'. Here Rowbotham describes how Melvina Walker, a stalwart of the East London Federation of Suffragettes, attended the first Labour Women's Conference after the war. Walker described the tension between the educated middle-class women on the platform and the rank-and-file working women on the floor. Walker felt that the middle-class women had usurped working-class women and taken their rightful place in the workers' party. She quoted 'a tram-wayman's wife who argued that more working-class women should speak: "... if I was in the chair I wouldn't be guided by no-one but myself, and I wouldn't want to hear so much of the platform but more of the rank and file"' (Rowbotham, 1973, p. 159).

Walker's outrage summed up how I felt about the Women's Liberation Movement in the early 1980s. Liberation feminism in the late 1970s and early 1980s tended to posit an essential womanness that we were all supposed to share regardless of the class, racial, ethnic, sexual and cultural differences between us. Like the movement earlier this century, it called to a common sisterhood that sought to override difference. The effect of this essentialist stance was to silence many women. I was silenced in my particular group through my lack of higher education, my accent and my ignorance of certain cultural and social knowledge. It was a benevolent silencing but it was silencing nonetheless. Once again, I found myself on the margins, my difference masked by a gloss of sisterhood which we were not supposed to question because men were the real problem; class was superficial and, for some women, posed no problem at all. However, my experience in my conscious-ness-raising group triggered something in me and subconsciously I began to formulate my plan to return to education and study women's history. This did not come into fruition for several years, during which I studied for 'A' levels which I did not take (memories of schooldays) and studied history with the Workers' Education Association which I enjoyed. I also became involved in feminist and green politics – 'right to choose' campaigns, Greenham, anti-nuclear power groups, rape crisis, reclaim the night and so on.

On Being a Working-Class Feminist Academic

Ironically, it was two men with whom I shared a house in Brighton who finally persuaded me to apply for a place at the University of Sussex. I began my academic career as an undergraduate studying History in 1983 with the added complication of being the single mother of a 3-month-old daughter. Since then, I have gained my BA and funded myself through part-time teaching and other work to complete a Master's degree and Doctorate. I have recently stopped seeing myself as a survivor of the class system and began perceiving myself as a success in my own terms. Most of my women academic friends would count themselves as outsiders because of class, ethnicity or sexuality or because, like me, they studied as mature students rather than following the conventional pathway into higher education (HE). However, I would not describe my entry into academia as unproblematic. At the back of my mind there has been the voice from the past telling me that all this is 'not for the likes of us'. Indeed, some of my family have felt that I was out of my mind to go to university, especially as I had a small child. For myself, I always saw my undergraduate study as paid work. I worked set hours, dictated by my daughter's needs, and paid myself my grant monthly, like a salary cheque. When I started teaching part-time to subsidize my postgraduate studies, my extended family were shocked that I was continuing to study but mollified that I had a part-time job. This fitted in with their notions of women's proper work.

I see my role in academia as on the margins. I am employed part-time and on a temporary basis. Most of my work is situated in a marginal department, the Centre for Continuing Education (CCE) at the University of Sussex. On one level, I could view myself as undervalued and exploited – which I am. However, I am, at the moment, not seeking actively to change my situation. I am used to living on the breadline and I do not perceive success in terms of material possessions. Although it would be nice to have some conventional recognition of my worth, I have no desire to 'play the game' in order to climb an academic career ladder, despite acknowledging that it is important that some women do this. I have not become a 'good girl'. I am still a rebel and I see my work as politically motivated. As the convenor of Women's Studies in the CCE, I meet women from similar backgrounds to my own. Some are meeting feminist ideas for the first time, others have been seriously let down by the education system and lack confidence to pursue a higher education. I hope that I can help them overcome their fears by my own example. I try not to be to evangelical in this. I do not regard a women's decision not to pursue entering HE as a failure. I hope I offer them a practical insight into what HE entails and sometimes women decide it is not the right move for them but still have learned a lot about both practical and theoretical feminisms which they can use in their lives.

In my work as an academic practitioner in a class-ridden, sexist, and racist institution, I think it is important to reflect on how far I become caught up with those structures and in what ways I can challenge them. What do I prioritize –

my commitment to feminism or the struggle within a male-defined career hierarchy? As I have said, I have chosen the former. This position raises the question of how we work with women less privileged than ourselves without exacting a price from them? How do we help them empower themselves? These are questions I struggle with and will continue to struggle with both in my teaching and research and in my role in feminist networks.

For feminists, silence means repression and finding a voice is a strategy in our struggle against patriarchy. The notion of sisterhood, of a homogeneous identity, allows some women to assume they speak for all women. Recent feminist theorists have begun to unpack this notion. However, there is still much work to do if we are going to put these theoretical insights into practice. On scanning the books on my shelf to write this article, I was pleased to find articles on being a black/gay/woman in academia but very little on being working-class, especially a working-class mature student. Being an educated working-class white woman is a slippery, shifting identity. To our students, our education can mask our class. However, I can still feel intimidated by students who have an authoritative voice and stance (Holloway and Stuart, 1995). In our relationships with our colleagues, the rhetoric of sisterhood often masks unequal power relations and assumptions can be made which leave us feeling like and being treated as, as Jo Stanley (1995, p. 170) has put it, 'working-class thickos'. The main problem I still face is the silencing I often experience at work. Women I admire in other respects often operate unconscious gatekeeping processes which keep out women who 'are not like them'. Networks operate that I, and others, do not have easy access to and if we dare voice our views we are met by puzzled looks which silence us again, restating our Otherness and marginality.

Despite my ambivalence about academic life, I shall remain part of it for the time being. I think it is important for working-class women to see that it is possible, that it is 'for the likes of us', to work in such elitist institutions without being subsumed by their culture. I still need to explore the dynamics of class, the process of silencing and finding a voice. I want to find ways in which women can organize that challenge internal as well as external power structures so that all women can find a voice regardless of colour, sexuality or, dare I say it, class.

References

CULLWICK, H. (ed. L. Stanley) (1984) *The Diaries of Hannah Cullwick, Victorian Maidservant*, London, Virago.

FELL, A. (1985) 'Rebel with a Cause', in HERON, L. (Ed.) *Truth, Dare or Promise: Girls Growing Up in the Fifties*, London, Virago.

HENNEGAN, A. (1985) '. . . And Battles Long Ago', in HERON, L. (Ed.) *Truth, Dare or Promise: Girls Growing Up in the Fifties*, London, Virago.

HERON, L. (Ed.) (1985) *Truth, Dare or Promise: Girls Growing Up in the Fifties*, London, Virago.

HOLLOWAY, G. and STUART, M. (1995) 'Mothers and Sisters: Power and Empowerment in Women's Studies', in STUART, M. and THOMSON, A. (Eds) *Engaging with Difference: The 'Other' in Adult Education*, Leicester, National Institute of Adult Continuing Education.

LEVINE, P. (1990) *Feminist Lives in Victorian England: Private Lives and Public Commitment*, Oxford, Blackwell.

LORDE, A. (1984) *Sister Outsider*, New York, The Crossing Press.

PHILLIPS, A. (1987) *Divided Loyalties: Dilemmas of Sex and Class*, London, Virago.

ROWBOTHAM, S. (1973) *Hidden from History: 300 Years of Women's Oppression and the Fight Against It*, London, Pluto.

STANLEY, J. (1995) 'Pain(t) for Healing: The Academic Conference and the Classed/Embodied Self', in MORLEY, L. and WALSH, V. (Eds) *Feminist Academics: Creative Agents for Change*, London, Taylor & Francis, pp. 169–82.

STEEDMAN, C. (1986) *Landscape for a Good Woman: A Story of Two Lives*, London, Virago.

STUART, M. and THOMSON, A. (Eds) (1995) *Engaging with Difference: The 'Other' in Adult Education*, Leicester, National Institute of Adult Continuing Education.

WALKERDINE, V. (1990) *Schoolgirl Fictions*, London, Virago.

Notes on Contributors

Kim Clancy was born in Lancashire in 1959. She was the first member of her family to attend university and has enjoyed a love/hate relationship with academia ever since. She is a writer and lecturer with particular interests in representation and cultural identity.

Shani D'Cruze took, after 'A' level, a secretarial diploma, which led to a series of white-collar jobs, eventually that of 'p.a. to the m.d.' in a small engineering firm. Divesting herself of a husband, a semi-detached with integral garage and the job in the course of a year, she went of Essex University. A history degree was followed by a MA and a PhD plus part-time teaching, here, there and everywhere. A post-doctoral research post took her north to Lancaster. Now she lectures at Crewe and Alsager Faculty of Manchester Metropolitan University. She is just completing a four-year term on the National Steering Committee of the Women's History Network and is co-editor of *Women's History Notebooks*.

Gail Fisher is 29 and lives in East Anglia with the regulation one husband and two kids. Having satisfied that persistent convention, she feels free to be as perverse and bloody-minded about the rest of her life as comes naturally.

Valerie Hey is a researcher based at the Social Science Research Unit, Institute of Education, University of London. She is currently writing up (with colleagues) a project exploring the gendered construction of special educational needs. Her book on girls' friendship is due to be published in November 1996 by the Open University Press as *The Company She Keeps: An Ethnography of Girls' Friendships*. She lives in London. She has a particular interest in issues of subjectivities and difference in the context of education and civil society.

Gerry Holloway is a woman of many parts. She convenes and teaches on the Certificate and Diploma in Women's Studies at the Centre for Continuing Education at the University of Sussex. At the moment she also has a tutorial fellowship in the School of Cultural and Community Studies at Sussex where she teaches Women's History and Cultural Studies. Her research interest largely lies in the way women organize and following on from this interest she is on the committees of the National and Southern region of the Women's History Network. She also works as the administrator for *History Workshop Journal*. More importantly, she likes to be with her family, travel, walk, swim, read and go to the cinema and art exhibitions.

Meg Maguire teaches at King's College, London. Previously she taught in inner-city primary schools. Her publications include work on women in education and initial teacher education.

Pat Mahony is Professor of Education at Roehampton Institute, London. She has published extensively in the areas of teacher education and sexism in school. Her books include *Schools for the Boys?* (1985), *Learning our Lines* (with Carol Jones, 1989) and *Promoting Quality and Equality in Schools* (with Ruth Frith, 1994). She is joint Irish and British Editor of *Women's Studies International Forum*.

Louise Morley has recently joined the Institute of Education at the University of Sussex. She was previously at the University of Reading. Her research interests focus on gender, equity and change in professional and higher education. She has published widely on policy, pedagogy and empowerment, in particular in relation to the micropolitics of women's studies and feminism in the academy. Recent publications include *Feminist Academics: Creative Agents for Change* (Edited with Val Walsh, Taylor & Francis, 1995) and *Breaking Boundaries: Women in Higher Education* (Edited with Val Walsh, Taylor & Francis, 1996).

Janet Parr has been associated with further and higher education as a mature student and lecturer in a range of institutions on both a direct and a distance learning basis. Her interest in the experiences of mature women students led first to a Master's Degree in Education and subsequently to a PhD. She is currently lecturer on the Master's Degree programme in Continuing Education and in Training and Development in the Division of Adult Continuing Education at the University of Sheffield.

Diane Reay is a research associate at King's College, London, engaged in research on social justice and education. Her doctoral research explored the influences of social class and 'race' on mothers' involvement in their children's primary schooling. Prior to undertaking a PhD she worked for twenty years as a primary teacher in inner London.

Monika Reinfelder teaches Women's Studies and politics at the University of London. Of German working-class origin, she has lived and travelled widely in Latin America and Africa. She is active in the international lesbian feminist movement and is the editor of *Amazon to Zami: Towards a Global Lesbian Feminism*.

Tracey Reynolds was born and educated in southwest London. After completing a Social Science degree at Goldsmiths' College, University of London, she worked for a couple of years before returning to full-time education. Tracey is currently completing her PhD at South Bank University, London. Her research focuses on mothering amongst African-Caribbean women in Britain today.

Karen Sayer is a lecturer in the Faculty of Humanities at the University of Luton. She took her first degree at Portsmouth Polytechnic, her second at the University of Sussex, and she published her first monograph, *Women of the Fields*, with Manchester University Press in 1995. She is currently working on a social and cultural study of the country cottage as domestic space.

Beverley Skeggs is co-director of the Centre for Women's Studies at Lancaster University. She has written widely on the media, education and ethnography. Her books include *The Media*, *Feminist Cultural Theory* and *Becoming Respectable*.

Jo Stanley is a writer, journalist, historian and traveller. Currently she teaches on the University of Sussex's unique Diploma in Life History and writes about seafaring women's work history. Her most recent books are *Bold in her Breeches: Women Pirates across the Ages* (Pandora, 1996) and *Cultural Sniping: The Art of Transgression* (Routledge, 1995), an anthology by the late Jo Spence which she edited. She is preoccupied by fiction and art as ways to profoundly represent hidden aspects of the self.

Bogusia Temple is a Senior Research Fellow in the Pharmacy Department at Manchester Victoria University. Her writing and research are concerned with methodological issues, particularly in research with women.

Val Walsh is a freelance writer, researcher, editor and teacher, with many years' experience of equal opportunities activism and teaching interdisciplinary and multi-media courses in higher education. She co-edited, with Mary Kennedy and Cathy Lubelska (1993), *Making Connections: Women's Studies, Women's Movements, Women's Lives*; with Louise Morley (1995) *Feminist Academics: Creative Agents for Change*; and (1996) *Breaking Boundaries: Women in Higher Education*; and she is series editor for a new mini-series on Gender and Higher Education. Her abiding interest is women's creativity as both self-care and politics.

Christine Zmroczek is Senior Lecturer in Women's Studies at Roehampton Institute, London, and Managing Editor of *Women's Studies International*

Forum. She has published widely on women and technology, Women's Studies and social studies of science and technology. She is passionate about extending knowledge of working-class women's lives through both oral history and women's experiences and theorizing in their own words and voices. She is currently working on a volume about domestic material culture and together with Pat Mahony is editing a series, Women and Social Class, with Taylor and Francis and a book on *International Feminist Perspectives on Social Class* (forthcoming 1997).

Index

academia
  class relations in 116–17
  discourses of oppression in 25
  internalized oppression in 114–15
  marginalization of social class in
    18–19, 113, 123
  position of black women in 13–14
  status of teacher training in 96, 98
  women's status and position in 97
  see also higher education;
    working-class women
accent
  advantages for researchers 146–7
  in Boddington's advertisement
    140–1
  learning middle-class 49
  and north/south divide 163
  used in cultural language games
    3, 142–3
Acker, S. 90, 94
Anglo-Indians
  British status 71–2
  history in India of 67–70
autobiography
  academic credibility of 109, 169
  articulation of life histories 166–7,
    190–1
  historical specificity of 88–9
  intellectual auto/biographies of
    researchers 78–9
  see also narrativity

Bhabba, H. 143
biography, link with
    autobiography 79

black feminist theory 9, 13
black people, class differences
    between 10
black women
  constructions of 8–9, 11–12, 14
  diversity amongst 10, 15
  educational achievements 11–12,
    13
  experiences of school 12–13
  position within academia 13–14
  routes to higher education 12
Boddington's advertisement 140–1
Bourdieu, Pierre 91, 115, 127–8,
    129

Campaign for Nuclear Disarmament
    (CND) 180, 181
capitalist individualism, impact on
    working-class 23
capitals
  Bourdieu's model of 127–30
  of working-class women 128–9,
    130–2, 133
Casey, Kathleen 24
castes and classes in India 68–9
Catholicism
  importance for Irish migrants
    91–2
  as unifying factor at Catholic
    grammar schools 93
Chisholm, Lynn 20–1
class
  attitudes to 4
  categorizations and definitions of
    creation of 124–5, 126